D1526165

GALICIA:
A MULTICULTURED LAND

Edited by Christopher Hann and Paul Robert Magocsi

Habsburg Galicia, an area in central Europe covering territory presently ruled by Poland and Ukraine, was distinctive for its multi-ethnic character. With the unravelling of the Austro-Hungarian Empire following the First World War, a new political map of Europe emerged, one based on the principle of the nation-state. The very concept of the nation-state, however, was problematic in culturally pluralistic regions like Galicia.

The essays in this volume examine Galicia beyond the traditional paradigm of national history, in an effort to understand better the region as a place where different ethnic communities – Poles, Ukrainians, Jews, Austro-Germans – lived in peaceful co-existence. With the recent expansion of the European Union, increased migration, and the demise of the nation-state, a look back to see how cultural diversity was managed in a pre-nationalist age is of more than antiquarian interest. The contributors to this multidisciplinary volume pursue a wide range of approaches that shed fresh light on this unique region.

CHRISTOPHER HANN is a director of the Max Planck Institute for Social Anthropology in Halle/Saale, Germany.

PAUL ROBERT MAGOCSI is a professor in the Department of History and in the Department of Political Science at the University of Toronto, where he holds the chair of Ukrainian Studies.

GALICIA

A Multicultured Land

Edited by
Chris Hann and Paul Robert Magocsi

UNIVERSITY OF TORONTO PRESS
Toronto Buffalo London

© University of Toronto Press 2005
Toronto Buffalo London
Printed in Canada

Reprinted 2011

ISBN 0-8020-3943-X (cloth)
ISBN 0-8020-3781-X (paper)

Printed on acid-free paper

Library and Archives Canada Cataloguing in Publication

Galicia : a multicultured land / edited by Chris Hann
and Paul Robert Magocsi.

Includes bibliographical references and index.
ISBN 0-8020-3943-X (bound).   ISBN 0-8020-3781-X (pbk.)

1. Pluralism (Social sciences) – Galicia (Poland and Ukraine) –
Congresses.   2. Galicia (Poland and Ukraine) – Ethnic relations –
Congresses.   I. Hann, Chris   II. Magocsi, Paul R.

DK4600.G34G34 2005   943.8'6004   C2005-900644-7

University of Toronto Press acknowledges the financial assistance to its
publishing program of the Canada Council and the Ontario Arts Council.

University of Toronto Press acknowledges the financial support for its
publishing activities of the Government of Canada through the Canada
Book Fund.

Contents

Preface

The Habsburg Empire disappeared in 1918. Any map depicting its various administrative units, among them the imperial province of Galicia, thereby immediately became obsolete. A new political map was drawn, intentionally based on the principle of the nation-state. Boundaries, as well as the precise names, of many of the former empire's territories were later readjusted, particularly in the mid-1940s and the early 1990s. Yet, even if a perfect congruence of the cultural unit and the political unit could seldom be attained in practice, the Wilsonian principle of "self-determination for nations" has stood its ground and retained its explanatory powers and moral legitimacy into the twenty-first century. Why, then, should a multinational province of a defunct empire still be of interest to scholars and a wider public almost a century after its demise?

Answers accounting for the ongoing interest in Galicia are provided by the studies in this volume. First, there is the professional concern of historians and other academics. This region of central Europe straddles two contemporary states, Poland and Ukraine. Often it is poorly served, and its features are easily distorted, by the dominant paradigms of national history. Until recently this region has been referred to in scholarly and popular accounts alike as either Polish Galicia or Ukrainian Galicia, even German Galicia, by some. Little effort has been made to depict the rich multicultural and multireligious fabric of traditional Galician society. What happened to Galicia's diverse cultural and religious groups, and how is their legacy being played out today? As expansion of the European Union proceeds, it is surely desirable to know most about the past of a region lying at the crossroads of the continent and split in two by the present boundary between East and West.

The period of Habsburg rule in Galicia, which lasted from 1772 until 1918, is the focus of most chapter in this volume. Some attention is also given to earlier periods, when Galicia had quite different boundaries. Several chapters examine the period after 1918, when Galicia had ceased to exist as a distinct administrative entity with the end of the Habsburg Empire. Yet a Galician legacy persists. This legacy is observable in the patterns of behavior among the region's present-day inhabitants on both sides of the Polish-Ukrainian border. It persists in the ideas and memories lying behind their distinctiveness. Analogous to the work of distinguished Romanian historian Nicolae Iorga on the Byzantine legacy in southeastern Europe, one might argue that the time has come for a new synthesis on our topic, perhaps entitled "Galicia après Galicia."

Second, the history of Galicia is pertinent as an aid in grappling with some of the central problems confronting societies and communities in many parts of the contemporary world. Our subtitle provides the clue to our perspective: We are particularly interested in examining the ways in which different communities lived together, or at least alongside each other – peacefully – in the Galicia of the past. Moreover, we would like to understand the forces that undermined this "multiculturalism" during a certain period in history, primarily as a result of the rise in emphasis on mutually exclusive nationalisms. Some commentators suggest that, in the current era of accelerating globalization, the golden age of the nation-state is over. If so, a glance back to see how cultural diversity was managed in a pre-nationalist age might offer guidance and inspiration for the future. In addition to their intrinsic value to historians and to area studies specialists, then, the essays presented here should be of interest to a wide range of social scientists and policy makers in the two countries in which Galicia is situated today.

The authors of the eleven chapters in this book represent several disciplines, as well as different countries and diverse preconceptions about their subject. Interdisciplinarity and "academic multiculturalism" characterized the conference at which most chapters were first presented in their earlier version. Entitled "Galicia: A Region's Identity?" the conference was held in May 1998, in Århus, Denmark, as part of the celebrations of the fiftieth anniversary of the founding of the Department of Slavonic Studies at the University of Århus. We welcome this opportunity to once more express our thanks to the conveners of the conference, Thomas Petersen and Joel Nordborg Nielsen, not only for organizing a memorable meeting but also for the preliminary work they did in gathering the papers together for a publication. When they were unable to continue with their plans, we were pleased to accept their invitation to see the project through to completion.

The present volume includes many but not all of the papers presented at Århus. Most have been substantially revised, even entirely rewritten. In addition, we also solicited several new contributions in order to achieve more complete coverage of the topics that interest us most: the formation and maintenance of collective identities.

The preparation of a volume of essays by eleven different authors living in seven different countries across two continents inevitably poses certain technical problems. In an effort toward consistency, we have standardized place names throughout the book, adopting the main forms used in Paul Robert Magocsi, *Historical Atlas of Central Europe*, revised and expanded edition (Toronto and Seattle, 2002), We also use American English throughout and use the Library of Congress transliteration system to render in the Latin alphabet titles and words that originally appeared in the Cyrillic alphabet. (Moreover, we have tried to reflect the original orthography, so that older letters in Ruthenian/ Ukrainian are rendered as follows: ъ = î; ы = ŷ; ô = ô). Some terms posed special problems and challenged the logical inclination toward consistency. Particularly problematic were the terms *Ruthenian* and *Ukrainian*, which some authors may consider synonyms and others view as distinct concepts. In general, Ruthenian refers to the East Slavic population of Galicia and neighboring lands at a time when that population had not yet adopted a consciousness associated with a particular nationality. Ukrainian implies that the given East Slavic population (or portion thereof) had adopted a clear Ukrainian national identity. This process was a gradual one that occurred during the late nineteenth century and first decades of the twentieth century. Therefore, in general, Ruthenian is used here to describe the East Slavs of Galicia until the end of the "historic" nineteenth century (1914), and Ukrainian thereafter.

We are particularly grateful to the Max Planck Institute for Social Anthropology in Halle, Germany, which provided the home base to coordinate our editorial work. Special thanks are due to Sevdalina Wiezorrek, Ralph Orlowski, and Berit Westwood, who with good cheer and admirable patience input with great accuracy several revisions of each chapter. Our final appreciation is extended to the publisher of this volume.

Chris Hann
Paul Robert Magocsi
June 2004

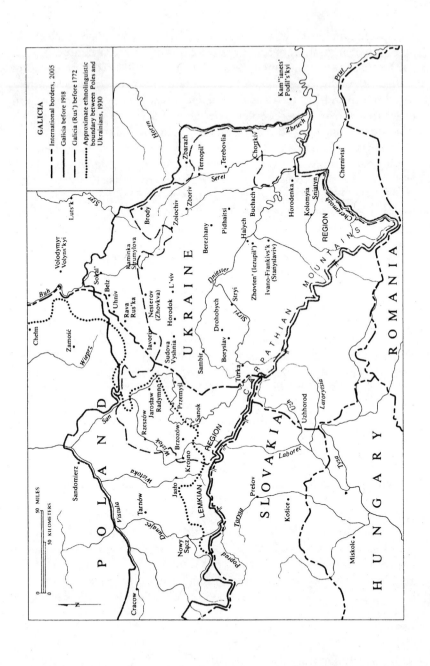

GALICIA

- – · – International borders, 2005
- –––– Galicia before 1918
- ——— Galicia (Rus') before 1772
- ·········· Approximate ethnolinguistic boundary between Poles and Ukrainians, 1930

POLAND

UKRAINE

SLOVAKIA

HUNGARY

ROMANIA

CARPATHIAN MOUNTAINS

CHERNIVTSI REGION

LEMKIAN REGION

Cracow
Nowy Sącz
Tarnów
Sandomierz
Jasło
Krosno
Brzozów
Sanok
Rzeszów
Radymno
Jarosław
Przemyśl
Sudova Vyshnia
Iavoriv
Nestorov (Zhovkva)
Rava Rus'ka
Uhniv
Belz
Sokal'
Zamość
Chełm
Volodymyr Volyns'kyi
Luts'k
Kaminka Strumylova
Brody
Zolochiv
Zboriv
Zbarazh
Ternopil'
Terebovlia
Chortkiv
Zhoven' (Iezupil')
Kam"ianets' Podil's'kyi
Chernivtsi
Sniatyn
Kolomyia
Horodenka
Halych
Ivano-Frankivs'k (Stanyslaviv)
Berezhany
Pidhaitsi
Buchach
Stryi
Drohobych
Boryslav
Sambir
Horodok
L'viv
Turka
Uzhhorod
Prešov
Košice
Miskolc

Rivers: Prut, Zbruch, Seret, Dniester, Styr, Buh, San, Wisłok, Wisłoka, Dunajec, Vistula, Wieprz, Torysa, Tysa, Laborec, Latorytsia, Uzh, Poprad, Tisa

50 MILES
50 KILOMETERS

N

GALICIA:
A MULTICULTURED LAND

1 Galicia: A European Land

PAUL ROBERT MAGOCSI

Most informed sources suggest that there are anywhere from 3,500 to 4,000 distinct languages spoken throughout the world.[1] It follows that there are at least as many distinct cultures and peoples. Yet, there are only about 200 states. Simple mathematics would force us to conclude that most, if not all, countries have within their borders more than one, if not several, different languages and peoples. Put another way, in their composition, most countries worldwide are multinational.

Multinational states are the norm for Europe. The exceptions can be counted on the fingers of one hand, with countries like Iceland and Portugal coming immediately to mind. France, or Spain, or the United Kingdom – not to mention all the countries of central or east-central Europe and the former Soviet Union – are the kind of multinational states that are the most common in Europe. Among them are countries that are often thought to be ethnically homogeneous, but that actually are not. An example is Germany, which includes within its borders Danes, Frisians, and Lusatian Sorbs.[2] No matter how we might define Galicia, one thing is indisputable: throughout a millennium of recorded history Galicia has been inhabited by a multiplicity of peoples – among them Ukrainians, Poles, Jews, Germans, Armenians, Lemko-Rusyns, and more recently, Russians. Galicia is in this sense a typical European land.

Geographical and Historical Context

In the context of central Europe the term *Galicia* is usually understood to mean the imperial Austrian province – formally the *Königreich Galizien und Lodomerien* – according to its boundaries until the demise of the Habsburg Empire in 1918. This territory stretched from the source of the Vistula River in the far west to the Zbruch and Cheremosh rivers in the east and was bounded by the crests of the Carpathian Mountains in the south. Divided more or less in half by the San River, it had two major cities: Cracow in the west and L'viv in the east. The San River also roughly coincided with the ethnolinguistic boundary between Poles and Ukrainians, so that it was not uncommon during the Habsburg period to refer to a Polish-inhabited western Galicia and a Ruthenian (Ukrainian)-inhabited eastern Galicia.

Habsburg Galicia is a relatively modern concept and strictly speaking should be distinguished from what may be called historic Galicia.[3] Before 1772, when the Habsburgs annexed the territory, Galicia had existed for nearly seven centuries, first as a distinct principality and later as a palatinate known variously as Halychyna, Galician Rus', Chervona Rus' / Rus' Czerwona, or the Rus' palatinate / Wojewódz-two Ruskie. Historic Galicia during this long era coincided more or less with what later became the eastern "half" of Habsburg Galicia. This same territory after World War II was incorporated into the Soviet Union; since 1991 it forms part of the sovereign state of Ukraine. With regard to the past, it is perhaps useful to keep in mind five dates (981, 1340, 1772, 1918, and 1939), as markers that delineate the basic periods in the historical evolution of Galicia.

The first documented mention of Galicia appears in the year 981 in the *Rus' Primary Chronicle (Povest vremennykh let)*.[4] Over the following 360 years Galician territory functioned first as a principality and later a kingdom within the medieval polity known as Kievan Rus'. Medieval Galicia essentially coincided with what later was called eastern Galicia, although its borders stretched slightly farther west than the San River and somewhat farther east than the Zbruch (the eastern border of Habsburg Galicia). The principality and kingdom of Galicia shared more or less the same legal and governing structure and the same Eastern Christian culture as the rest of Kievan Rus'. Historic Galicia moved into a new era in the 1340s, when it was subjected to nearly four decades of invasions by Poland, Hungary, and Lithuania. In 1387, Poland annexed the former Rus' kingdom of Galicia, which was transformed into a palatinate (wojewodztwo) within the Kingdom of Poland. Polish administrative structures and Polish laws were gradually introduced. Polish cultural influence, effected by the use of the Polish language and the presence of the Roman Catholic Church, grew in importance, most especially in L'viv (Lwów), the region's political center.

The First Partition of Poland, in 1772, saw Galicia annexed to the Habsburg Empire. As a Habsburg crown land, imperial administrative practice and law were introduced, and German became the province's official language. During the Habsburg era, Galicia's boundaries also changed markedly, expanding in 1795 to the north. The province's boundaries were stabilized only after 1815. From that time, and in contrast to historic Galicia, Habsburg Galicia also included the area west of the San River and south of the Vistula, as far as the city of Cracow (including the adjacent countryside on the northern bank of the river), all of which was inhabited mainly by Poles.

When the Habsburg Empire collpased in late 1918, Austrian Galicia was incorporated into the revived state of Poland. During the "second" Polish period, which was to last only two decades, Galicia ceased to exist as a distinct administrative and territorial unit. It was divided into the palatinates of Kraków/Cracow, Lwów/L'viv, Tarnopol/Ternopil', and Stanislawów/Stanyslaviv. The interwar period was characterized by an increase in usage of the Polish language and by a large influx of Polish settlers into what had been predominantly Ukrainian-inhabited eastern Galicia.

The most recent period began in 1939 with the destruction of Poland and, thus, the outbreak of World War II. At the end of the war, Galician territory that was to the east of the San River – that is, the territory that we have been calling historic Galicia – was annexed to the Ukrainian Soviet Socialist Republic. The Ukrainian period, which covers sixty years down to the present, was interrupted from June 1941 to September 1944 by Nazi Germany's invasion of the Soviet Union and its annexation of Galicia. The Red Army returned in late 1944, and a Soviet regime was re-established, with its centralized command economy and the subordination of all aspects of political, social, and cultural life to the directives of the Moscow-led Communist party.[5] During this period a concerted effort was made to eliminate all vestiges of the region's Polish past. This included the forced deportation of many Poles and the introduction of government-approved Soviet cultural and educational models that were nominally Ukrainian, but in practice largely Russian. Historic Galicia became four Soviet oblasts (later three: L'viv, Ternopil', and Ivano-Frankivs'k). This administrative-territorial structure has remained in place even after the fall of the Soviet Union and the establishment of an independent Ukraine in 1991.

In summary, Galicia existed as a distinct territorial unit from about 980 to 1918 – that is, for 938 years. The Habsburg period represents a mere 136 years or 14.5 percent of Galicia's historical existence. Yet despite its relative brevity, the Austrian period has come to determine in the popular mind what Galicia was, in terms of both territory and cultural identity. We should not forget, however, that for most of its history, for eight centuries (980–1772) *Galicia* essentially meant the lands east of the San River, territory that since the 1940s has been within the boundaries of Ukraine. This is the territory we will refer to as historic or eastern Galicia. Let us now turn to three aspects of the region that may help provide a better understanding of its character: trade and commerce, ethnic diversity, and the Habsburg heritage.

Trade and Commerce

Like many parts of Europe, Galicia is a borderland that links different geographical regions and has served as a meeting place for various peoples and religions. The name *Galicia* is considered by some scholars to be derived from the Indo-European root for the word salt (*hal*). From this root word came the name of the town and later capital city, Halych, as well as the name for the entire region. Galicia is the Latin form of the Rus'-Ukrainian name *Halychyna*.[6] Mines near Halych yielded significant amounts of salt, which was highly valued in the medieval period as a food preservative. Galician salt found its way eastward to Kiev for centuries, after that city's traditional source in the Crimea was cut off by nomadic invasions.

Trade patterns in the region shifted gradually from east-west to north-south following the decline of Kievan Rus' and Poland's annexation of Galicia. By the sixteenth and seventeenth centuries, the cities and towns of historic Galicia were a major destination for traders along routes that connected Poland's royal capital, Cracow, with the Kingdom of Hungary to the south. Galicia's own agricultural and artisanal productions were transported northward and westward via the Vistula and Bug rivers to Warsaw and Gdańsk/Danzig on the Baltic Sea, as well as southward across the Carpathian passes to the towns of northern Hungary (present-day Slovakia).

During the Habsburg era, which began in 1772, Galicia's economy and its status as a transit zone for international trade declined. This was a direct result of the Austrian Empire's economic policy. To the Habsburgs Galicia was primarily a source of raw materials and a market for industrial goods from the empire's western provinces of Bohemia, Moravia, and Lower Austria. As the empire's "internal colony," Galicia, whose trade routes had been enhanced from the 1850s by new railways, was now obliged to direct them south and west. Thus, commerce became directed towards the imperial capital of Vienna, via Cracow, and towards Budapest in Hungary. In the Soviet Ukrainian period after World War II, as in the medieval period, Galician trade patterns were directed eastward. Once again, the region became an important transit zone for international trade. This time the main transit products were gas and oil exports from the Soviet Union, including some extracted in Galicia itself, to its Communist-bloc allies Czechoslovakia, Hungary, Poland, and East Germany, and eventually to western Europe, as well.

Ethnic Diversity

International trade encouraged movement and interaction between people of different cultural backgrounds. The second salient feature of Galician society is therefore its ethnic and cultural diversity. In terms of demographic composition, Galicia was typical of much of central and eastern Europe. Its small towns and cities were usually inhabited by peoples of several different nationalities and religions, most of whom differed from those living in the immediate countryside. The ethnic diversity of Galicia's cities was promoted from the medieval period onward by what might be called demographic engineering on the part of ruling regimes. As early as the thirteenth century, Germans were encouraged by the Galician Rus' princes to settle in their realm. Poland's rulers continued this practice, so that by the fifteenth century Poles, Armenians from the Crimea, and in particular Jews from other parts of Poland and central Europe were all offered incentives to settle in Galicia. In the early 1780s and early 1800s, the Habsburg regime encouraged new waves of Germans from the Rhineland Palatinate and other southwestern German states to settle in compact colonies in the countryside of eastern Galicia. But numerically, the three most important groups in Galicia during the nineteenth century were the Poles, Ruthenians, and Jews.

What were their numbers? This question is impossible to answer because dealing with statistical data about nationality or linguistic groups is intrinsically difficult. Very often governments, whether deliberately or not, manipulate census data to suit their own political purposes. This happened in Habsburg-ruled Austria-Hungary when, during the second half of the nineteenth century, its authorities began to collect population data. Hence, the following figures must be considered at best to be estimates.[7] Galicia had 7.9 million inhabitants in 1910:

45.4 percent were Poles, 42.9 percent Ruthenians, and 10.9 percent Jews. Within historic (eastern) Galicia, Ruthenians formed a majority (62 percent), although there were also significant proportions of Poles (25.3 percent) and Jews (8.2 percent). It is important to note that by the end of the nineteenth century eastern Galicia was by no means exclusively Ruthenian. This is mainly because of the large influx of Poles, who had been encouraged by the Habsburg provincial authorities to settle in urban areas as well as in some rural districts. Between 1869 and 1910 the number of Poles in eastern Galicia almost doubled as a consequence, from 754,000 to 1.3 million.

Galicia's multiethnic character underwent profound changes in the twentieth century. Already during World War I some of the most destructive battles and sieges on the Eastern Front took place on Galician soil (Rava Rus'ka, Przemyśl, Gorlice-Tarnów). These resulted in a large number of civilian casualties, either because of the military conflict or because of the forced deportation and voluntary evacuation of certain elements of the population, in particular Ruthenians of Russophile national orientation, who were suspected by the Habsburg authorities of aiding and abetting the tsarist Russian enemy.[8] The subsequent collapse of the Habsburg Empire precipitated a new war that lasted from November 1919 to June 1919 between Polish and Ukrainian armies for control of eastern Galicia, during which a certain number of Polish and Ukrainian civilians were killed. Having succeeded in annexing all of Galicia in 1919, Poland then proceeded to change the demographic mix of the eastern half of the former Habsburg province. During the 1920s the government encouraged the settlement of over 73,000 Poles from other parts of Poland in areas that had until then been inhabited primarily by Ruthenians/Ukrainians; at the same time an estimated 150,000 Ukrainians emigrated abroad, mostly to Canada, Argentina, and France.[9]

During the brief life of the Nazi-Soviet Pact (August 1939 to June 1941), which eliminated Poland as a country and divided Galicia along the San River, Nazi Germany and the Soviet Union signed agreements on population exchanges. These agreements allowed the Hitler regime to resettle Galician Germans en masse from eastern Galicia to territories closer to the German heartland, in particular Warmia (German: Wartheland). At the same time, the Soviet authorities deported an estimated 400,000 Poles from eastern Galicia to forced labor camps in the Gulag. In June 1941, when Nazi Germany invaded the Soviet Union and annexed eastern Galicia to an administrative entity called Generalgouvernment Polen, virtually the entire Jewish population of Galicia was killed. The last years of the war (1944–1945) witnessed further violence as a result of the Soviet-German military conflict and the simultaneous clashes between Polish and Ukrainian partisans, which led to civilian deaths on both sides and the flight of more Poles from eastern Galicia. In September 1944, the Soviet Union and the restored state of Poland signed agreements on the mutual exchange of populations. The result was the resettlement of over 810,000 Poles, mostly from eastern Galicia, to various parts of postwar Poland, and the resettlement of 482,000 "Ukrainians, Russians, and Rusyns," largely from Galicia west of the San River to eastern Galicia. Finally, in 1947, nearly 140,000 East Slavs who were still living in Poland and who had not joined the exodus to the Soviet Union were forcibly removed and resettled in the northern (Pomerania) and western (Silesia) parts of Poland that had previously belonged to Germany.[10] In effect, old Habsburg Galicia west of the San River became ethnically homogeneous within a few years of the end of World War II.

Basically the same can be said for historic or eastern Galicia. The region's Jews and Germans were eliminated during the war years, and by 1959 the number of Poles had dropped to 93,000, less than 7 percent of their prewar numbers. The postwar years were to witness, however, the arrival of an entirely new group in eastern Galicia: Russians (and russified Ukrainians) from various parts of the Soviet Union. Whereas before the war there may have been at most one thousand Russians in historic Galicia, by 1989 Russians numbered 279,000, or 5.3 percent of the population. But the most marked demographic development in the postwar years has been the steady increase in the proportion of Ukrainians, from 90.6 percent of the population in 1959 to 94 percent in 1989. This trend has continued since Ukraine gained independence in 1991. The results of independent Ukraine's first census (2001) reveal that in historic Galicia the number of Poles has declined further to only 22,700; the number of Russians has dropped to 131,000, less than half what it was only a decade before; while the proportion of Ukrainians has increased to 96.2 percent. Put another way, historic Galicia at the outset of the twenty-first century is less ethnically diverse than at any time in its entire history.[11]

The Habsburg Heritage

Despite it being relatively short, the concept of Galicia in most scholarly as well as popular and fictional literature is associated with the Austrian period. Habsburg Galicia lasted from 1772 to 1918. This was a time of vibrant social change, marked by the first steps toward a modern society. The vast majority of the population was liberated from the impediment of serfdom in 1848. During the second half of the nineteenth century, the Habsburg regime created structures of representative government at the local, provincial, and national levels. This allowed ever larger numbers of citizens to participate in political life. Education, cultural institutions, and publications in a variety of languages flourished. Galicians of all national backgrounds began to have access to new worlds, whether as students and scholars drawn to the province's expanding urban centers of Cracow and L'viv and the cosmopolitan imperial capital of Vienna, or as peasant farmers seeking to improve their economic lot by migrating abroad, notably to the United States and Canada. Finally, the peoples of Galicia were for virtually the entire Habsburg period exposed to the ideology of nationalism, whereby self-designated leaders encouraged them to learn about and to value their national distinctiveness.

It is worth emphasizing that Austrian Galicia was not unique in terms of its cultural diversity. Other European regions such as Alsace, Bohemia, and Silesia were equally diverse, and the Vojvodina, Transylvania, and Macedonia were even more so. In all of these places, the interaction between varying peoples and cultures produced rivalry and competition that had both a positive as well as negative impact on the political, economic, and in particular, cultural status of each group.

Habsburg Galicia had five clearly discernible national groups, two of which, the Armenians and Germans, were numerically much smaller than the other three. The Armenian community, which dated from the thirteenth century, had over time largely assimilated to Polish culture. By the outset of the nineteenth century Galicia's Armenians numbered only 1,500. In subsequent decades, the Armenian presence remained only in the form of the Armenian Rite Catholic Church with its archdiocesan seat in L'viv.[12] Galicia's Germans numbered 65,000 in 1910. The vast majority of them lived in rural settlements, and they did not have much influence on the political or cultural life of the province. It is true that German-speaking Austrian officials dominated the provincial administration in L'viv, Cracow, and to a lesser degree in smaller towns, but few of these officials settled permanently in Galicia.[13] Moreover, many were not Austro-Germans at all, but rather Czechs from Bohemia and Moravia who, because of their official status, were considered to be Germans by the local populace.[14]

Galicia's Jews, or *Galitsiyaner*, were much more important in terms of their numbers and economic, cultural, and political influence than either the Germans or Armenians.[15] During the Habsburg period, the number of Galicia's Jews increased by more than sixfold, from 144,000 (in 1776) to 872,000 (in 1910). This increase was attributable to a high birth rate and to a steady influx of refugees fleeing the neighboring Russian Empire, where a series of pogroms began in the 1880s. Galicia's Jewish population continued to grow, despite the fact that many, both locals and recent immigrants, were moving away to northern Hungary, Budapest, Vienna, or North America. Three-quarters of Galicia's Jews lived in the eastern part of the province, concentrated in towns that were almost entirely Jewish (Brody, Belz, Buchach, Rohatyn, Peremyshliany, Deliatyn, Sokal') and in cities such as L'viv, Zhovkva, Drohobych, Stanyslaviv, Ternopil', and Kolomyia, where they constituted roughly one-third of the population. Their urban presence allowed Jews to dominate large sectors of the Galician economy, in particular trade and small-scale retail sales, as well as to maintain an extraordinarily creative religious and cultural life.

Jewish people have had no one answer to the question of their place in a non-Jewish world, which often came down to the question of whether to assimilate or not to assimilate. Traditionalist rabbis and Talmudic scholars (the *mitnaggedim*) and, most especially, the Hasidim, rejected assimilation into the larger society. Hasidism was the popular religious movement led by several dynasties of spiritual leaders, or rebbes, such as those founded by Shalom Rokeah at Belz, the Hayyim ben Leibush (Halberstam) dynasty at Nowy Sącz, and David Moses Friedman of Chortkiv, that eventually came to dominate Jewish life in Galicia.

For some Jews, the answer was to transform themselves into Habsburg subjects whose religion was Judaism, and in this way enable themselves to participate fully in a secular, non-Jewish society. This group first took its cue from the Haskalah, or Enlightenment movement, with its secular school system centered in the town of Brody. The Haskalah reached its high point during the first half of the nineteenth century. Like the traditionalists, assimilationists were internally divided between those who favored adopting the German language and those who saw adopting Polish (the language of prestige in Galicia) as the best means by which to become full-fledged subjects of the Austrian Habsburgs. Eventually, the Polish option came to prevail among Galicia's Jewish elite. The Ruthenian/Ukrainian option was never seriously considered, because the Ukrainian language and culture lacked the prestige Jews believed was essential for upward social mobility in Habsburg society. With time, "enlightened assimilators" could be found among the elites of Galician society. By 1897, for example, 58 percent of the province's civil servants and judges were of Jewish origin.

Despite the prominent Jewish presence in economic and political life, the vast majority of Galicia's Jews lived in conditions of poverty. This made little difference, however, in the way others looked at them. Poor Jews and rich Jews alike were lumped together and often blamed for the economic woes of the Polish and Ukrainian populations. Galicia's Jews responded in different ways to mounting criticism. Those who remained committed to living where they were tried to change the social structure by joining the socialist and labor movements that emerged in the second half of the nineteenth century. Others, notably the Zionists, argued that a safe and prosperous future for Jews could be secured only by abandoning Galicia altogether and starting new lives in Palestine. Activists, regardless of their orientation, had to mobilize potential supporters in a language the recruits could understand. Both socialists and Zionists therefore supported the movement to transform Yiddish – the Germanic "jargon" in the words of its detractors – into a literary language. By the beginning of the twentieth century, Austrian Galicia was one of the most important centers of the Yiddish language. L'viv (Yiddish: Lemberik/ Lvuv) in particular, became home to both a Yiddish literary movement Jung Galizia and to the first Yiddish daily newspaper, *Lemberger Togblat* (established in 1904).

While it is certainly true that Austrian Galicia was a vibrant center of Jewish life, in the end it was the Poles and Ruthenians who defined the political agenda and ultimately the future of the province. It would, of course, be naive in the extreme to assume that either the Poles or Ruthenians formed monolithic communities, each of which was united behind a common purpose. Like the Jews, these people, too, were internally divided by a wide variety of social and political orientations, and even definitions of what constituted the national cause could differ significantly.[16]

Galicia's Poles were primarily divided between the nobility, consisting of former magnates and gentry, and the peasantry. Indeed, for most of the nineteenth century, it was assumed that the only Poles were those who belonged to the nobility; the remaining Polish-speakers were simply Roman Catholic peasants. This was a gulf that the Polish national movement tried to overcome in the course of the nineteenth century, by insisting that Polish identity should in the future be based on ethnolinguistic and not social criteria.

Ever since the partitions and the disappearance of the Polish state in 1795, Polish political activists (almost exclusively of aristocratic origin) had had as their goal the restoration of an independent Poland from lands they considered to have been occupied by Russia, Prussia, and Austria. From their point of view, all of Habsburg Galicia was historic Polish land waiting to be reunited as part of an independent Poland. The Poles were not successful, however, in changing the political status of their homeland. Indeed, after the abortive Polish revolt against Russia in 1863, some Polish leaders became convinced that further armed revolt could be harmful to the national cause. Some even argued that independent statehood was not the only form of national existence. Such views were inspired by the conservative, Cracow school of Polish historiography, which argued that Poland had been partitioned because of its own social irresponsibility and political anarchy, and that Polish society had to be strengthened through organic cultural work and political calculation, not armed uprisings. These attitudes came to dominate politics in Galicia, led primarily by conservative aristocrats and their supporters, the so-called Stańczyks.[17] For its part, the Austrian government was anxious to reach a political modus vivendi with Galicia's Poles. Given this convergence of political interests, from the 1870s, in return for their loyalty to the Habsburgs, the Poles were left to transform Galicia into a stronghold of Polishness – a potential Piedmont or base for a new Polish state based on nationalist criteria.[18]

But Galicia was also to become a Piedmont for the Ruthenians/Ukrainians. Austrian Galicia, in its entirety, accounted for only about 15 percent of the entire Ukrainian population in 1897. Almost all of the rest lived in the southern provinces of the Russian Empire, from its western borders with Habsburg Austria to the Kuban river east of the Sea of Azov. Nevertheless, while at this time there may have been as many as 21.5 million Ukrainians in the Russian Empire, most had only a vague or even non-existent sense of a distinct national identity. True, there was a handful of intellectuals who argued that Ukrainians formed a distinct people with their own language. But the vast majority of Ukrainians in the Russian Empire were unaware of their Ukrainianness as such. This situation was in large part the result of imperial politics, which denied the existence of Ukrainians. Instead, they were called "Little Russians," and treated as a branch of a single Russian people. In contrast to developments among other stateless Slavic and non-Slavic peoples in central and eastern Europe, who were also experiencing national awakenings during the second half of the nineteenth century, Ukrainians in the Russian Empire had no schools in their own language, no Ukrainian newspapers and no Ukrainian cultural organizations. Furthermore, Ukrainians belonged to an Orthodox Church that denied their nationality, and they lived under a regime that promulgated decrees (in 1863 and 1876) banning the publication or importation of materials in the Ukrainian language.

The contrast with the status of Ruthenians/Ukrainians in Austrian Galicia could not have been greater. In the course of the 1848 revolution the Habsburg authorities, concerned by Polish demands for greater control in Galicia, gave support to the Ruthenians and recognized them as a distinct nationality. Thereafter, Ruthenians established their own cultural organizations, newspapers, and political parties, as well as a system of state-supported elementary, secondary, and post-secondary schools and also several departments (*katedry*) offering Ruthenian-related subjects. The Ukrainian national idea in Habsburg Galicia was not limited to urban-based intellectuals and the school system. It was also propagated throughout the Ruthenian population by a large network of priests, monks, and nuns of the Greek Catholic Church. Indeed, by the outset of the twentieth century, under the leadership of Metropolitan Andrei Sheptyts'kyi, the church had become as effective a promoter of the Ukrainian national idea as any secular organization.[19] Over time, all Ukrainian activists, whether in the Russian Empire or the Austro-Hungarian Monarchy, came to see Galicia as a kind of Piedmont, a land where a sociologically complete, or nearly complete Ruthenian/Ukrainian society had been created. Galicia, they believed, would be the solid base on which to build a political unity that would eventually also encompass Ukrainians in the Russian Empire.[20]

The significance of Galicia as a seedbed for the Polish, as well as the Ukrainian, national movements was evident in the intense commitment both attached to the province's administrative centre – called Lemberg in German, L'viv in Ukrainian, and Lwów in Polish. Indeed, as the literary scholar George Grabowicz contends, perceptions of this city in Ukrainian and Polish history and culture "go to the very heart of national memory and constitute a powerful symbolic narrative of national identity."[21] Lwów was home to such important Polish national institutions as the Ossolineum (Ossoliński National Foundation), the Polish Academy of Arts, the Polish Historical Society, and the Polish Theater, as well as serving as the seat of a Polish Roman Catholic Archdiocese. The university remained a predominantly Polish-language institution. Cheek by jowl with these centers of Polishness along the city's same narrow streets were the largest and most influential

Ukrainian institutions anywhere in the world. These include the popular enlightenment Prosvita Society, the scholarly Shevchenko Scientific Society, the Dniester Insurance Company, and the archeparchial seat of the Greek Catholic Church. Finally, it is not an exaggeration to say that the Polish and Ukrainian presence in L'viv was literally embedded in the soil. The final resting place for generations of both Poles and Ukrainians was the extensive Lychakiv/Łyczakowie cemetery, whose large monuments erected over the tombs of famous Polish and Ukrainian cultural and political figures have been sites of pilgrimage and national inspiration for both peoples down to the present.

Habsburg Galicia, then, was not just another piece of real estate where Poles and Ukrainians lived. In the course of the nineteenth century it became a sacred ground for both the Polish and Ukrainian nationalities. Whereas Ukrainians were, with the exception of the small mountainous strip of land known as the Lemko Region, not interested in Galicia west of the San River, the Poles claimed the entire province as part of their national patrimony. This included not only the city of L'viv/Lwów, soon to be transformed by Polish ideologues into an almost mythological site ever faithful to the idea of Poland (Lwów semper fidelis),[22] but also the rest of eastern Galicia up to the Zbruch River. This meant that one of the legacies of the Habsburg period – that of mutually conflicting claims to the same territory – led after the collapse of the Austrian Empire in 1918 to nearly three decades of conflict between Poles and Ukrainians that ended with forced deportations after World War II.

Another legacy of the Austrian period was a deeply rooted Ukrainian patriotism that persisted despite the efforts of the interwar Polish regime and post-World War II Soviet regime to eliminate it. In the late Soviet period western Ukraine – more precisely former eastern Galicia – still had a reputation as the region most committed to Ukrainian independence. Ever since independence, the Galicians are still perceived by other citizens of Ukraine to be the most committed to the idea of a strong centralized, nation-state that is Ukrainian in content as well as in name.[23]

Conclusion: Regional versus National Identity

Galicia was a historically distinct territory with relatively stable borders for nearly eight centuries until 1772, after which time it expanded primarily in a westward direction. In an effort to distinguish these two territories, this essay has proposed the concept of a pre-1772 historic Galicia and a post-1772 Habsburg Galicia. As long as Habsburg Galicia existed, one can speak of the existence of a regional identity among its inhabitants. The fact that such a Galician identity was expressed in different languages – Polish, Ukrainian, German, or Yiddish – does not make it any less real. Each of these groups used regional prefixes in describing itself and was described as such by co-nationals living elsewhere: Galicia's Poles were *Galicyjanie*, Galicia's Ukrainians were *Halychany*, Galicia's Jews were *Galitsiyaner*, and Galicia's Germans were *Galiziendeutsche*.[24] A Galician identity was celebrated by many writers before and after 1918. Some illustrious examples are writings of the Pole Jan Lam, the Ukrainian Ivan Franko, the Austrian Leopold von Sacher-Masoch, and the Austrians of Jewish background, Karl Emil Franzos and Joseph Roth. Each tried to depict the specificity of the Galician environment and mentality. In both the United States and Canada, Slavic immigrants from this region continued for generations to identify themselves to census-takers not as Poles or Ukrainians, but rather as Galicians.

We should not, however, overstate the case for regional loyalties. The political activists of the largest groups in the region, Poles and Ukrainians, never seriously considered creating a distinct Galician state. Rather, they called for its incorporation either into an independent Poland or an independent Ukraine. It is true that there was a call for the resurrection of an independent Kingdom of Galicia-Volhynia at the close of World War I, but this was short-lived and more a desperate attempt to acquire statehood on however small a part of Ukrainian territory than a rejection by Galician Ukrainians of their otherwise deep commitment to an independent greater Ukraine (Soborna Ukraïna). Galician particularism was revived in the post-Soviet end. As early as 1991, Ukrainian nationalists established a Galician Assembly to strengthen their lobbying influence with the central government in Kiev. This assembly was soon disbanded, however, for fear its existence would encourage further demands from other regions that would result in a "weak" federal structure for the new country.[25] Nevertheless, at the outset of the twenty-first century there is still a small but active group of intellectuals in L'viv – accused by their critics of being separatists – who want to transform Galicia into "an autonomous republic within the framework of Ukraine."[26]

One might ask whether awareness of a historic Galician identity has any validity today, other than as a vehicle for nostalgia. What is the relationship between regions and nation-states during the current era of increased European integration? Many historic regions, Galicia included, are divided between two or sometimes more nation-states. European integration should, in my view, be accompanied by an increase in the self-governing status of such regions and a corresponding decrease in the power of nation-state central governments. At the same time, the international boundaries that now separate countries and that divide historic or geographical regions such as Galicia must be made permeable.[27]

The revival of cultural identities based on historic regions – in other words, the realization that a place like Galicia is historically both a Polish *and* a Ukrainian land – may help the citizens of neighboring countries overcome the unhealthy tendency to equate a given state with a single so-called national culture. It may also help them realize that in order for the New Europe to survive and prosper it must consist of multinational states linked by permeable borders. It is in this sense that a better understanding of historic regions like Galicia may contribute to the further integration of Europe and the future well-being of European civilization.

Notes

1 David Crystal, *The Cambridge Encyclopedia of Language* (Cambridge, 1987), pp. 284–285.
2 There is also an increasingly strong movement calling for Low German (Plattdeutsch), or Low Saxon, to be recognized as a distinct West Germanic language. See the exchange of views on this topic in *Contact Bulletin*, XIV, 1 (Brussels, 1999), pp. 3–4. Of course, ethnic and linguistic diversity is far greater in most European countries when, in addition to the indigenous populations, the new immigrant populations are taken into account.
3 For further details on nomenclature and territorial conceptualization as well as references to other topics discussed in this essay, see Paul Robert Magocsi, *Galicia: A Historical Survey and Bibliographical Guide* (Toronto, Buffalo, and London, 1983).
4 Like most "origins," the date 981 is somewhat arbitrary. Fortified centers and seats of political power (Halych, Zvenyhorod, Cherven) already existed on Galician territory at the outset of the tenth century. It was not until the 1080s that Galicia really began to function as a unified political unit.
5 The Soviet-Polish border agreed to at the close of World War II was slightly different from the 1939 Soviet-Nazi German demarcation line along the San River. In 1945, the boundary was fixed slightly to the east of the San

River, leaving the entire city of Przemysl (Ukrainian: Peremyshl') within Poland.

6 The salt etymology was put forth by the Ukrainian archaeologist, Iaroslav Pasternak, "Zvidkilia nazva Halych," *Students'kyi prapor*, II (L'viv, 1944), pp. 9–15. An alternative view, the so-called heraldic hypothesis, argues that Halych is derived from *halychchia*, a Ukrainian word meaning jackdaw, a crow-like bird similar to that which appears in the coat-of-arms of Galician Rus', devised in 1642 and later used as the official emblem of the Habsburg province until 1918. See Iaroslav B. Rudnyts'kyi, "Nazvy 'Halychyna' i 'Volyn'," *Onomastica Ukraïns'koï vil'noï akademiï nauk*, no. 3 (Winnipeg, 1952), pp. 9–16.

7 The figures given here are derived from the author's calculations on the basis of Austrian statistical data concerning both language and religion. Cf. Paul Robert Magocsi, *A History of Ukraine* (Toronto, London, and Buffalo, 1996), pp. 423–424. Other figures are drawn from Magocsi, *Galicia*, p. 225.

8 As the tsarist Russian Army advanced into Galicia between September and December 1914, nearly 8,000 Ruthenians were interned in an Austrian concentration camp at Thalerhof (near Graz). When the Russian Army and civilian administration evacuated the province in the spring of 1915, an estimated 10,000 Russophile Ruthenians, frightened of Habsburg revenge, fled eastward, settling near Rostov-na-Donu. Only a portion of the Thalerhof detainees and Rostov evacuees were ever able to return to Galicia. On these little-known developments, see V.R. Vavrik, *Terezin i Talergof* (Moscow, 2001) and Anna Veronika Wendland, *Die Russophilen in Galizien* (Vienna, 2001), p. 540ff.

9 The figures given here are from Volodymyr Kubiiovych/Kubijovyč, *Etnichni hrupy pivdennozakhidnoï Ukraïny (Halychyny) na 1.I.1939 / Ethnic Groups of the South-Western Ukraine (Halyčyna-Galicia) 1.I.1939* (Wiesbaden, 1983), pp. xxii–xxiii.

10 There is an extensive literature about the Soviet-Polish population exchanges and the 1947 forced deportation of East Slavs (known as the Vistula Operation / Akcja Wisła) to other parts of Poland. A useful introduction to the problem is found in Bohdan S. Kordan, "Making Borders Stick: Population Transfer and Resettlement in the Trans-Curzon Territories 1944–1949," *International Migration Review*, XXXI, 3 (Staten Island, N.Y., 1997), pp. 704–720.

11 The numbers provided here are based on data in Serhii Chornyi, *Natsional'nyi sklad naselennia Ukraïny v XX storichchi: dovidnyk* (Kiev, 2001); and Stanisław Stępień, "Polacy i inne mniejszości narodowe na Ukrainie w świetle spisu z 5 grudnia 2001 r.," *Biuletyn Ukrainoznawczy*, No. 8 (Przemyśl, 2002), pp. 215–232.

12 The Armenian Rite Catholic Church dates from 1635, when adherents of
the Armenian Apostolic (Gregorian) Church united with Rome and recognized the pope instead of the Armenian Orthodox *Catholicos* as the head of
their church. Scholarly literature on Armenians in Galicia is indicated in
Magocsi, *Galicia*, pp. 244–248.

13 Aside from the older literature on Germans discussed in Magocsi, *Galicia*,
pp. 249–252, see the collection of conference papers in *Nimets'ki kolonïï v
Halychyni / Deutsche Siedlungen in Ostgalizien* (L'viv, 1996).

14 Some writers have suggested it was the period of Habsburg Galicia that
largely created the still existing negative stereotype that Poles have of
Czechs. The nineteenth-century Galician Polish writer Jan Lam captured
the resentment Polish nobles felt toward those germanized Austrian Czech
officials who helped to undermine the centuries-old Polish order in the
province. The attempt in 1859 to replace the Cyrillic alphabet with a Polish-
based Latin alphabet, which provoked the ire of Ruthenian intellectuals
regardless of national orientation, was formulated by a Habsburg official of
Czech nationality, Josef Jireček. But there were also Czechs living in Habsburg Galicia, like Karel Vladislav Zap and František Řehoř, who supported
the national aspirations of the local Ruthenians and promoted awareness of
them in Czech society. On these little-known aspects of Galician interethnic
relations, see Antoni Kroh, "The Pole and the Czech: Two Brothers," in
Teresa Walas, ed., *Stereotypes and Nations* (Cracow, 1995), pp. 45–48; Florian
Zapletal, *Rusíni a naši buditelé* (Prague, 1921); and the essay by Nadja
Valášková on Řehoř, in Stella Hryniuk and Jeffrey Picknicki, *The Land They
Left Behind* (Winnipeg, 1995), pp. iv–vi.

15 Aside from the extensive literature on the Jews of Austrian Galicia in
Magocsi, *Galicia*, pp. 227–244, see Piotr Wróbel, "The Jews of Galicia under
Austrian-Polish Rule, 1869–1918," *Austrian History Yearbook*, XXV (Minneapolis, 1994), pp. 97–138; and the series of essays in Israel Bartal and Ant-
ony Polansky, eds., *Polin: Studies in Polish Jewry*, vol. 12: *Focussing on Galicia:
Jews, Poles, and Ukrainians, 1772–1918* (London and Portland, Ore., 1999),
pp. 3–176.

16 For example, among Galicia's Ukrainian population at the time there
existed the so-called Old Ruthenian and Russophile orientations, whose
spokespersons and institutions denied that there was a distinct Ukrainian
nationality. Instead, they held that Galicia's East Slavs were a branch of the
Russian nationality. See Paul Robert Magocsi, "Old Ruthenianism and Russophilism: A New Conceptual Framework for Analyzing National Ideologies in Late 19th Century Eastern Galicia," in Paul Debreczyn, ed., *American
Contributions to the Ninth International Congress of Slavists*, vol. II, *Literature,*

Poetics, History (Columbus, Ohio, 1983), pp. 305–324; and Anna Veronika Wendland, "Die Rückkehr der Russophilen in die ukrainische Geschichte: Neue Aspekte der ukrainischen Nationsbildung in Galizien, 1848–1914," *Jahrbücher für Geschichte Osteuropas*, XLIX (Stuttgart, 2001), pp. 389–421.

17 The following discussion is based largely on the views of Piotr Wandycz, "The Poles in the Habsburg Monarchy," *Austrian History Yearbook*, III, 2 (Houston, 1967), pp. 261–286.

18 The Piedmont idea is based on the example of Italy, which in 1859 came into being on the basis of the Kingdom of Piedmont-Sardinia, which had already functioned as an independent state and led the way to Italian unification. On Galicia as the Polish Piedmont, see Józef Buszko, *Galicja, 1859– 1914: Polski Piemont, Dzieje narodu i państwa polskiego*, vol. III (Warsaw, 1989).

19 On the pre-World War I activity and views of Sheptyts'kyi, see the chapters by Wolfdieter Bihl and John-Paul Himka in Paul Robert Magocsi, ed., *Morality and Reality: The Life and Times of Andrei Sheptyts'kyi* (Edmonton, 1989), pp. 15–46.

20 Of the many studies on Ruthenians/Ukrainians in Austrian Galicia, a good introduction is Ivan L. Rudnytsky, "The Ukrainians in Galicia under Austrian Rule," *Austrian History Yearbook*, III, 2 (Houston, 1967), pp. 394–429. See also Paul Robert Magocsi, *The Roots of Ukrainian Nationalism: Galicia as Ukraine's Piedmont* (Toronto, 2002).

21 George G. Grabowicz, "Lviv/Lwów Mythical Refractions of a Contested City," unpublished manuscript for the University of Toronto Literary History Project: East Central Europe, 1999, p. 1.

22 L'viv/Lwów attained this inspiring Latin descriptor during the successful efforts of Polish armed forces (ostensibly with the help of Polish civilians) to hold on to the city after the departure of Habsburg authorities on November 1, 1918, and the immediately ensuing outbreak of a Polish-Ukrainian military conflict for control of eastern Galicia.

23 Both before and after the declaration of an independent Ukrainian state in August 1991, the L'viv, Ternopil', and Ivano-Frankivs'k oblasts (historic Galicia) consistently returned the highest percentages in various referenda and elections that indicated strong support for independence and for other causes favored by Ukrainian nationalists. Ukraine's Communist and other leftist parties continue to accuse the post-independence Ukrainian governments of bowing to the demands of "the fascists in the Ukrainian Piedmont" – i.e., Galicia – and of trying to "Galicianize" all of Ukraine. See Andrew Wilson, *Ukrainian Nationalism in the 1990s: A Minority Faith* (Cambridge, 1997), p. 135.

24 It is perhaps the Germans who have maintained, at least in name, the clear-

est sense of a regional identity. In 1946 Galician-German émigrés of the Lutheran (Evangelical) faith living in the western zones of Germany formed the Aid Association of Galician Germans (Hilfskomitee der Galiziendeutschen) to keep alive the memory of their ancestral homeland (*Heimat*) among its members. Its various activities include the publication of an annual almanac (initially using the old Gothic type): *Zeitweiser der Galiziendeutschen* (Stuttgart, 1958–). On the Galician-German communities in Germany as well as in Austria, Sweden, Canada, and the United States, see Julius Krämer, *Aufbruch und Neubeginn: Heimat der Galiziendeutschen*, vol. 2 (Stuttgart-Bad Cannstatt, 1977), esp. pp. 364–619.

25 See the discussion in Wilson, *Ukrainian Nationalism*, pp. 163–168.

26 For a wide-ranging discussion of the various proposals for greater self-rule in Galicia, or western Ukraine, including the desirability of adopting the Latin alphabet instead of Cyrillic for the Ukrainian language, see the special issue entitled "The Federal Republic of Ukraine," *Ï: nezalezhnyi kul'turolohichnyi chasopys*. no. 23 (L'viv, 2002).

27 These ideas are developed more fully in Paul Robert Magocsi, "The End of the Nation-State? The Revolution of 1989 and the National Minorities of East Central Europe," in Valerie Heuberger et al., eds., *Nationen, Nationalitäten, Minderheiten* (Vienna and Munich, 1994), pp. 232–235.

2 Confessional Relations in Galicia

JOHN-PAUL HIMKA

The long-term history of relations among religious groups in the region of Galicia, especially the evolution of tolerance and intolerance, and the most appropriate periodization of this history, are examined in this essay. A survey, albeit brief, of about eight and a half centuries makes possible discernment of larger patterns, with all the imperfections that generalization entails. As is typical for a historical narrative, this survey emphasizes conflictual and transformative moments. It should be kept in mind, however, that until the middle of the twentieth century the developments outlined below took place within a long-standing and fairly stable structure of coexistence among the people of various faiths and nationalities inhabiting Galicia.

The Medieval Principality and Kingdom, c. 1150–1340

The principality of Galicia (Galicia-Volhynia from 1199 and a kingdom after 1253) originated as a Rus' state of the Orthodox faith.[1] As a prosperous commercial center – situated at the crossroads of many cultures – Galicia soon attracted a steady trickle of foreigners of diverse faiths and nationalities, including Jews, Karaites, Sudavians, Lithuanians, Prussians, Iatvingians, Pechenegs, Torks, Polovtsians, Berendeys, Germans, and Poles.[2] The influx of foreigners grew in intensity during the reign of King Iurii II (r. 1323–1340). We may assume that in this period anti-Latin and anti-Judaic texts of Byzantine origin were known to Rus' ecclesiastical and learned circles. Still, there seems to have been a general tolerance on the part of the Rus' state towards other religions. For example, the Orthodox King Lev Danylovych (r. 1264–1301) built a Roman Catholic chapel for his Hungarian wife.

A different tenor was introduced into the medieval principality by the Latins / Roman Catholics in the crusading spirit of the thirteenth century. In 1204 Latin crusaders conquered Constantinople. At about this time the Teutonic Knights began to transfer their activities from the Holy Land to central and eastern Europe. Throughout Europe the mendicant orders preached not only a new piety but also an intolerance that was directed particularly towards Jews.[3] They also engaged in missionary work alongside the crusading orders that invaded Livonia. The Dominicans were established in Galicia in the thirteenth century; they were later joined by the Franciscans.[4] The first serious collisions between Latins and Orthodox in Galicia took place when, during a period of Hungarian rule over Galicia-Volhynia (1219–1234), Roman Catholics allegedly drove out the Rus' clergy and hierarchy.[5] A characteristic episode concerns the negotiations between Prince (later King) Danylo (r. 1238–1264) and the papacy.

Pope Innocent IV (r. 1243–1254) was interested in Danylo's conversion. At first he wanted Danylo to bring Rus' entirely over to the Latin faith, eradicating Greek (Orthodox) rites and customs. However, later he allowed that Rus' could retain a married clergy and use leavened bread in the eucharist. In exchange for Danylo's conversion, the pope offered to organize a large crusade against the Mongols. Danylo carried on the negotiations until it became clear that the pope would be unable to keep his end of the proposed bargain. Relations between Danylo and Rome broke down, and by the mid-1250s Pope Innocent's successor was trying to organize a new crusade, this time not against the Mongols but against Danylo. This mixture of conversion and crusading was typical of the thirteenth century. Tensions between Western and Eastern Christians in the kingdom lingered on, and were perhaps responsible for the poisoning of King Iurii II in 1340.[6]

Red Rus' from 1340 to the Reformation

The Kingdom of Galicia-Volhynia collapsed in 1340 and its territory was integrated at first into Hungary and then into Poland. The ethnoreligious demography of what was now known as Red Rus', and later as the Ruthenian palatinate, underwent a major transformation as a result of massive colonization, particularly by Germans, Poles, and Jews. Others also immigrated into Galicia at this time, including non-Chalcedonian, "monophysite" Armenians, who built their own cathedral in L'viv. Armenians recognized the authority of their Catholicos in

Sis in Cilicia.[7] A small population of Karaites also settled in Halych. The period to the Reformation was characterized by two contradictory impulses: the crusading spirit and the need to integrate the Orthodox nobility.

This was the period in which Roman Catholic dioceses were fully organized on the territory of Galicia.[8] It was also a period in which the Orthodox church of Rus' was subject to persecution. Orthodox cathedrals in L'viv, Przemyśl, and Halych were seized and their buildings and property transferred to the Catholics. Orthodox monasteries were also seized, and some of them were then transferred to the Dominicans. Other persecutory measures were also taken against the Orthodox: In 1370 the governor of Galicia ordered the closure of the Orthodox eparchies, an order soon rescinded by King Kazimierz. In 1375 a Catholic metropolitan province was created in Halych for the purpose of replacing the Orthodox hierarchy there. In 1381 a Roman Catholic inquisitor was appointed for Galicia and Muntenia (Wallachia), and in 1390 Queen Jadwiga founded a Benedictine monastery in Cracow for missionary work among the Orthodox.[9] By the end of the fourteenth century it seems that, outside Przemyśl, the Orthodox hierarchy in Galicia had virtually collapsed.

The Polish state, however, recognized that it was in its interests to integrate the Orthodox nobility, not only of Red Rus' but especially of Lithuania. This was particularly imperative after the death of the Lithuanian ruler Vytautas, in 1430, and the outbreak of a civil war which endangered the Polish-Lithuanian union. In this context a number of concessions were made: In 1432 the Orthodox parishes of L'viv received a charter guaranteeing them the right to practice their religion. In 1433 a statute proclaimed equal rights for the Orthodox clergy, and another statute guaranteed equal rights for the Orthodox nobility. An Orthodox brotherhood was established in 1439 at the Dormition cathedral in L'viv. The period opened, then, with hard blows to the Orthodox Church, from which it slowly recovered, until a major turning point occurred in the 1430s. By the second half of the fifteenth century, an Orthodox hierarchy was once again functioning in Galicia.

In addition to developments in the ecclesiastical and political realms, certain social features emerged. These would have a profound and lasting effect on the balance of forces between the Latins and the Rus' for centuries. Magdeburg Law had already been introduced under Iurii II in the last years of the Galician-Volhynian kingdom, but during the fifteenth century its influence became much greater and more systematic. Magdeburg Law legitimized the ascendancy of Latins over both Orthodox and Jews in the cities. Urban crafts were increasingly dominated by guilds. Non-Catholics were largely forbidden membership in guilds: Orthodox Ruthenians (formerly called Rus') could join only a select few guilds. Armenians were first allowed into guilds in 1600, while Jews were completely excluded until the middle of the eighteenth century.[10]

The Ruthenian Palatinate from the Reformation to the Reconquista

This period, too, was initially characterized by two contradictory impulses. The first was the spirit of religious contestation that characterized the Reformation throughout Europe, of which the intolerance of the victorious Polish Counter-Reformation is a good example. In Galician Rus' this confessional turbulence manifested itself in the polemics surrounding the Union of Brest of 1596. Although the union between the Kievan and Roman churches achieved at Brest was rejected in Galician Rus', debates over the issue were heated and divisive. In L'viv the Rus' bishop remained Orthodox and no Uniate parish was formed in the city until the second half of the seventeenth century. A Uniate bishop was appointed for Przemyśl in 1611, but he was resisted by the local population. The rival Orthodox claimant regained the Przemyśl see by force, but then was arrested and imprisoned.[11]

This was also, however, an era in which the state sought to accommodate the Orthodox nobility. On the eve of the Union of Lublin, which in 1569 joined Poland and Lithuania into a single commonwealth, the privileges of the Orthodox nobility were formally confirmed, in 1563 and again in 1568. Moreover, at this time there was greater tolerance of religious differences in Poland than was usually the case in other places. Many nobles embraced Calvinism and even more radical variants of Protestantism. In the commonwealth the power of the nobility was such that no other authority could limit that estate's choices, even in matters of religion. Thus, the Confederation of Warsaw of 1573 was able to approve a formal guarantee of religious liberty for the land. Protestants appeared in Galicia at this time, but they did not form long-lasting communities.

As in the previous period, *religious* issues divided the population, while *political* considerations mitigated the tensions. Later it would often be the other way around. The Zaporozhian Cossack revolts to the east influenced matters in Galicia. These revolts, which were often framed as a defence of Orthodoxy, exacerbated Catholic-Orthodox tensions throughout the commonwealth, and endowed confessional relations with profound social and political dimensions. For example, Ruthenians and the Armenians both fell under suspicion of disloyalty in 1648 when the Cossack Hetman Bohdan Khmel'nyts'kyi besieged L'viv.

The Jews of L'viv were subjected to frequent harassment, particularly by students running riot in the Jewish section of the city. From 1603 to 1608 the Jews and Jesuits of L'viv engaged in a bitter legal conflict over property.[12] In the countryside, Jews were drawn more deeply into the role of intermediary between landlord and peasant, and this exposed them to the resentment of the latter. Outbreaks of peasant violence against Jews were rare in Galicia itself, but the mass murder of Jews by the Cossacks – the peasants' co-nationals and co-religionists – must have instilled insecurity among Galician Jews. Social relations were hardening along religious and ethnic lines, since landlords were predominantly Roman Catholic Poles and serfs were predominantly Orthodox Ruthenians. Jews leased estates and their appurtenances from landlords and sold liquor to and bought produce from peasants. Each social stratum had its own language, customs, religion, and calendar.

The Cossack revolt, led by Khmel'nyts' kyi, touched off decades of strife and resulted in major territorial losses for the Commonwealth of Poland and Lithuania. By the time the dust settled, at the end of the seventeenth century, Poland had forfeited all of Left-Bank Ukraine to Russia. It did manage to reconquer Right-Bank Ukraine and also to retain Galicia. On these territories the Poles abolished Cossack formations, reintroduced and intensified serfdom, and saw to it that the remaining Orthodox eparchies accepted union with Rome, that is, Przemyśl in 1692, followed by L'viv in 1700. The Orthodox (Stauropegial) Brotherhood accepted union with Rome in 1708. Only one Orthodox monastery survived (Maniava Skete), otherwise Galician Rus' was entirely Uniate.[13]

The Ruthenian Palatinate, 1700–1772

Uniatism was imposed on Galician Rus' a century after the original union within the context of a general reconquest of Ruthenian (Ukrainian) territories by Poland. It therefore lacked the more creative, idealistic vision of church unity that had prevailed in Belarus and other East Slavic regions from 1596 to the middle of the seventeenth century.

Instead, Uniatism in Galicia proved, at first, to be an instrument of latinization. The Uniates were treated as second-class Catholics by the
Poles. Their church was run by monks of the Basilian Order, who, while
of the Byzantine-Greek rite, were of Polish Roman Catholic origin or at
any rate thoroughly immersed in Polish culture.[14] In 1720 the Uniates
of the entire commonwealth gathered for the provincial synod of
Zamość, which was largely dominated by the Basilians and where many
latinizations were approved for the Rus' church.

The early eighteenth century was the heyday of Sarmatism among
the Polish gentry. Sarmatism was a cultural style and political attitude
that was convinced of the superiority of Polish institutions and customs, deliberately rejected Western values and culture, and displayed a
religious bigotry unusual for Poland. This was an era in which suspected witches and Jews were cruelly persecuted.[15] At the end of this
period, however, the Polish Enlightenment and the reforms of the
1760s once more strengthened tolerance throughout the Polish and
Lithuanian Commonwealth.

The Habsburg Kingdom of Galicia and Lodomeria, 1772–1918

With the three partitions of Poland and its transfer to Austrian rule,
Galicia – now officially renamed the Kingdom of Galicia and Lodomeria – was exposed to the intense enlightened-absolutist impulses of
the Habsburg monarchs. Maria Theresa (r. 1740–1780) proclaimed the
Roman Catholic and Uniate churches to be equal and renamed the latter the Greek Catholic Church. Her son Joseph II (r. 1780–1790) continued her policies, and issued a series of patents of toleration, which
expanded freedom of religion in the empire. Since the Roman Catholic
Church had previously enjoyed many advantages, it experienced this
equalization as a loss and therefore opposed many of the imperial measures taken on behalf of the Greek Catholics. Roman and Greek Catholic priests vied with one another to gain adherents to their rites, and the
Austrian government had to intervene to regulate this competition for
souls. A major result of the Habsburgs' improvement of the status of
the Greek Catholic Church was the emergence of an educated Ruthenian clergy that later assumed leadership of a national movement.[16]

Joseph II's policy toward the Jews, notably in his patent of 1789,
mixed emancipatory goals with practical restraints on their activities.
For example, Jews were forbidden to live in the countryside unless
they worked as farmers; the intent was to move the Jews out of com-

merce and money-lending and into a "productive" branch of the economy. Both Maria Theresa and Joseph II regulated and reformed the
relations between landlords and peasants. Since the landlords were
mainly Roman Catholic, while many of the peasants were Greek Catholic, this had implications for relations between the confessions as well.
But the attempts of these two enlightened absolutist rulers to alleviate
social tensions only came to fruition in the next historical period.

There can be no doubt that a fundamental transformation of social
relations took place in the later Habsburg period. The abolition of serfdom in 1848 reduced landlord-peasant tensions, but the unfinished
business of who should get the forests and pastures after emancipation
embroiled landlords and peasants in court cases and extra-legal conflicts for decades thereafter. Further legislation in the 1860s aimed at
fostering commerce and industry, and the building of the railways, set
the stage for the rapid development of a money economy in Galicia.
Jewish participation in the new economic environment seems to have
increased tensions between Jews and Christians.

Antagonisms between Roman Catholics and Greek Catholics intensified. After the revolution of 1848–1849 they had mainly a political basis,
as a reflection of the Polish-Ruthenian power struggle. An attempt was
made by Rome to settle the differences between Roman and Greek
Catholics, the Concordia of 1863, but it had little practical effect.[17] Until
the 1880s most of the Ruthenian intelligentsia had a pro-Russian
orientation, which went hand in hand with an attraction to Russian
Orthodoxy.[18] This Russophilism developed primarily as an anti-Polish
reaction.

Many Galician Russophiles emigrated in the 1860s and 1870s to the
Kholm/Chełm eparchy, the last remaining Uniate eparchy in the Russian Empire. There the ethnically Ukrainian inhabitants belonged to a
highly latinized, highly polonized version of the Uniate church. The
Galician newcomers helped the tsarist authorities in their brutal suppression of Polonism, latinization and, by the mid-1870s, Uniatism itself
within the Kholm eparchy. The Kholm events added to the conflict in
Galicia between Poles, who were Roman Catholics, and Ruthenians,
who were Greek Catholics. When a Russophile priest encouraged a
Greek Catholic parish in Galicia to convert to Orthodoxy in 1882, the
Polish administrative and ecclesiastical elite in Galicia seized upon the
occasion to raise the alarm in Vienna and the Vatican. Over the course of
the next decade there was massive intervention from above into the
affairs of the Greek Catholic Church in Galicia. Measures adopted to

"sanitize" the Church ranged from forcing the Metropolitan of Halych to resign to deploying Jesuit missionaries into the Ruthenian countryside. Most Greek Catholics felt that Rome and Vienna had overreacted, and they blamed the local Poles for what had happened.[19]

Increasingly, as in the incidents outlined above, secular interests intruded into church affairs. Polish nationalists, the National Democrats, sought to expand the number of Roman Catholic parishes in the eastern, Ruthenian-inhabited part of Galicia. Their sole aim, in which the Roman Catholic archbishop of L'viv proved cooperative, was to strengthen the Polish element in the region.[20] Ruthenian national populists often had a secular outlook but they too had a clear goal in the ecclesiastical realm: the construction of a national church, dependent on neither the Poles nor the Russians.

Christian-Jewish conflict also intensified, partly because the Jews of Galicia were fully emancipated in 1868.[21] Jewish tavernkeepers and usurers were excoriated in the populist press, both Polish and Ruthenian. Modern anti-Semitic doctrines filtered into Galicia in this period and made inroads also among the clergy. Both Christian churches found themselves at odds with the Jews over issues connected with the secularization of society: Jews generally supported liberal policies aimed at constructing a society in which no one confession was favored above others. The Christians fought for the maintenance of Christian values and Christian influence in the educational system and in legislation regulating family matters and holidays. Catholics of both the Greek and Roman rite accused the Jews (and Masons) of guiding the godless socialist movement.

Finally, this period saw the return of Orthodoxy as a factor in confessional relations, and not just because of the Ruthenian Russophiles. After Austria's annexation of Bosnia, certain circles in the Russian Empire developed a proactive policy of winning Ruthenians over to pro-Russian positions and persuading Greek Catholics to convert to Orthodoxy.[22] The Austrian government was able to curtail conversions in Galicia. It could do nothing, however, to prevent Galician emigrants to the Americas from accepting Russian Orthodox priests as their pastors. This development eventually had significant consequences in the homeland.

At the outset of World War I, tsarist Russian forces occupied eastern Galicia. From September 1914 to the spring of 1915 the Greek Catholic Church was persecuted and the Orthodox Church promoted in its place. Greek Catholic Metropolitan Andrei Sheptyts'kyi was arrested and exiled to the Russian interior. Tsarist soldiers perpetrated pogroms against the Jewish population.

With the end of the war and the collapse of Austria-Hungary in late 1918, hostilities broke out between Poles and Ukrainians over the future of Galicia. The church hierarchies tended to side with their own people, as the correspondence between the Roman Catholic Arch-bishop of L'viv Józef Bilczewski and the Greek Catholic Metropolitan Sheptyts'kyi attests.[23] The Polish forces in L'viv accused the Jews of sid-ing with the Ukrainians, and after taking the city they engaged in a pogrom – the intensity of which is assessed differently in Polish and Jewish historiography.[24]

"Eastern Little Poland" in the Second Polish Republic, 1919–1939

Animosity between Poles and Ukrainians continued after the end of the Polish-Ukrainian war, in June 1919, and the incorporation of Gali-cia into the restored Polish state. The ongoing Polish-Ukrainian con-flict had numerous manifestations in the ecclesiastical sphere. Greek Catholic priests were fined for filling out baptismal certificates with names transliterated from Cyrillic, instead of using the equivalent Pol-ish forms. The Polish state prevailed upon the Vatican to restrict the jurisdiction of the Greek Catholic Church to the territory of Galicia, although Greek Catholic parishes had been formed in Volhynia during World War I and its revolutionary aftermath. Ukrainians in Galicia, although Greek Catholics, protested the expropriation and destruction of Orthodox churches in the nearby Kholm/Chełm region and Podla-chia, in which both state authorities and the Roman Catholic hierarchy were complicit. Anti-Semitism intensified among both Poles and Ukrainians,[25] and anti-Semitic parties maintained close relations with the Roman Catholic Church. Poland's primate, Cardinal Hlond, even went so far as to issue a pastoral letter identifying the Jews with com-munism.

World War II, 1939–1944

Soviet forces occupied Galicia in September 1939. They installed an atheistic regime which singled out the Greek Catholic Church for per-secution. Soviet security forces began to involve the Russian Orthodox Church in plans to liquidate Greek Catholicism. The Roman Catholic Church also suffered under Soviet rule and many of its members were deported to the Soviet Gulag. The anti-church momentum was interrupted in the summer of 1941 by Operation Barbarossa, Nazi Germany's invasion of the Soviet Union.[26] Germany annexed what it called the Distrikt Galizien to the Generalgouvernement Polen.

In the bloody period of Nazi rule, between 1941 and 1944, most Jews of Distrikt Galizien were murdered on so-called racial, not religious grounds. The record of the Christian churches during the Holocaust is mixed. Some priests collaborated in one way or another in the extermination process. But a recent study argues that the churches were actually the most important institutions trying to prevent the murder of Jews in eastern Galicia.[27] The efforts of Metropolitan Sheptyts'kyi to save Jews were exceptional.[28] Poles were murdered, too, above all by Ukrainian nationalists in Volhynia, but also in Galicia. This led to bloody reprisals by the Polish Home Army. The violent Polish-Ukrainian conflict, although primarily an issue of nationalist politics, had ecclesiastical repercussions, and once again the Roman Catholic and Greek Catholic archbishops of L'viv corresponded, each defending the perspective of his own people.[29]

The Western Oblasts of the Ukrainian SSR and Independent Ukraine, 1944 to the Present

Most of the Poles who remained in Galicia under Soviet Russian rule were soon forcibly resettled to Poland. Ukrainians living on the other side of the new Polish border were also forcibly resettled, either to Soviet Ukraine or to the formerly German territories of southwestern and northern Poland.[30] Ukrainian Greek Catholic and Orthodox churches on the Polish side of the border were often turned into Roman Catholic churches. With the Poles gone, and the Jews dead, the biological basis for relations among the confessions in Galicia had been removed. Previously, conflict had not endangered cohabitation – now it had destroyed it.

The Soviets, with the aid of the Russian Orthodox Church, abolished the Greek Catholic Church in Galicia. The process was forcible and bloody, and those who survived underground as Greek Catholics were left extremely bitter towards the Orthodox. Some Greek Catholics preferred to worship in the reduced number of surviving Roman Catholic churches, rather than go over to the Orthodox.

In 1989, during the waning days of the Soviet Union, the Greek Catholic Church was able to emerge from underground. It was no longer, however, the church to which virtually all Galician Ukrainians belonged. Now it was challenged, particularly by the emergence of the

Ukrainian Autocephalous Orthodox Church. The first years of religious freedom were marred by intense, and occasionally violent interconfessional rivalry, especially when Catholic and Orthodox each laid claim to the single church in any one village. Now the population, especially in the countryside, was relatively homogeneous ethnically and socially, but religion remained a profound source of division. These problems were to continue in some cases after Ukraine became an independent state in 1991.

Even within the Greek Catholic Church, which achieved dominance in the three western oblasts of L'viv, Ivano-Frankivs'k, and Ternopil', there were divisions between those who had worshipped underground and those who had accepted Orthodoxy, and between those who were pro-Latin and those who favoured "easternizing." Within the hierarchy and consistories tensions existed between the locals, that is, those who had lived in Ukraine all along, and those who had come from the diaspora – to occupy the most important positions.

The Roman Catholic Church was also able to develop as a result of the new freedoms, and the L'viv archdiocese of the Latin rite was revived in 1991.[31] The expansion of the Roman Catholic Church in Galicia is viewed with distrust by many Ukrainians, who see this as the first step toward the restoration of Poland's claim to Galicia. Just across the border, relations between Greek and Roman Catholics in Przemyśl have deteriorated badly, with the main bone of contention being ownership of the former Greek Catholic cathedral.[32]

The factors shaping the history of inter-confessional relationships in Galicia over the last millennium were a reflection of larger developments in European history: conversion, Crusades, Reformation, Counter-reformation, Enlightenment, nationalism, Communism, Nazism, and Fascism. Galicia was anything but isolated. A peculiarity of the region for most of its history was the close association of particular religions to particular peoples. The relations between the confessions sometimes affected and sometimes were affected by relations between the nationalities. Increasingly over time an accretion of non-religious factors, especially social and political ones, encumbered relations among the confessions. The long perios in which inter-confessional relationships were also inter-nationality relationships ended during World War II and its aftermath. Perhaps the historically formed culture of inter-confessional conflict explains why it broke out again in post-Communist Galicia, despite the fact that the region was more homogeneous and more secular than it had ever been in the past.

Notes

1 I use the contemporary terminology to refer to the Ukrainians in different historical epochs: Rus' for the Middle Ages, Ruthenians for the early modern and Austrian periods (although for the early modern period, the term also included the Belarusan inhabitants of Poland-Lithuania), and Ukrainians for the twentieth century.

2 I.P. Kryp'iakevych, *Halyts'ko-volyns'ke kniazivstvo* (Kiev, 1984), p. 20.

3 Heiko Oberman, "The Travail of Tolerance," in Ole Peter Grell and Bob Scribner, eds., *Tolerance and Intolerance in the European Reformation* (Cambridge, 1996), p. 23.

4 Władysław Abraham, *Powstanie organizacyi kościoła łacińskiego na Rusi*, vol. 1 (L'viv, 1904), pp. 111, 169–70.

5 Abraham believes that the chronicle account is untrue, but supposes that the Roman Catholic clergy indeed acted aggressively at that time. Ibid., p. 102.

6 Francis Dvornik, *The Slavs in European History and Civilization* (New Brunswick, N.J, 1962), pp. 214–215.

7 Jerzy Kłoczowski, *Histoire religieuse de la Pologne* (Paris, 1987), pp. 113–114.

8 Tadeusz M. Trajdos, *Kościół Katolicki na ziemiach ruskich Korony i Litwy za panowania Władysława II Jagiełły (1386–1434)*, vol. 1 (Wrocław, 1983), pp. 169–290.

9 Osyp Zinkewych and Andrew Sorokowski, eds., *A Thousand Years of Christianily in Ukraine: An Encyclopedic Chronology* (New York, Baltimore, Toronto, 1988), pp. 68–69.

10 Trajdos, *Kościół Katolicki*, pp. 287–90. Ia. P. Kis', *Promyslovist' L'vova u period feodalizmu, XIII–XIX st.* (L'viv, 1968), p. 70.

11 Frank E. Sysyn, *Between Poland and the Ukraine: The Dilemma of Adam Kysil, 1600–1653* (Cambridge, Mass., 1985), pp. 91–92, 101–102.

12 Vladimir Melamed, *Evrei vo L'vove (XIII-pervaia polovina XX veka): sobytiia, obshchestvo, liudi* (L'viv, 1994), pp. 81–84.

13 Antonii Petrushevych, "Iosyf Shumlianskii, pervyi l'vovskii uniiatskii epyskop," *Halychanyn*, I, 1 (L'viv, 1862), pp. 117–124.

14 John-Paul Himka, "The Conflict between the Secular and the Religious Clergy in Eighteenth-Century Western Ukraine," *Harvard Ukrainian Studies*, XV, 1/2 (Cambridge, Mass., 1991), pp. 35–47.

15 Melamed, *Evrei vo L'vove*, pp. 92–93.

16 Oleh Turii, "Die Griechisch-Katholische Kirche und die Entstehung der ukrainischen nationalen Bewegung in Galizien," *Ostkirchliche Studien*, XLVII (Würzburg, 1998), pp. 3–21.

17 The text of the Concordia is published in *Collectanea S. Congregations de Propaganda Fide seu decreta instructiones rescripta pro apostolicis missionibus*, vol. 1 (Rome, 1907), doc. 1243, pp. 685–688.

18 Oleh Turii, "Konfesiino-obriadovyi chynnyk u natsional'nii samoidentyfikatsï ukraïntsiv Halychyny v seredyni XIX stolittia," *Zapysky Naukovoho tovarystva im. Shevchenka, CCXXXIII: NTSh, Pratsi istorychno-filosofs'koï sektsiï* (L'viv, 1997), pp. 69–99.

19 For details, see John-Paul Himka, *Religion and Nationalism in Western Ukraine: The Greek Catholic Church and the Ruthenian National Movement in Galicia, 1867–1900* (Montreal and Kingston, Ontario, 1999).

20 Janusz Gruchała, *Rząd austriacki i polskie stronnictwa polilyczne w Galicji wobec kwestii ukraińskiej (1890–1914)*, Prace Naukowe Uniwersytetu Śląskiego w Katowicach, no. 981 (Katowice, 1988), pp. 64, 128.

21 Filip Friedmann, *Die galizischen Juden im Kampfe um ihre Gleichberechtigung 1848–1868* (Frankfurt am Main, 1929).

22 Rich archival materials on this subject are available in Vienna, in the Allgemeines Verwaltungsarchiv: Ministerium des Innern, Präsidiale, 22 Russophile Propaganda in gen. 1903 [sic; should read 1908]–1912.

23 *Nieznana korespondencja arcybiskupów metropolitów lwowskich, Józefa Bilczewskiego z Andrzejem Szeptyckim w czasie wojny polsko-ukraińskiej, 1918–1919* (L'viv and Cracow, 1997).

24 There is a detailed account in Frank Golczewski, *Polnisch-jüdische Beziehungen 1881–1922: Eine Studie zur Geschichte des Antisemitismus in Osteuropa* (Wiesbaden, 1981), pp. 185–205.

25 Shimon Redlich, "Jewish-Ukrainian Relations in Inter-War Poland as Reflected in Some Ukrainian Publications," *Polin*, Vol. XI (London and Portland, Oreg, 1998), pp. 232–246.

26 Bohdan Rostyslav Bociurkiw, *The Ukrainian Greek Catholic Church and the Soviet State, 1939–1950* (Edmonton and Toronto, 1996).

27 Dieter Pohl, *Nationalsozialistische Judenverfolgung in Ostgalizien 1941–1944: Organisation und Durchführung eines staatlichen Massenverbrechens* (Munich, 1997), p. 322.

28 Shimon Redlich, "Sheptyts'kyi and the Jews during World War II," in Paul Robert Magocsi, ed., *Morality and Reality: The Life and Times of Andrei Sheptyts'kyi* (Edmonton, 1989), pp. 145–162.

29 Józef Wolczański, "Korespondencja arcybiskupa Bolesława Twardowskiego z arcybiskupem Andrzejem Szeptyckim w latach 1943–1944," *Przegląd Wschodni*, II, 2 [6] (Warsaw, 1992–1993), pp. 465–484.

30 Iurii Slyvka, ed., *Deportatsiï: zakhidni zemli Ukraïny kintsia 30-kh – pochatku*

50-kh rr.: dokumenty, materialy, spohady u tr'okh tomakh, vol. 1, *1939–1945 rr.* (L'viv, 1996); and vol. 2, *1946–1947 rr.* (L'viv, 1998).

31 By 1998, the L'viv Roman Catholic Archdiocese had 230 churches and chapels. "Pol's'ka Rymo-katolyts'ka Tserkva na zakhidn'o-ukraïns'kykh zemliakh," *Sivach* (Stamford, Conn.), June 21, 1998.

32 For details, see Chapter 11 of this volume.

3 Ethnic Communities in the Towns of the Polish-Ukrainian Borderland in the Sixteenth, Seventeenth, and Eighteenth Centuries

JERZY MOTYLEWICZ

For the purpose of this chapter, the Polish-Ukrainian borderland is defined as a region which covers an area extending approximately a hundred kilometers on either side of the present Polish-Ukrainian border. The political history of this territory was very complicated during the "tribal" period of the seventh to ninth centuries, and the difficulties continued throughout the Middle Ages. Events during these early periods had important consequences for the national composition of the population in the region. Settlement patterns were influenced in different ways by each of the various states that exercised power in various parts of this borderland region, whether Kievan Rus', Piast Poland, Lithuania, or Hungary.[1] Initially, migrations were largely spontaneous. But from the late Middle Ages on they were decisively shaped by the political and economic objectives of the Polish-Lithuanian and Hungarian states. The settlement policies of secular landlords and of Western and Eastern church administrations also played significant roles.[2] Immigration by German-speakers from Silesia and southern Germany was mostly promoted by kings and by secular nobles. Finally, there was also the long, systematic, and intensive process of Jewish settlement, which increased at the end of the fifteenth century – although some Jewish communities had been established by the eleventh century, and possibly even earlier.

Among the forty-six more important towns and cities of the Polish-Ukrainian borderland were Przemyśl, L'viv, and Stanyslaviv. Immigration to urban areas by members of other nationalities (Armenians, Scots, Vlachs, Czechs) always remained primarily a matter of individual choice.[3] As a result of such migration, most towns in the region, both old and new, became ethnically mixed. The surrounding villages, by contrast remained monoethnic, even after the "incorporation laws" of the

Table 3.1 Religious composition of select towns in the Polish-Ukrainian borderland in the mid-eighteenth century.

Town	Roman Catholic		Greek Catholic		Jewish	
	n	%	n	%	n	%
Dynów	1332	73.1	79	4.2	435	23.5
Drohobycz	1274	34.0	263	7.0	2200	58.8
Jarosław	2683	53.7	1196	23.9	1116	22.3
Leżajsk	1628	57.1	484	16.9	738	25.8
Łańcut	1368	62.0	–	–	809	37.1
Mościska	1230	62.2	238	12.1	494	25.1
Przemyśl	1202	39.5	147	4.8	1692	55.6
Przeworsk	2802	75.9	–	–	887	24.0
Radymno	860	79.4	196	18.2	26	2.4
Rzeszów	1661	50.1	–	–	1648	49.8
Sambor	4016	68.1	378	6.4	1500	25.4
Sanok	346	48.7	184	14.7	259	36.4
Stryj	3559	88.8	225	5.6	220	5.4
Wisznia	462	59.9	248	32.1	61	7.9

Source: Jerzy Motylewicz, *Miasta ziemi przemyskiej i sanockiej w drugiej połowie XVII i XVIII wieky* (Przemyśl and Rzeszów, 1993), Table 18.

Middle Ages, which stipulated settlement conditions according to "German (or Magdeburg) law." The later development of the feudal system eventually impeded further large-scale migration. The most ethnically mixed areas, where Polish and Ruthenian populations became intertwined, were concentrated in the area between the Upper Dniester and the Upper and Middle San rivers.[4] The Polish population predominated in the western part of this area and the Ruthenian population in its southeastern part. Historical research has not yet provided sufficient information concerning the population distribution of the different ethnic groups in all of the region's towns. We can, however, formulate some hypotheses, relying mostly on detailed research carried out in certain western districts.[5] Here Poles formed the majority, representing about 60 percent of the population for towns in the Przemyśl area and 56 percent in the Sanok area. By contrast, Ruthenians were no more than 30 percent of the population in these same areas, as becomes evident in Table 3.1 (in which it seems safe to assume that the category "Roman Catholic" is basically the equivalent of ethnic Poles and "Greek Catholic" of Ruthenians).

Unfortunately, we do not possess comparable information for areas situated further east, which were very much influenced by Ruthenian, Moldavian, and Vlach migrations. Nevertheless, it seems that the further east we look the larger is the Ruthenian speaking population. Certain groups that were present in these eastern areas were almost entirely absent from the western part of the region. The term *Ruthenian* was often applied to all people communicating in an East Slavic language and belonging either to the Orthodox or Greek Catholic Church, regardless of their precise ethnic origin.[6] For example, it could apply to Orthodox or Greek Catholic groups such as Moldavians and Vlachs as well as to ethnic Ruthenians.

Towns incorporated between the second half of the sixteenth and the end of the eighteenth centuries were settled mostly by people coming from nearby villages. Therefore, the newly founded towns in the northwestern area of the Polish-Ukrainian borderland, where Poles represented the majority of the population, were also settled mostly by Poles. By contrast, in the southeastern parts of the borderland region, where ethnic Ruthenians formed the majority of the population, they came to represent a majority of the population in thirteen of the forty-six towns.[7] Until the beginning of the seventeenth century, Polish and Ruthenian groups formed the basic elements of the urban population in the majority of these towns. This situation changed in the course of the eighteenth century, when Jews, despite regulations to impede their settlement, became the second most numerous group, after the Poles.

Germans

Germans, indicated in the sources as *alemanicum*, settled mostly in the western districts of the borderland region, but also in some towns further east. Exact ethnic origins and figures are difficult to determine, but it is unlikely that they ever exceeded one-third of the population of the towns in which they settled.[8] Germans were invited with a view to the specific economic or defensive roles they might play. As a result, the municipal administrations of some towns in the sixteenth century were predominantly German-speaking, although their proportion fell sharply by the beginning of the following century. In every town where they settled, from the thirteenth century onwards, members of this ethnic group implemented the so-called German Law (Magdeburg Law), which affected all aspects of local government. Terms such as *hajn czynsz* (real estate tax) and *szragen czynsz* (commercial tax) and the use of German language in the first town books reveal the extent of German influence in the sixteenth century.[9]

German Law buttressed the identity and durability of the group, which maintained its own self-government, its justice, and its crafts organizations, not to mention its religion and accompanying value system. This was especially important for Germans of the Roman Catholic faith, who enjoyed full civic rights from the very beginning. In the early sixteenth century, however, many German Catholics converted to the Lutheran faith. The religious conflicts which culminated in the Counter-Reformation led eventually to the disappearance of Germans as a distinct community. This trend was enhanced by the fact that German speakers were not residentially segregated. Hence, there were no barriers to mixed marriages and to the assimilation of the Germans, most of whom eventually adopted the Polish language and identity.

Poles

As towns became formally incorporated, the Polish community, like the German, obtained a legal basis for its civic rights, without any of the constraints that were imposed upon other groups. The legal status of Polish burghers rested on the dominant position of the Roman Catholic faith, which was enshrined in the incorporation privileges and in other supplementary documents.[10] Their privileged position was also evident in voting rights, which were not fully available to other ethnic groups. Polish burghers came to exercise a dominant position in the municipal administration and the guilds (at least in all those guilds in which Poles were active). Poles became the economically dominant element, not only in trade but also in craft production. Whereas the Polish language ranked behind Latin as an administrative language, it was first in terms of everyday use as a lingua franca among various groups. All other languages were restricted to use at home and for religious practices – Ukrainian, Yiddish/Hebrew, and Armenian.

The urban settlement pattern of Poles began to change in the middle of the seventeenth century. Prior to this it was concentrated in the town centers, with only a few enclaves elsewhere. Residential segregation gradually gave way to a general ethnic mingling, a result not only of the arrival of Jews but also of changing patterns of real estate ownership. The habits and value systems of the Polish group were closely linked to its religious faith, which marked a visible boundary from most other groups. Polish culture certainly influenced other ethnic groups, especially the Ruthenians, but its strength began to diminish in the late seventeenth and eighteenth centuries. There were a number of reasons for this, including physical dispersal, the loss of its dominant economic position, demographic decline because of warfare, the flight of many citizens, rising mortality rates, and the increasing limitations imposed on urban self-government.[11]

Ruthenians

The location and social structure of the Ruthenian population derived largely from its religious status. Orthodoxy was considered by Latin-rite Roman Catholics to be a "schismatic" faith, and it had no legal position whatsoever. Although Orthodoxy was not actively repressed, adherents of the Orthodox confession nonetheless occupied a much worse position than those of the dominant Roman Catholic faith. Before the Union of Brest, 1596, and even for some time afterwards, Catholic and Orthodox populations were usually to be found close by one another but in separate churches, with the latter tending to inhabit the more peripheral zones. Thus, the majority of the Ruthenian population was to be found in the suburbs, where it was easier for them to engage in agriculture. This situation cannot be attributed entirely to their new legal status following incorporation, since the same pattern can be observed in the medieval period when Rus'/Ruthenian princes were still the leading political force in the country.

In the early modern period a certain religious, geographical, and mental "isolationism" became evident among all groups, and the Orthodox population was no exception. As already noted, the term *Ruthenian* was commonly applied to all Eastern Christians, regardless of their actual ethnic origin. Isolationism was less conspicuous in economic life, but even here there was to some extent an ethnic division of labor in the way each group created its own organizational forms. All guilds were dominated by Roman Catholics, that is, by ethnic Poles. Ethnic divisions were stronger in the larger towns and the cities, where each group was numerous enough to build up strong internal links and even a degree of economic self-sufficiency. In smaller towns it was essential to maintain external links, so the internal unity of each group was correspondingly weaker.

In the Polish-Ukrainian borderland region the Reformation gave birth to a new set of relations between the Roman Catholic Church and the Orthodox. On the one hand, not only did both churches emphasize their internal unity, but at least in some fields Roman Catholics found cause to treat the Orthodox as their equals. On the other hand, the Reformation and Counter-Reformation led also to greater division and strife, in particular among priests at the lower levels of church life. In Roman

Catholic circles, it was common to consider Orthodoxy as a sectarian faith comparable to the new Protestant churches, and such attitudes inevitably soured relations.[12] If the Orthodox were excommunicated, then any kind of relations with them, such as employment or entering into a relation of godparenthood, was considered undesirable and forbidden. In this way the Roman Catholic clergy accentuated the division between Poles and Ruthenians and contributed to the isolation of the latter. Ruthenians did sometimes have rights to take part in the election of municipal administrations. But they were more often than not excluded from these rights, it seems, as a consequence of earlier rules that prevented them from settling in the town center and from becoming full members of guilds or occupying any position in the administration. Although exceptions could be made for specific families, the Orthodox never obtained a general right to be elected to the municipal council or to the administration of the guilds.[13]

In smaller towns, where the proportion of Ruthenians was higher, the owners of workshops – most often for economic reasons – did not insist on their right to restrict guild recruitment of artisans according to nationality. Sometimes Ruthenian artisans received the same rights as other members of the guilds, including the obligation to take part in funeral ceremonies.[14] Yet, even when equal rights were introduced, Ruthenians might still be ineligible for offices in the municipal administration.[15] Regulatory practice varied from one town to another. In some, the sons of Orthodox families were not granted access to certain crafts.[16] In other cases, town elders proclaimed the unity of the population and pledged to observe the principle of equal rights for Poles and Ruthenians.

It took a long time after 1596 before the Orthodox population of these borderlands could be integrated into the new Uniate (Eastern-rite Catholic) Church. How this affected their participation in the life of the town varied considerably. Latin-rite Roman Catholics often felt threatened by this evolution. They were reluctant to share their rights with the Uniates, whom they continued to despise to the same degree as when they had been Orthodox. For their part, the Uniates aspired to full equality. A decree issued in 1611 by King Sigismund III, apparently under Roman Catholic pressure, certified that it was forbidden for Uniates to hold municipal office unless they had previously received this right as a special privilege.[17] Royal inspectors recommended that four councillors of Roman Catholic faith be selected for each single Uniate selected, but these decrees and privileges were not always implemented.

The position of those who remained loyal to Orthodoxy even after the emergence of the Uniate Church was particularly difficult. The severe conflicts between the Orthodox and the Uniates often turned violent. These conflicts were usually initiated by the Orthodox, who were frustrated by the loss of a large part of their believers and by the diminution of the administrative and territorial structure of their church. They tried, through Orthodox nobles in the Polish Diet, to obtain laws granting them equal status to the Uniate townspeople. Initially, these attempts were rarely successful, although in some places the Orthodox were granted equal rights and became eligible to hold office in the administration or in guilds and to carry on trade activities.[18] This new interpretation of the laws was eventually extended to all Ruthenians, Orthodox as well as Uniate. In spite of the church union, Latin-rite Roman Catholics continued to perceive the two eastern confessions (Uniate and Orthodox) to be comprised of members of a single national group, which of course they were. This is attested by the fact that in numerous documents the term *Ruthenian* is not qualified by a precise indication of religious denomination. The emergence of the Uniate Church did not alter the long-standing conviction that Ruthenians occupied a lower position in the hierarchy of nationalities and that the entire Ruthenian community was still considered schismatic.

Those Ruthenians who accepted the church union finally succeeded in gaining representation in the municipal government.[19] The Polish opposition then concentrated its efforts on circumscribing the electoral rights of Ruthenians and on trying to obstruct their access to power. Ruthenians were still not free to settle in the town center, and it was difficult for them to learn certain trades or to be employed in workshops belonging to Polish artisans. Under these conditions it was also difficult for Ruthenians to celebrate their faith.[20] In some privately held towns belonging to lords who were either Uniates themselves or who supported the idea of union, conditions were more favorable, in spite of negative reactions from some sections of the Latin-rite Catholic Church.

The seventeenth century was a dynamic but very complicated period in the history of the Uniate Church. The Uniates not only consolidated their own urban base but also influenced indirectly the life of the Orthodox. This process culminated in the definitive adoption of the Union by the Orthodox bishops of Przemyśl and L'viv in 1691 and 1702 respectively. About the same time, royal edicts issued by King Jan III Sobieski (14 October 1695) and King August II (17 December 1697) granted Uniates the right to be elected to all municipal offices, including the highest.[21] As a result, by the end of the 1740s the Uniates were represented in every town council of the Rus'/Ruthenian palatinate, in two or three urban administrations, and in the direction of the guilds. This happened not only in eastern districts of the borderland region, where they formed the majority of the population, but also in western districts, where they were outnumbered by Poles. In many urban courts Ruthenians were numerous, not because of any specific legal regulations but simply through the working of the electoral mechanisms. It was a similar story concerning the representation of lower class urban citizens, among whom the proportion of Uniates was always high. Uniates frequently occupied the position of guild sub-master since the position of guild master was usually held by a Pole, irrespective of the ethnic composition of the guild in question.[22]

The increased prominence of the Uniates within urban society is particularly evident in the changing customs of guilds. Compromises were introduced to allow both Roman Catholics and Uniates to combine their different rituals, and, supported by the clergy of both denominations, to observe and even participate in each other's major religious holidays. In several towns the guilds themselves sponsored the most important religious feasts in which, it seems clear, the entire society was expected to take part. Agreements were also concluded concerning minor holidays, when some labor was permitted, but within specified time limits. Many artisan groups organized regular or exceptional church services in both rites. For instance, the old (Julian) calendar of the Uniates gained such significance that it was often used to determine market days for all groups regardless of church affiliation. In fact, during the seventeenth century, almost 80 percent of all markets were organized according to the old calendar, the proportion tending to be even higher in the towns of the eastern districts. Transformations such as these also influenced the internal cohesion of the Ruthenians and their integration into the wider urban society.

Nonetheless, the church union had several different and even contradictory consequences. On the one hand, Ruthenians wished to protect their identity and therefore preserved their rite, their separate cemeteries, religious brotherhoods, schools, public holidays, and so forth. On the other hand, social and economic changes outside the realm of religion tended to undermine links *within* the ethnic community and to promote its integration into the town as a whole. The legal equalization of the Eastern and Western Catholic rites promoted more frequent contact between the groups, but it also contributed to a reduction in internal group cohesion. The possibility of joining the society's political and economic elite tended to open up internal divisions. The established (usually Polish) elites had good economic reasons for cultivating links with other groups and for practising mixed marriages.

Another factor that contributed to undermining the Ruthenian community was its rapid dispersal throughout all the towns in the borderland region after the adoption of the church union. Scattered among different ethnic groups, Uniate adherents adopted new ways of living so that both the old boundary markers and group identity as such became less noticeable. The Ukrainian language became less important as a means of everyday communication, and it gradually became confined to religious services. In this way, and because it divided the East Slav community politically, church union weakened the integrity of Ruthenians as a group and promoted a new cultural mixture in all urban areas of the Polish-Ukrainian borderland.[23]

Jews

Initially concentrated in compact groups in the suburbs, in the course of the seventeenth and eighteenth centuries Jews were increasingly able to buy houses and land in the vicinity of the central marketplaces. In towns that have so far been studied, it seems that an average of 9 percent of all properties belonged to Jews.[24] Jews were, of course, formally outside municipal law, for religious reasons. Despite their right to settle throughout the Polish-Lithuanian Commonwealth, in practice, religious difference caused the Jewish community to maintain a high degree of isolation. Jews in towns developed their own legal and administrative organizations composed of communes, local diets, and tribunals with formal links to other judicial institutions of the municipality and the state. They also had their own tax system, which was partly linked to the financial economy of the rest of the town.

Christian groups did not initially see Jews as a threat; they settled in outlying areas and worked in non-prestigious economic sectors. Later, however, when Jews began to take control of central areas, Christians urged these towns to adopt a decree known as *de non tolerandis Judaies*, which was intended to ban Jews from settling in the towns and from buying any property there. While Jews were economically dynamic, religious and legal restrictions hindered their acceptance into Christian artisan and trade organizations. In a few privately held towns, however, Jews did obtain rights to join the guilds (though they did not necessarily enjoy voting rights); and in those places where Jewish artisans

were numerous and other labor was unavailable, they sometimes succeeded in creating their own autonomous guilds.[25] Life in the Jewish
communities in the privately held towns was very strictly regulated by
their owners, and this had indirect influence on the communities in
other towns.[26]

Their faith, embodied in the Torah and Talmud, was responsible for
the exceptionally durable social cohesion of the Jews as a group. Judaism exercised a pervasive influence on the everyday life of all Jews. Talmudic principles were inculcated in the family and also in a highly
formalized education system, which gave this group the capacity to
resist external influences and to preserve its own language in community life (for external communication, the Polish language and, in rare
cases, Ruthenian, was used). Jewish culture and values were little influenced by changing economic and social conditions. Nevertheless, the
emergence of Hasidism in the seventeenth century did threaten group
cohesion and undermine Jewish self-government in several towns,
leaving the community more exposed to the influence of the municipal
administration or the landed estate.[27] The economic crises throughout
Poland-Lithuania in the seventeenth and early eighteenth centuries, an
increase in the group's territorial dispersion, and the emergence of new
social divisions and new forms of contact with the Christian population
were all factors that combined to weaken the integrity of the Jewish
community. This was no different, however, from other ethnic groups,
who were also adapting to changing circumstances. The Jewish community retained a very strong self-identification as a consequence not
only of its religious and cultural alienation, but also of the very acute
conditions of economic competition in which it was embroiled. Unlike
the case with other groups, Jewishness depended strictly on birth, and
marriages outside the community were extremely rare.[28]

"Ethnic" Streets

Before concluding this examination of the principal ethnic groups of
the towns of the Polish-Ukrainian borderland during the early modern
period, it might be useful to look more closely at two basic spatial elements: the overall urban settlement pattern and, in particular, the individual street, which together formed a topographical unity. In most
small towns, where the ethnic groups were not large, each one was
concentrated in the main in a single street, whereas in larger towns
such as Przemyśl, Sambir, and Drohobych, entire districts were com-

monly identified in "ethnic" terms. This development took place following a town's incorporation, when both occupational and religious-cultural structures were taking shape. Not surprisingly, the Ruthenian Street was usually located close to an Eastern-rite (Orthodox or Uniate) church. Every important concentration of Ruthenian, or Jewish, population was linked to a particular street, which therefore constituted a basic part of the given group's identity. This became clear when Jews acquired property in the center of town, which they tended to use for economic purposes only. They usually carried on living in the Jewish street, sometimes in very simple houses.

In addition to their "ethnic" character, most streets had a second designation: the street "under the wall," "behind the enclosure," "perpendicular," or "behind the gate." Often, these streets were not linked to the main streets of the town and sometimes they were laid out alongside the city walls. This had consequences not only for housing construction, but also for the infrastructure, especially sanitation and running water. Waste from the town center was dumped here, and the sewage channels laid out behind the houses gave these "ethnic" streets a distinct stench.

Synagogues served not only the religious life of the Jewish community. They also housed educational, administrative, and judicial offices. Some even contained their own jail. Other public buildings of the Jewish Street included baths, hospitals for the poor, and the ritual soap manufacturers and slaughterhouses.[29] The construction of these streets diverged significantly from other parts of town. Buildings here were narrower, often not more than half of the size generally found in the center. They were usually made of wood and had only one or two floors. The Jewish streets were particularly animated and, largely beyond the reach of the municipal authorities, they had a very irregular layout. Demographic pressure and lack of space forced people to erect numerous outbuildings wherever possible, often directly against the town walls.[30] Simple, improvised constructions were consistent with the generally low-prestige economic activities of the Jewish population. The interiors corresponded to the particular needs of the owner. Many houses were augmented with large, well-built cellars, used not only for storage but also as a place to take refuge in times of trouble.

In terms of occupational structure, the Jewish streets were dominated by artisans and shopkeepers. Typically, between 40 and 60 percent of Jewish households derived their income from crafts, and a further one-third from trade. There was a distinct group of rich Jews known as the "streetmen." They owned all or at least a part of their houses, worked as managers for noblemen, and held the right to sell alcohol. They also traded in imported goods, owned workshops that dealt in fine cloths or gold, and practiced the "free" professions, for example, as doctors or barbers.[31] This elite lived in brick houses facing directly on the main streets. In the seventeenth century, these same premises doubled as workshops, but in the early eighteenth century, because of overcrowding, the richest merchants and artisans transferred their economic activities to peripheral properties, which they either rented or purchased.

The Ruthenian Street, too, was often to be found near the town boundary, adjacent to the town walls, and in places of lower prestige. After the church union, it was possible for Ruthenians to build churches within the town walls, but most were erected well away from the center, in the zone of the Ruthenian Street. Like the Jewish streets, Ruthenian streets too were commonly muddy and unsanitary. In addition to churches and belfries, there were houses for the priests, as well as schools and hospitals, mostly built of wood or half-timber. Rather than cellars, these buildings had caves dug into the earth, which people could enter through specially constructed corridors or grottos. They were used mostly to store agricultural products. Various outbuildings such as sheds and pigsties also served agricultural activities. Unlike with Jewish houses, Ruthenian interiors were exclusively residential and all workspace for subsidiary artisan activities was located outside the home. Many houses had a substantial courtyard, with perhaps a vegetable garden and orchard. Elaborate entrances to these courtyards were known as *miedzuchy*.[32] The professional and social structure of the inhabitants of the Ruthenian streets was less complicated than that found in the Jewish streets. Ruthenians were mainly occupied in agriculture, although certain trades provided the principal or at least supplementary source of money income for some. For this reason, and because they were usually fewer in number, Ruthenians were economically less differentiated than was the Jewish population.

Conclusions

The ethnic and religious structures of the Polish-Ukrainian borderland region, which took their basic shape in the Middle Ages, were consolidated in the course of later settlement processes, especially large-scale Jewish immigration. There was some dislocation and interethnic friction, in particular in those towns that received large numbers of foreign settlers in the early modern period. Ethnic groups in these towns developed both a heightened internal cohesion and a sharper consciousness of the other groups in urban society. Religious differences, including confessional differences among Christians, were fundamental to group relations. Those outside the dominant church were limited in their access to offices in the municipal government and in guilds – and might not even be allowed to join the latter. Furthermore, there were legal restrictions in the economic sphere and on their settlement in the city.

The various ethnoreligious groups also differed in terms of their internal cohesion. The smaller ones, such as the Germans and the Armenians, did not develop enduringly strong bonds, but were quickly assimilated into the Polish and Ruthenian communities. Jews, Poles, and Ruthenians formed the three basic national communities, each with its own religion, language, culture, and internal cohesion that defined the group's place in urban society. These identities were so strong and lasting that even religious divisions could not weaken them, as demonstrated with particular clarity in the case of the Ruthenians after the establishment of the Uniate Chuch. The groups were partially segregated and sometimes concentrated in particular "ethnic streets." Their houses were also differentiated, both externally and internally, and this was linked closely to their occupational differentiation.

The overall outcome of these manifold differences, above all religious and economic differences, was to provide a solid basis for the rivalries and antagonisms which manifested themselves with increasing vigor from the middle of the nineteenth century on. Their effects are still felt in the Polish-Ukrainian borderland region today.

Notes

1 Heinrich Feliks Schmid, *Das Schöffenbuch der Dorfgemeinde Krzemienica* (Leipzig, 1931), pp. 45–72; Kurt Luck, *Deutsche Aufbaukräfte in der Entwicklung Polens* (Plauen, 1934), pp. 12–32; Andrzej Janeczek, *Osadnictwo pogranicza polsko-ruskiego: województwo bełskie od schyłku XIV do początków XVII w.* (Wrocław, 1991), pp. 124–196; Nikolai Kotlar, *Formirovanie teritorii i vozniknovenie gorodov galitsko-volynskoi Rusi IX–XIII st.* (Kiev, 1985); Franciszek Persowski, *Studia nad pograniczem polsko-ruskim X–XI w.* (Wrocław, 1962).

2 Henryk Paszkiewicz, *Polityka ruska Kazimierza Wielkiego* (Warsaw, 1925), pp.

28–34; Janeczek, *Osadnictwo pogranicza*, pp. 125–180; Andrzej Janeczek, "Ekspansja osadnicza w ziemi lwowskiej w XIV–XVI w.," *Przegląd Historyczny*, LIX (Warsaw, 1978), pp. 597–622; Władysław Dworzaczek, *Hetman Jan Tarnowski: z dziejów możnowładztwa małopolskiego* (Warsaw, 1985), pp. 32–35.

3 See Sadok Barącz, *Żywoty sławnych Ormian w Polsce* (L'viv, 1856); Władysław Loziński, *Patrycjat i mieszczaństwo lwowskie z XVI i XVII wieku* (L'viv, 1899), pp. 194–223; Czesław Chowaniec, *Ormianie w Stanisławowie* (Stanislaviv, 1928).

4 Until the end of the nineteenth century the Ukrainian nationality was known by the term *Ruthenian*, and that usage will be largely followed in the present discussion.

5 Zdzisław Budzyński, *Ludność pogranicza polsko-ruskiego w drugiej połowie XVIII wieku* (Przemyśl and Rzeszów, 1991); Jerzy Motylewicz, *Miasta ziemi przemyskiej i sanockiej w drugiej połowie XVII i XVIII wieku* (Przemyśl and Rzeszów, 1993).

6 Stanisław Gierszewski, *Obywatele Polski przedrozbiorowej* (Warsaw, 1973), p. 75.

7 Motylewicz, *Miasta ziemi przemyskiej i sanockiej*, p. 98.

8 I find the estimate given by Zenon Szust, *Średnowiecze Łańcuta* (Katowice 1957), p. 29, to be much more plausible than that of Schmid, *Das Schöffenbuch*, p. 22.

9 Jerzy Motylewicz, "Łańcut w XIV–XVIII," *Rocznik Przemyśki*, XXVIII (Przemyśl, 1991–1992), Table 4.

10 Andrzej Janeczek, "Exceptis Schismaticis: upośledzenie Rusinow w przywilejach prawa niemieckiego Wiadysława Jagiełły," *Przegląd Historyczny*, LXXV (Warsaw, 1984), pp. 527–542.

11 Motylewicz, *Miasta ziemi przemyskiej i sanockiej*, p. 99.

12 August Stanisław Fenczak, "Z dziejów stosunków między obrządkami Kościoła katolickiego na obszarze greckokatolickiej diecezji lwowskiej w XVIII wieku," *Slavia Orientalis*, XXXVIII, 3–4 (Warsaw, 1989), p. 586.

13 This question was regulated by a law of King Sigismund August, *O obsadzaniu urzedow miejskich na Rusi* (On access to town administration in Ruthenia), in which it was clearly specified that "people belonging to the Ruthenian faith could neither be appointed nor freely elected."

14 Jerzy Motylewicz, "Społeczność unicka w miastach województwa ruskiego w XVII i XVIII wieku," in Stanisław Stępień, ed., *Polska–Ukraina 1000 lat sąsiedztwa*, vol. 4 (Przemyśl, 1998), p. 192.

15 Jan Ptasnik, *Miasta i mieszczaństwo w dawnej Polsce* (Warsaw, 1949), p. 278.

16 Tsentral'nyi Derhavnyi Istorychnyi Arkhiv Ukraïny u Lvovi (hereinafter TsDIA-L), f. 15, sign. 321, pp. 53–55.

17 Motylewicz, *Miasta ziemi przemyskiej i sanockiej*, p. 99.

18 Archiwum Państwowe w Przemyślu, Akta miasta Przemyśla (hereafter APP AP), sign. 587, p. 58. The basis of the privilege issued by King Władysław IV was apparently a royal document from 1497, which granted Orthodox Ukrainians the same rights as Catholics. See Andrzej Janeczek, "Miasta Rusi Czerwonej w nurcie modernizacji: kontekst reform XIV–XVI w.," *Kwartalnik Kultury Materialnej*, no. 1 (Warsaw, 1995), p. 13, n. 51.

19 *Lustracja Województwa Ruskiego 1661–1665*, pt. 1: *Ziemia przemyska i sanocka*, ed. Kazimierz Arłamowski and W. Kaput (Wrocław, 1970), p. 142; TsDIA-L, f. 35, op. 7, p. 356.

20 Archiwum Państwowe Miasta Krakowa i Wojewodztwa Krakowskiego (hereafter APMKiWK), sign. 860, p. 72; Jerzy Motylewicz, "Przywileje Żydow dobromilskich z 1612 i 1756 roku," *Rocznik Przemyski*, XXXII, 1 (Przemyśl, 1996), p. 132.

21 Aleksander Kuczera, *Samborszczyzna*, vol. 1 (Sambir, 1935), APP AP, sign. 560, no. 19.

22 Iaroslav Isaievych, "Administratyvno-pravovyi ustrii Drohobycha v dobu feudalizmu (kintsa XVIII st.)," in *Z istoriï ukraïnskoï SSR* (Kiev, 1962), pp. 3–19.

23 Jerzy Motylewicz, "Społeczność miejska a grupy narodowościowe w miastach czerwonoruskich w XV–XVIII w.: problem przemiań w trwałości więzi społecznych," in *Miasto i kultura ludowa w dziejach Białorusi, Litwy, Polski i Ukrainy* (Cracow, 1996), p. 102.

24 The range is from 0.4 percent up to 42.6 percent. APMKiWK, Wawel section, Schneider collection, sign. 839.

25 Maurycy Horn, "Chronologia i zasięg terytorialny żydowskich cechów rzemieślniczych w dawnej Polsce (1613–1795," in *Żydzi w dawnej Rzeczypospolitej* (Wrocław, 1991), p. 201.

26 Władysław Depczyński, *Tarnogród 1567–1967* (Tarnogród, 1970), p. 146; Barbara Wyrozumska, "Ordynacja Żydow sokołowskich z 1772 r.," in *Żydzi w dawnej Rzeczypospolitej*, pp. 85–90.

27 Chone Shmeruk, "Chasydyzm i kahał," in *Żydzi w dawnej Rzeczypospolitej*, p. 65.

28 On economic competition in Samogitia, see Elmantas Meilus and Adomas Butrimas, "Przemiany etniczne i wyznaniowe w miastach i miasteczkach Żmudzi w XVII–XVIII wieku," in *Miasto i kultura ludowa w dziejach Białorusi, Litwy, Polski, Ukrainy*, p. 115.

29 Jacek Krochmal, *Krzyż i menorah: Żydzi i chrześcijanie w Przemyślu w latach 1559–1772* (Przemyśl, 1996), pp. 75–76.

30 Kazimierz Arłamowski, "Rozwój przestrzenny Przemyśla," *Roczniki Dziejów Społecznych i Gospodarczych*, no. 15 (Poznań, 1953), p. 164.

31 Jerzy Motylewicz, "Ulice etniczne w miastach Ziemi przemyskiej i sanockiej w XVII i XVIII wieku," *Kwartalnik Historii Kultury Materialnej*, nos. 1–2 (Warsaw, 1999), p. 154.

32 Jerzy Motylewicz, "Żydzi w miastach ziemi przemyskiej i sanockiej w drugiej połowie XVII i XVIII wieku," in Feliks Kiryk, ed., *Żydzi w Małopolsce* (Przemyśl 1991), p. 115.

4 Borderland City: Przemyśl and the Ruthenian National Awakening in Galicia

STANISŁAW STĘPIEŃ

Przemyśl lies roughly mid-way between Cracow and L'viv, in the zone where western and eastern Slavic cultures meet. The city had an important position in the multinational Commonwealth of Poland and Lithuania. Before that, it served from 1067 to 1147 as the administrative and political center of a separate principality within the western part of Kievan Rus'. Przemyśl developed into an important economic hub during the early Middle Ages, as it lay at the crossroads of major trade routes. It was a cultural center and its cathedral school was affiliated with the university in Cracow. An Eastern Christian eparchy was founded there before 1218, and a Roman Catholic diocese followed after 1340.[1] Przemyśl's cosmopolitan society included numerous famous priests, writers, architects, and musicians. The Christian communities were later augmented by a Jewish population that was similarly dynamic and creative.

A Jesuit college was founded in 1617, and soon became celebrated for the quality of its teaching. The college's theater and library were very influential in shaping the city's cultural development. In 1678 a Roman Catholic seminary was established. Students of these two institutions were also able to profit from several monastic libraries. The Roman Catholic Bishop Wacław Hieronim Sierakowski created Przemyśl's first public library in 1754. Possibly this is an indication that the proportion of educated people was already rather high. This was only the second public library within the Polish-Lithuanian Commonwealth; the first was Warsaw's Załuski library, established in 1747. A particularly important element in the intellectual history of Przemyśl was the printshop established there in 1754 by Adam Klein, a native of Cracow.[2] Klein's printshop served both Christian communities, and it maintained a reputation for excellence even after Klein sold his business to the Jesuits in 1757.

For all these reasons, when the southeastern lands of the Polish-Lithuanian Commonwealth were annexed to the Austrian Empire in 1772, the new Habsburg authorities at first considered making Przemyśl the capital of their new province, which they named the Kingdom of Galicia and Lodomeria (Königreich Galizien und Lodomerien).[3] The city's central location and its good communication links to the imperial capital of Vienna strengthened the case to make it the provincial capital. Eventually, however, L'viv was chosen, and Przemyśl had to content itself with the status of district center. Nevertheless, it continued to play an important role in the political and cultural life of all three of Galicia's main nationalities (Poles, Ruthenians, Jews). According to the first Austrian census, taken in 1775, Przemyśl's population numbered 3,421 Christians (Roman Catholics and Greek Catholics combined) and 1,558 Jews.[4] Then, as later, religious divisions more or less coincided with national divisions, that is, the Poles were Roman Catholics and the Ruthenians (Ukrainians) were Greek Catholics. In the early period of Habsburg rule the numbers of Poles and Jews grew quickly. As the imperial government developed its administrative apparatus, it brought in people of other nationalities, mainly Czechs, Austro-Germans, and Hungarians to the city. Ruthenians, however, continued to form a sizeable community, comprising nearly one-quarter of the entire population. The next census, carried out in 1830, recorded 7,538 inhabitants, of whom 1,508 were Greek Catholics – a significantly larger number than in most other centers in Galicia.[5]

The clergy formed an important element. This was not only because they served the Eastern-rite Greek Catholic eparchial see, but also for their links to several other institutions, especially schools. Priests were the dominant group within the Ruthenian intelligentsia. Since celibacy was not a requirement for the clergy in the Greek Catholic Church, "priest dynasties" would develop, and church offices were often handed down from father to son. In the early 1800s, about 95 percent of all Ruthenians were peasants. For complex historical reasons this ethnic group was almost entirely deprived of a noble or aristocratic class, and thus the clergy came to play a key role in the early phases of the Ruthenian national movement.[6]

The intellectual formation of the Greek Catholic priesthood was decisively influenced by the policy and the patronage of the Empress Maria Theresa and her son Joseph II. The Habsburg-ruled centralized state undermined the position of the nobles, municipal authorities, and the Roman Catholic clerical elite. Yet the empire needed an efficient bureaucratic staff. In practice such officials could only be trained by religious institutions, and so church-run schools had to improve their standards. This especially applied to the Greek Catholic Church, whose priests were mostly illiterate and often unfamiliar with even the basic principles of their faith.

In a concerted effort to transform this church, the Habsburg government granted it identical status to the Roman Catholic Church. In 1774 the name was changed from *Uniate* to *Greek Catholic*, and the Eastern term *pop* to designate a priest was formally replaced by *sviashchennyk*. The Habsburgs also took the important decision to allow the sons of priests who held a function in the bishop's administration the same right of access to state offices as the sons of nobles. Between 1775 and 1784 a Greek Catholic seminary known as the Barbareum functioned in Vienna; later it was replaced by a seminary in L'viv that had been established in 1783. These institutions were responsible for the education of Greek Catholic priests throughout the empire. Between 1787 and 1809 Greek Catholic priests could also be educated at the Studium Ruthenum, established by Joseph II within the German-speaking university at L'viv.

Seminarians at all these institutions were highly motivated to emulate Latin-rite priests. Furthermore, they recognized the importance of raising the educational level of their congregations. These seminarians were also influenced by the pan-European ideology of Romanticism and the developing Polish independence movement. Poles often drew on Ruthenian themes, and there were intensive discussions regarding the emancipation of serfs.[7] National consciousness among Ruthenians was still decidedly underdeveloped at this time. The strongest source of self-identification was with one's own church (rite) and social group, which the people themselves described with the adjectival form derived from the noun, *Rus'*. Thus, *rus'kyi narod* for Rus'/ Ruthenian people, *rus'ki khlopy* for the Rus'/Ruthenian peasants, *rus'kyi obriad* for Rus'/ Ruthenian rite, and *rus'ka besida* for Rus'/Ruthenian speech.[8] It was still quite easy to change one's nationality by passing from the Ruthenian to the Polish national group, or vice versa. Many people of Ruthenian origin developed a Polish consciousness through their education, speaking Polish not only publicly but also at home. Polish was the administrative language of the Greek Catholic Church, and in towns its priests used this language in their preaching and teaching. At the same time, many peasants of Polish origin used the "Ruthenian dialect" as their everyday tongue, and wherever Roman Catholic churches were inaccessible, they attended Greek Catholic churches. This ultimately led many peasants into a process of "Ukrainianization."

The Ruthenian national awakening was a product both of the political situation and of the ideals of the Enlightenment. The Habsburgs sought to unify their vast domains. They endeavoured to consolidate their rule in Galicia, which derived historically from Hungary's claim to the region that dated from the Middle Ages.[9] Linguistic and religious similarities among Ruthenians in Galicia and the Russian Empire as well as with Russians, prompted Habsburg interest in reinforcing the cultural and religious distinctiveness of the Ruthenians in Galicia. The Greek Catholic Church was an excellent means to this end.

Within the framework of Habsburg absolutism both Catholic churches performed a bureaucratic role and also contributed to general social stability by legitimating the state to the lower classes. Thus, it was very important that priestly education be state-supervised. Graduates of the Barbareum and the seminary in L'viv were the most westward oriented of the clergy within the Greek Catholic Church. These priests played a leading role in the Ruthenian national movement.[10]

Bishop Snihurs'kyi and His Circle

Among early promoters of the Ruthenian national awakening in Galicia were Bishop Mykhailo Levyts'kyi / Michal Lewicki and the eparchial canon Ioann Mohyl'nyts'kyi / Jan Mogilnicki.[11] At their initiative the first Ruthenian educational and religious organization came into being in Przemyśl in 1815: the Societas Presbyterorum graeco-katholici Galicensium (Association of Greek Catholic Priests in Galicia).[12] Legally recognized in 1816, the new association's name suggests that it aimed to cover all of Galicia. It recruited well-educated Greek Catholic priests both from within and beyond the Eparchy of Przemyśl. One of its first recruits was Ioann Snihurs'kyi / Jan Snigurski, then the resident priest at the Greek Catholic parish of St Barbara in Vienna. In 1818 he became bishop of Przemyśl and a very active patron of the arts.[13] The essential objective of the association was to diffuse religious knowledge, but this could not be achieved without language reform and a general effort to improve the educational and cultural level of the rural population. The form of the Ruthenian literary language was not yet settled: some favored using Church Slavonic as its base, others the spoken vernacular.

Local state authorities considered the language of Galicia's Ruthenians to be a branch of Russian and at first would not agree to its use in the schools. But after Ruthenian activists petitioned the Habsburg court in Vienna, the Galician administration agreed to permit religious instruction in their own language for Greek Catholic children.[14]

Canon Mohyl'nyts'kyi, as inspector of schools for the eparchial consistory, was well aware of the disadvantaged position of Ruthenians, particularly in rural parishes. To address these problems, the Przemyśl eparchy arranged for the publication of a catechism and elementary primer in language based on the spoken vernacular, and had both books distributed to public and parish schools.[15] In 1818 the state decided to permit teaching in the national language for pupils in the elementary-level parish schools.[16] This required textbooks and teachers able to use them. The Institutum Cantorum et Magistrorum Scholae (Institute for Deacons and Teachers) in Przemyśl, had opened the previous autumn, under the directorship of Canon Mohyl'nyts'kyi. This was the first pedagogical college in Galicia. The curriculum included basic theology, language (Church Slavonic, Polish, German, and Ruthenian), calligraphy, arithmetic, logic, and Slavo-Byzantine singing. Approximately twenty-four students studied at the college each year. Alongside Mohyl'nyts'kyi, the staff included Ioann Lavrovs'kyi / Jan Ławrowski, Petro Nazarevych / Piotr Nazarewicz, and numerous parish priests from the vicinity.[17] They taught not only for the Greek Catholic Church, but also for the public schools (which were under the church's control). The Philosophical and Theological Institute, also in Przemyśl, was established in January 1818 for students of both Polish and Ruthenian nationality. It had a broader character and recruited professors from both Christian communities to teach theoretical and practical philosophy, pedagogy, theoretical and practical mathematics, physics, general history, religion, and Greek. Courses lasted three years, and most graduates went on to become teachers at the secondary level.[18]

Ioann Snihurs'kyi studied theology at the University of Vienna; he received his doctorate there in 1811 and then was made a professor of theology at the university. He also served as an assistant and then resident priest at St Barbara's Church during this time. After his appointment in 1818 as bishop of Przemyśl, Snihurs'kyi very quickly succeeded in gathering around himself the most talented priests from near and far. Ioann Lavrovs'kyi, until then rector of the L'viv seminary, settled in Przemyśl in 1820. As a close associate of the bishop, Lavrovs'kyi was nominated a canon and the cathedral preacher. In addition to his work at the Institute for Deacons and Teachers, Lavrovs'kyi taught at the city's Roman Catholic seminary. There he maintained contacts with Polish scholars such as Samuel B. Linde, Zorian Dołęga-Chodakowski, Piotr Kepper, and Alexander Vostok. Lavrovs'kyi was made an honorary member of the Cracow Scholarly Society (which later became the Academy of Arts).

In 1825, after graduating from the Barbareum in Vienna, Father Iosyf Levyts'kyi / Józef Lewicki, one of Galicia's most distinguished linguists and publicists, arrived in Przemyśl. He became the confessor of Bishop Snihurs'kyi and taught Church Slavonic at the Greek Catholic seminary. Father Iosyf Lozyns'kyi / Josef Lozinski returned to his native Przemyśl in 1830, having finished his university studies in L'viv; he wrote several articles on Ruthenian orthography. Antonii Dobrians'kyi / Antoni Dobrianski, parish priest at Walawa, also taught Church Slavonic at the seminary; he was a leading Ruthenian activist and protégé of the influential Austrian Slavist of Slovenian origin, Jernej Kopitar. And in 1835 Ioann Harasevych / Jan Harasiewicz, a teacher and vice-rector of the L'viv seminary, and author of a study about the Studium Ruthenorum, settled in Przemyśl.[19]

Books, Publishing, and the Language Question

Religious and cultural life in Przemyśl's Eastern Christian eparchy centered around Bishop Snihurs'kyi and these close associates.[20] Certain developments, however, preceded his arrival. The Greek Catholic library began in 1804, when Przemyśl inherited part of the private library of Father Ieronym Strilets'kyi / Hieronim Strilecki, parish priest at Vienna's St Barbara's Church.[21] This was the beginning of a collection that was to be greatly extended over the years, particularly through gifts by Father Lavrovs'kyi, who had brought his own valuable library with him in 1820.[22] Lavrovs'kyi's impact is comparable to that of Józef Maximilian Ossoliński, the great Polish librarian in L'viv. By 1822, Przemyśl's Lavrovs'kyi collection already had some 33,000 books, 300 manuscripts, seventy paintings, several graphics, and 200 coins, as well as some other materials.[23] Of these items, 14,139 were transferred to the Przemyśl library, while the remainder went to the Greek Catholic library of the L'viv metropolitan cathedral chapter. The Przemyśl library also profited from the gift of 2,096 volumes from the personal collection of Bishop Snihurs'kyi. Soon the combined bequests came to be known popularly as the "Snihurs'ko-Lavrovs'kyi collection."[24] Further donations were made by canons and priests of the Przemyśl eparchy, and by 1851 Father Dobrians'kyi could catalogue about 17,024 volumes.[25] This was a very significant collection. To a great extent it made up for the transfer of the Roman Catholic library in 1774 (in connection with the suppression of the Jesuit Order) to the University of L'viv.[26]

After the suppression of the Jesuits in 1773, the printshop established by Adam Klein continued to serve both rites under its new owner, Antoni Matyaszowski. Apart from books, mostly religious, he printed the highly popular Polish and Ruthenian almanac, *Kalendarz polski i ruski,* every year from 1780 to 1794. In addition to Polish and Latin, Matyaszowski published German and even Hebrew books.[27] Later, the business passed to Jan Gołębiowski, who continued the city's publishing traditions, issuing numerous volumes of sermons, schoolbooks, church debates, and school reports. In 1829, after Gołębiowski's death, the printshop was acquired by Bishop Snihurs'kyi, and it became known as Typohrafiia Iepyskops'ka (the Bishop's Printshop).[28] It was transferred to the cathedral chapter in 1840, and from that time it was called the Typohrafiia (or Drukarnia) Sobornoï hreko-katolyts'koï Kapituly or Typohrafiia Iepyskops'koho Sobora Kryloshan' (Greek Catholic Cathedral Chapter Printshop).

At the beginning of the nineteenth century the only other Galician printing facility using Cyrillic letters belonged to the Stauropegial Institute in L'viv, and its situation had become ruinous. Consequently, books intended for the liturgy had to be printed in Pochaïv on the Russian side of the border, while many other texts and schoolbooks were simply handwritten.[29] Father Iosyf Levyts'kyi became the first director of the Greek Catholic Cathedral Chapter Printshop. He purchased the necessary Cyrillic letters and printed not only prayerbooks and catechisms but also many other books for use in rural schools.[30] Levyts'kyi was also responsible for the publication, in 1834, of the first Ruthenian hymnal in Galicia. Consisting mainly of baroque compositions, his *Pisny nabozhnŷia yz Bohohlasnyka Pochaievskoho peredrukovannŷia* had a great impact on the contemporary debate about whether or not to create a Ukrainian literary language based on spoken dialects.[31] This discussion influenced the kind of language used by Levyts'kyi in his Ruthenian grammar (*Grammatik der ruthenischen order klein-russischen Sprache in Galizien,* 1834).

Przemyśl scholars also contributed to contemporary debate about the alphabet most appropriate for Galician-Ruthenian publications. As an important cultural location, with a high concentration of intellectuals centered around the local Greek Catholic bishop, Przemyśl became the scene for the outbreak in 1834 of "the first alphabet war" (*persha azbuchna viina*) and in 1859 "the second alphabet war" (*druha azbuchna viina*). Iosyp Lozyns'kyi, a parish priest in the nearby village of Medyka, promoted use of the Latin alphabet. He published an article in the Polish-language L'viv periodical, *Rozmaitości*, entitled "O wprowadzeniu abecadła polskiego do pismiennictwa ruskiego" (Concerning the Introduction of the Polish Alphabet in Ruthenian Writings) in 1834. The following year, he published in Przemyśl in the Latin alphabet an ethnographic study called *Ruskoje wesile* (The Ruthenian Wedding). Lozyns'kyi completed his grammar, written in Polish with the titled *Gramatyka języka ruskiego (małoruskiego)* (Grammar of the Ruthenian [Little Russian] Language), in 1834, but it was published (in Przemyśl) only thirteen years later. The question of the alphabet was intimately connected to the question of which linguistic form to select for the literary language. Several of Lozyns'kyi's close collaborators took part in this discussion, including Iosyf Levyts'kyi, Ioann Lavrovs'kyi, and Markiian Shashkevych. In a much debated brochure, *Azbuka i abecadło* (The Cyrillic and Polish Alphabets), published in Przemyśl in 1836, Shashkevych argued decisively against Lozyns'kyi and in favor of the Cyrillic alphabet. Quite apart from emotional attachment toward the Cyrillic literary tradition, which goes back to the times of Kievan Rus', it was argued that adoption of the Latin alphabet would separate Galician Ukrainians from the Ukrainians – larger in number – in the Russian Empire. Lozyns'kyi reaffirmed his pro-Latin views,[32] but the supporters of the Cyrillic alphabet were in the majority, and eventually they won the day.

The language debate was enriched by several other works published in Przemyśl. Father Antonii Dobrians'kyi's Church Slavonic grammar (*Gramatyka języka starosławianskiego, jakiego Słowianie obrządek grecki wyznający w księgach swych cerkiewnych używają*) came out in 1837. This Polish-language text met with such success that it was republished two decades later in a Ruthenian version.[33] Another priest, Ioann Lavrovs'kyi in 1838 published, in Polish, a textbook for elementary schools (*Elementarz ruski, niemiecki i polski dla szkół parafialnych w Galicyi*). Of particular significance in the field of lexicography was the appearance of a Church Slavonic-Ruthenian dictionary compiled by Iakiv Doskovs'kyi and printed at the Cathedral Chapter Printshop.[34]

In 1848 the Cathedral Chapter Printshop issued a volume of romantic poetry (*Stykhotvoreniia*) by Ioann Hushalevych.[35] That same year Father Hushalevych wrote the popular *Mir Vam bratia* (Peace Unto You, Brother). This song served as a national anthem for Ukrainians at least until the mid-1860s. For those East Slavs of Galicia who were either of Old Ruthenian or Russophile orientation it retained its popularity for several more decades.[36]

The language and choice of alphabet debates gained new strength in 1858–1859. This "second alphabet war" was mainly inspired by the state authorities in Vienna and L'viv. It was also shaped by three volumes of poetry published in Przemyśl. Their author was Leon Eugeniusz Węgliński, a Pole who wrote in the Ruthenian language but used the Polish form of the Latin alphabet. The controversy was short-lived, and in the end the idea of adapting the Latin alphabet to the Ruthenian language was abandoned. As did other East and South Slavic peoples, the Ruthenians of Galicia continued to use the Cyrillic alphabet, although in the form of the somewhat simplified civil script (*grazhdanka*), which from the 1860s steadily increased in popularity. Nevertheless, some religious literature continued to be published in the traditional Slavonic script (*kyrylytsia*) for those elements in the population accustomed to the "old" writing.

The language used in Greek Catholic Church services had a great effect on the development of the Ruthenian language in Galicia. Sermons in the vernacular were pioneered at St Barbara's Church in Vienna by Father Ieronym Strilets'kyi. This innovation was continued by Father Ioann Ol'shavs'kyi and by Bishop Snihurs'kyi, who put enormous energy into promoting use of the vernacular, arguing that God's words had to make sense to ordinary people. Sermons written in the vernacular by the celebrated parish priest in Rava Rus'ka, Havriïl Paslavs'kyi/ Gabriel Paslawski, were published in the 1840s.[37] After that, other such sermons were published: by Dmytro Zyblikevych,[38] Iuliian Hankevych,[39] and Antonii Dobrians'kyi.[40] In 1850 Dobrians'kyi began issuing the annual almanac *Peremŷshlianyn*, which contained a wide range of information about literature, history, and the domestic economy. He also published the first sketches of the history of Przemyśl and its Greek Catholic eparchy.[41]

Church Music

In the 1820s Przemyśl became a center for the revival and development of Byzantine-Slavonic chant, which at the time was quite neglected throughout Galicia. The impulse for this activity came from Bishop Snihurs'kyi, who sought to emulate the example of St Barbara's Church in Vienna. After the liquidation of the Orthodox Church in Vienna, which had functioned under the auspices of the Russian embassy, members of its choir appealed to St Barbara's, whose priest (Father Ol'shavs'kyi) allowed them to participate in the Greek Catholic liturgy. Their choral repertoire was based mainly on works by the St Petersburg composer of Ruthenian descent, Dmytro Bortnians'kyi. Within a very short time, performances by this choir became so popular that not only local aristocrats but also members of the imperial family and foreign diplomats began to attend the liturgy at St Barbara's, where Snihurs'kyi was then the resident priest.[42] Accustomed to a high quality choral singing, as Bishop of Przemyśl, Snihurs'kyi decided to improve the poor quality of singing in his own cathedral church. Under his predecessor, Bishop Mykhailo Levyts'kyi, the singing had been in the L'viv manner (an archaic and very primitive form of chant) under the conductor Iakiv Neronovych.

Bishop Snihurs'kyi commissioned new Byzantine-Slavonic works from St Petersburg, mainly by Bortnians'kyi and Maksym Berezovs'kyi.[43] Father Levyts'kyi was charged with organization of the choir, with the bishop himself as its conductor. As lead bass, Snihurs'kyi chose a singer from the Roman Catholic cathedral choir, Wincenty Kuriański. The new choir premiered in the Greek Catholic cathedral church on the *Iordan* (Epiphany) feast in 1829. Among its members were the talented brothers (and cousins of the bishop), Mykhailo and Volodyslav Verbyts'kyi.

Mykhailo Verbyts'kyi, who also sang in Roman Catholic choirs, was especially gifted. In the late 1830s he taught singing at the convent of the Benedictine sisters, which had managed to escape the Josephine reforms, and sang tenor in the Roman Catholic cathedral.[44] After returning to Przemyśl, he maintained a close friendship with the head of the Roman Catholic cathedral orchestra, Franciszek Lorenz, who helped him to improve his instrumentation skills. In 1864 Mykhailo Verbyts'kyi set to music the poem *Shche ne vmerla Ukraïna* (Ukraine Has Not Yet Perished), by Pavlo Chubyns'kyi, which still serves as the national anthem of Ukraine.[45] Verbyts'kyi wrote mostly vocal Byzantine church music, but also instrumental works, music to accompany vaudeville and drama, and secular songs. His friend Ioann Lavrovs'kyi (nephew of the priest of the same name) also played an important role in the musical life of the Przemyśl eparchy.[46] Aside from religious works, Lavrovs'kyi set to music the texts of numerous contemporary Galician poets.

Lavrovs'kyi and Verbyts'kyi were the founders of what became known as the "Przemyśl School" of music, which became quite influential throughout Galicia.[47]

The Przemyśl Greek Catholic cathedral choir was favorably received, but it established no new or original direction for the development of Byzantine-Slavonic chant. Bishop Snihurs'kyi's musical training was insufficient for such a task, and he was keen to find a more suitable musician to replace him as conductor. The governor of Przemyśl district suggested that his daughter's music teacher, the Czech Alois Nanke, who had come to Przemyśl from Brno in Moravia, might be a suitable candidate. Father Iosyf Levyts'kyi came to Nanke's aid and explained to him all the texts of the Eastern liturgy and transcribed the necessary pieces into the Latin alphabet. Nanke conducted the choir for the Easter services in 1829. The organ, still in place when the choir performed for the first time at the *Iordan* feast, had by now, with the agreement of the bishop, been removed in order to facilitate a return to purer forms of liturgical celebrations (the organ seems to have been installed shortly after the 1720 Synod of Zamość, which opened the way to accelerated latinization). In addition to Greek Catholics, Nanke invited Roman Catholic Poles and even two Austrians to sing in his choir, and also the district governor's daughter and a captain in the Austrian army stationed in the city.

Alois Nanke established a reputation not only as a talented conductor but also as an instructor, and he began to teach music at the Institute for Deacons and Teachers. Bishop Snihurs'kyi agreed to Nanke's request for permission to hire a second conductor, singer from Brno, Vincenty Zrzavý. Overwhelmed by his increasing responsibilities, Nanke resigned briefly in 1833 and then permanently the following year because of illness. Zrzavý succeeded Nanke both as cathedral choirmaster and as teacher at the institute; he seems to have conducted the cathedral choir until his death in 1853.[48] The contributions of these two Czechs, Nanke and Zrzavý, to the development of Slavonic sacred music were enormous. The quality of their work became well known. Performances of the liturgy under their direction in the Przemyśl Greek Catholic cathedral were attended by school pupils, seminarians of both the Catholic rites, and also by both Polish and Austrian aristocrats.

Przemyśl and its musicians had an enormous impact on Ukrainian church music. Their innovations were rapidly adopted by the Greek Catholic cathedral in L'viv, where in 1838, after the organ was removed, a new choir was established. They spread to other cities, transmitted by graduates of the Institute for Deacons and Teachers and by former members of the cathedral choir.[49] One such member, bass Konstantin Matezonskii / Konstanty Bialorusin, moved to Uzhhorod in 1833, where he organized both a cathedral choir and a Byzantine-Slavonic singing academy.[50] In time, the Przemyśl singing style was adopted by parishes throughout Galicia, Bukovina, and Subcarpathian Rus'.

These musical developments were a catalyst for the more general renewal of the Greek Catholic liturgy, which had experienced far-reaching latinization and consequent impoverishment. Many masses and other rituals had faded entirely from use. Bishop Snihurs'kyi addressed this problem by publishing a large-format 700-page liturgical prayerbook (*Leïtorgïkon syrîch sluzhebnyk*) in 1840. This prayerbook was illustrated by the well-known Galician artist Ioann Vendzylovych (Jan Wedzilowicz) who was active in the Polish national movement. It contained the liturgies of St John Chrysostom, Saint Basil the Great, and St Gregory the Great, the Roman pope.[51] Four years later, simplified versions of rites and customs appeared in another prayerbook, and these were subsequently adopted in Przemyśl as well as in other Greek Catholic eparchies.[52]

Theater

Another important element in the Ruthenian national revival in Przemyśl was the establishment in 1848 of an amateur theater. Its first director was Matylda Saar, the Polish wife of a Galician provincial counselor and the sister of the well-known Galician-Polish politician Franciszek Smolka. The theater's manager was the Ruthenian Ioann Vytoshyns'kyi, who was a lawyer by training but known for his literary essays published under the pseudonym Ivan Aifalevych. In 1849 Vitoshyns'kyi staged an operetta – one-act adaptation of *Der Kosak und der Freiwillige* (The Cossack and the Volunteer), a play by the German writer August Kotzebue. Mykhailo Verbyts'kyi wrote the music. Apart from Ruthenian plays, among them classical works such as those of Ivan Kotliarevs'kyi, the Przemyśl theater performed works by Polish and German writers, as well as by local Greek Catholic priests Foma Polians'kyi, Iosyf Levyts'kyi, and Iustyn Zhelekhovs'kyi, and by the physician Mykhailo Polians'kyi. Among the Przemyśl musicians who wrote for the stage were cathedral choirmaster Zrzavý and two others of Czech origin.

As in the cathedral choirs, so too in the theater, Ruthenians, Poles, and people of other nationalities of the Habsburg Empire performed alongside each other.[53] In mounting works by Polish, Ruthenian, Austrian, German, and Czech playwrights, the Przemyśl theater raised considerably the cultural standards of the city and the surrounding area. The theater also served an integrative function, since the audience, too, comprised people from all nationalities living in the area – Poles, Ruthenians, Jews, and others – as well as government and military officials representing the various peoples of the Austro-Hungarian Empire.

The Political Dimension

In the period leading up to the revolutions of 1848, and the "Springtime of Nations," the Ruthenian national movement was in no way in conflict with the Polish independence movement. Most Ruthenian activists believed that the national consciousness of their people should be strengthened, and thereby form the third element of a revived multinational commonwealth – alongside Poles and Lithuanians. This view was expressed in the popular slogan, *Pol's'ka, Rus', Lytva, to iedna molytva* (Poland, Rus' and Lithuania, are a single prayer). The only exceptions were those members of Ruthenian society in Galicia, the so-called Russophiles, who believed that Ruthenians and Russians formed a single people.

In Przemyśl, Ruthenian activists participated in the Polish conspiratorial movement, and they worked alongside Poles in the scholarly and cultural life of the province. For these Ruthenians, Polishness was not something opposed to their East Slav identity. On the contrary, they felt part of a common heritage characterized by the multinational tradition of the first Polish-Lithuanian Commonwealth (Rzeczpospolita). The Poles, for their part, assisted the East Slavic national awakening through their patronage of Ruthenian culture and of the Greek Catholic Church, which included support for extensive publishing activities in the Ruthenian language.[54] Some Poles acknowledged that one reason for the loss of Poland's independence was the failure of Poles to recognize Ruthenian national aspirations; they were determined, therefore, that such a mistake not be repeated. Such sentiments derived partly from a general romantic sympathy and interest in the common people – as opposed to the rulers.

The Polish uprising of November 1830 against Russian rule politicized cultural life in Austrian Galicia. Many Greek Catholic seminarians of the Przemyśl eparchy joined the Polish Union of the Friends of the People / Związek Przyjaciół Ludu. When a branch of this organization was created in Przemyśl, in April 1834, Ruthenian seminarian Iosyf Konstantynovych / Józef Konstantynowicz was appointed its leader. Ruthenians were also very active in the Association of the Polish People / Stowarzyszenie Ludu Polskiego launched in 1835.[55] Even before this, in 1832, young people of both nationalities in Przemyśl had established Towarzystwo Uczonych (Society of the Educated). Also known as the Senate, this group organized many meetings to discuss cooperation between the two nationalities.[56] This activity was making the Habsburg authorities very nervous, and they observed that it was in Austria's interest to promote antagonism between Poles and Ruthenians. Yet, strong feelings of cultural proximity between these two peoples and the memory of common state institutions, especially among the intellectual elite, pulled in the opposite direction.

Ruthenians also joined Polish scholarly organizations and cooperated closely with individual Polish scholars. Priests from the Przemyśl eparchy's cathedral chapter, Ioann Mohyl'nyts'kyi and Ioann Lavrovs'kyi, maintained frequent contacts with the Polish scholars Zorian Dołęga-Chodakowski and Samuel Bogumil Linde. Chodakowski, for example, enabled Mohyl'nyts'kyi to distribute his school texts to the famous library of the Polish college at Kremianets'.[57] The revolutions of 1848 increased political tensions and ruptured the Ruthenian revival in Galicia.[58] From then on, the leading role in Ruthenian-Ukrainian political, social, and cultural life passed from Przemyśl to L'viv.

Conclusions

In accounting for the leading role played by Przemyśl in the Ruthenian national awakening during the first half of the nineteenth century, the following factors seem to have been critical. First, Przemyśl had the most western-oriented of all the Greek Catholic eparchies and, as such, both priests and lay intellectuals were very much influenced by their Polish colleagues. These contacts were mutually enriching, and there was a healthy process of competition. The Ruthenian national awakening was not considered a threat to Polish national interests. Moreover, representatives of other nationalities, especially Czechs, Austro-Germans, and Armenians, also played an active part in these developments. Second, the status of Przemyśl as a provincial city meant that Austrian censorship was weaker there than in L'viv, which was the seat of the provincial governor and other state institutions. Finally, Przemyśl was able to bring together a unique group of highly talented clergymen, including that outstanding patron of the arts, Bishop Ioann Snihurs'kyi. With their close ties to enlightenment Vienna, these priests eventually left a decisive mark on religious and social life not only in the Greek Catholic eparchy of Przemyśl but throughout eastern Galicia.

Especially in the 1820s, Przemyśl was much more significant than L'viv as a Ruthenian cultural center. This began to change only in the 1830s, as a result of the activities of the Ruthenian Triad and then, later, following the revolutionary events of 1848. Despite this shift, in succeeding decades, Przemyśl remained an important center for both Polish and Ruthenian culture. From the second half of the nineteenth century to the beginning of the twentieth, Przemyśl was also a significant cultural and religious center for the Jews of Galicia, but this is a topic for another study.

Notes

1 See August S. Fenczak and Stanisław Stępień, "Przemyśl jako regionalne centrum administracyjne: zarys dziejów," *Studia Przemyskie*, vol. 1 (Przemyśl, 1993), pp. 9–38.

2 Anna Siciak, "Dzieje pierwszej przemyskiej drukarni Adama Kleina, 1754–1757," *Res Historica*, XIII (Lublin, 2002), pp. 149–170.

3 Zbigniew Fras, Galicja (Wrocław, 1999), p. 19; Henryk Wereszycki, *Pod berłem Habsburgów: zagadnienia narodowościowe* (Cracow, 1986).

4 Walerian Kramarz, *Ludność Przemyśla w latach 1521–1921* (Przemyśl, 1930), p. 40.

5 Ibid., p. 54. On population expansion in the following years, see Leopold Hauser, *Monografia miasta Przemyśla* (Przemyśl, 1883), p. 176. On demographic developments in other small towns in Galicia, see Jadwiga Hoff, "Wygląd małych miast galicyjskich w XIX i na początku XX wieku," in Zbigniew Beiersdorf and Andrzej Laskowski, eds., *Rozwój przestrzenny miast galicyjskich położonych między Dunajcem a Sanem w okresie galicyjskiej* (Jasło, 2001), pp. 97–108.

6 See John-Paul Himka, *Galician Villagers and the Ukrainian National Movement in the Nineteenth Century* (Edmonton, 1998).

7 Włodzimierz Borys, "Z dziejów walk o wyzwolenie narodowe i społeczne w Galicji w pierwszej połowie XIX w: Ignacy Kulczyński w świetle zeznań

Juliana Horoszkiewicza i Kaspra Cięglewicza," *Przemyskie Zapiski Historyczne*, IV–V (Przemyśl, 1987), pp. 223–230.

8 Fras, *Galicia*, p. 41.

9 Anatol Lewicki, *Obrazki z najdawniejszych dziejów Przemyśla*, 2nd ed. (Przemyśl, 1994), pp. 144–145; Johann Christian von Engel, *Geschichte von Halitsch und Wladimir bis 1772*, 2 vols. (Vienna, 1792).

10 Fedir Steblyi, "Peremys'kyi kulturno-osviatovyi oseredok ta ioho diiachi epokhy ukraïns'koho natsional'noho vidrodzhennia (persha polovyna XIX st.)," in *Peremyshl' i peremys'ka zemlia protiahom vikiv* (Przemyśl and L'viv, 1996), pp. 103–130. On the beginnings of the Ukrainian scholarly activity in Przemyśl , see August S. Fenczak and Stanisław Stępień, "Ukraïnoznavchi doslidzhennia v Peremyshli," *Peremys'ki dzvony*, no. 3–4 and 5–6 (Przemyśl, 1993), pp. 14–15 and 24–27.

11 Before the partitions of Poland and during the period of Austrian-ruled Galicia, the Christian names and surnames of Ukrainians were written in two versions. If a document was in Polish, the names were written to reflect a Polish sounding form. In this chapter the first mention of each person of Ukrainian background is in Ukrainian followed by the Polish form. Names also depended on social status. Thus, names written in Polish, such as Jan, Dymitr, Bazyli, or Stefan, had two forms in Ukrainian: Ioann, Dmytryi, Vasylii, or Stefan if such individuals came from families of priests, nobles, or the intelligentsia; and Ivan, Dmytro, Vasyl', or Stepan, if the person came from peasant or poor townspeople's families.

12 The association's statute was published in Ivan Franko, "Pershe rus'ke prosvitne tovarystvo z rr. 1816–1818," *Zapysky istorychno-filosofychnoï sektsiï Naukovoho tovarystva im. Shevchenka*, V (L'viv, 1905), pp. 258–276. See also a discussion of the association's activity in Jan Kozik, *The Ukrainian National Movement in Galicia, 1815–1849* (Edmonton, 1986), pp. 53–56.

13 See Stefan Zabrowarny, "Dzieło biskupa Jana Snigurskiego," in Stanisław Stępień, ed., *Polska-Ukraïna: 1000 lat sąsiedztwa*, vol. III (Przemyśl, 1996), pp. 165–176.

14 On the problem of language, see Paul R. Magocsi, "The Language Question as a Factor in the National Movement in Eastern Galicia," in Andrei S. Markovits and Frank E. Sysyn, eds., *Nationbuilding and the Politics of Nationalism* (Cambridge, Mass., 1982), pp. 220–238.

15 *Nauka khrïstïanskaia po riadu katykhyzma normalnoho k polzî dîtei parafialnŷkh* (Buda, 1815); *Bukvar' slaveno-russkaho iazŷka* (Buda, 1816). Both text books carried the name of Bishop Mykhailo Levyts'kyi as author, although the Polish bibliographer Karol Estreicher suggests Canon Ivan Mohyl'nyts'kyi was author of the catechism.

16 For details, see Mieczysław J. Adamczyk, "Szkolnictwo ludowe w greck-okatolickiej diecezji przemyskiej w latach 1772–1867," in Stępień, *Polska-Ukraïna*, vol. 3, p. 143.

17 See Stanisław Stępień, "Rola Przemyśla w ukraińskim odrodzeniu narodowym w Galicji w pierwszej połowie XIX w.," *Warszawskie Zeszyty Ukrainoznawcze*, VIII–IX (Warsaw, 1999), p. 129.

18 Zygmunt Felczyński, "Rozwój kulturalny Przemyśla 1772–1918," in *Tysiąc lat Przemyśla*, vol. 2 (Warsaw and Cracow 1974), p. 164.

19 Ioann Harasevych, "O prepodavanïiakh na ruskom iazŷtsî i vseuchylyshchy l'vovskom zavedenŷkh vsemyslotyvîyshym Ïmperatorem Ïosyf II," *Zoria halytskaia*, IV, (L'viv, 1851), 61–64.

20 On the Greek Catholic priests linked to Bishop Snihurs'kyi, see W. Pilipowycz, ed., *Lirwak z-nad Sanu: peremys'ki druky seredyny XIX stolitia* (Przemyśl, 2001), pp. 427–446.

21 Archiwum Państwowe w Przemyślu (hereafter APP), Kapituła Greckokatolicka w Przemyślu (hereafter KGK), sign. 49, k. 7–16.

22 August Fenczak, "Zabytki pisma cyrylickiego w dawnych i współczesnych zbiorach południowo-wschodniej Polski," in *Paléographie et diplomatique slaves* (Sofia, 1980), p. 44.

23 APP, KGK, sign. 399, k. 64–66.

24 Antonii Dobrianskii, "Vîdomôst' ystorycheskaia o mîstî Peremŷshly y okruzî tohozhe ymeny," *Peremŷshlianyn*, III (Przemyśl, 1852), pp. 3–132; APP, Archiwum Biskupstwa greckokatolickiego w Przemyślu (hereafter ABGK), sign. 399, k. 64–66.

25 APP, KGK, sign. 49, k. 29–112. See also Leopold Hauser, *Monografia miasta Przemyśla* (Przemyśl, 1883), p. 14.

26 See Ludwik Grzebień, "Fundacje biskupa W.H. Sierakowskiego: biblioteka i drukarnia Jezuitów w Przemyślu,' *Roczniki Biblioteczne*, XXIX, 1–2 (Cracow, 1985), pp. 232–236.

27 For example, Matyaszowski's shop printed the work *Neues ABC voraus die Anfänge der Hebräischen Sprache*. See Karol Estreicher, *Bibliografia polska*, vol. 18 (Cracow, 1897), p. 70.

28 APP, ABGK, sign. 162, k. 1–3.

29 Dobrianskii, "Vîdomôst," p. 91.

30 In 1843 the school mathematics text by Levyts'kyi appeared under the title *Rukovodstvo ko rakhunkam dlia dîtei pochynaiushchykh vchytysia v trïvïal'nôi shkolî vo shklî rakhovaty*. This printer also issued books on economic development, such as V. Havryshkevych, *Rukovodstvo ko oumnozhenïiu i hodovaniyu sadovynŷ po selakh y mîstechkakh* (Przemyśl, 1844).

31 Stępień, "Rola Przemyśla," p. 132.

32 Iosyf Lozynskii, *O obrazovan̈iu iazŷka ruskoho* (Przemyśl, 1849).

33 Antonii Dobrianskii, *Hramatyka staroslavian'skoho tserkovnoho iazŷka* (Przemyśl, 1857).

34 Iakov Doskovskii, *Tserkovnŷi slovar' soderzhashcḧi perevod ... starodavnŷkh slavenskykh y ynoiazycheskykh recheni̇ i v pysani̇ i sviatom y knyhakh tserkovnŷkh* (Przemyśl, 1851).

35 Iaroslav Khordyns'kyi, "Naukova i literaturna pratsia ukraïns'kykh uchyteliv serednykh i vyshchykh shkil u Halychyni XIX i XX st.," in *25-littia Uchytel's'koï hromady* (L'viv, 1935), p. 64.

36 Volodymyr Trembits'kyi, *Ukraïns'kyi hymn ta inshi patriotychni pisni* (New York and Rome, 1973), pp. 40–41.

37 Havriyl Paslavskii, *Nauky parokhïal'nŷia na vsî nedîly tsîloho roku*, 2 vols. (Przemyśl, 1842–1846).

38 Dmytrii Zŷblykevych, *Nauka dukhovnaia, movlena z povodu vprovdzhen̈ia obshchestva vozderzhnosty* (Przemyśl, 1844).

39 Iulian Hankevych, *Nauky na nedîly tsîloho roku*, 2 vols. (Przemyśl, 1848).

40 Ant. D., *Povîsty z pys'ma sviatoho staroho zavîta* (Przemyśl, 1848).

41 Pilipowycz, *Lirvak*, pp. 247–266.

42 APP, ABGK, sign. 9620, k. 1; sign. 3509, k. 68, 86; and sign. 162, k. 165–168. See Z. Łys'ko, *Pionery muzychnoho mystetstva v Halychyni* (L'viv and New York, 1994), pp. 25–26.

43 M.V. yz M. [Mykhailo Verbyts'kyi], "O pîniiu muzŷkal'nom," *Halychanyn*, II, 2 (L'viv, 1863), pp. 136–141.

44 See Izydor Vorobkevych, "Mykaïl Verbyts'kyi," *Kalendar Prosvity* (L'viv, 1884), pp. 39–106.

45 Trembits'kyi, *Ukraïns'kyi hymn*, pp. 51–58.

46 Pilipowycz, *Lirvak*, pp. 407–408.

47 See Borys Kudryk, *Dzieje ukraińskiej muzyki w Galicji w latach 1829–1873* (Przemyśl 2001), p. 125.

48 Lys'ko, *Pionery*, p. 52.

49 Vasyl' Shchurat, "Iak piznaly Bortnians'koho v Zakhodnii Ukraïni," in *Muzychnyi lystok* (L'viv, 1925), pp. 9–10.

50 Matezonskii may be the alias of an émigré from the failed Decembrist Revolt of 1825 in Russia, who settled briefly in Przemyśl (where he was known as Konstanty Bialorusin) before moving on to Uzhhorod in what was then the Hungarian Kingdom. See Vasylii Hadzhega, "Konstantyn Matezonskyi (1794–1858)," *Podkarpatska Rus'*, VI, I (Uzhhorod, 1929), pp. 1–7.

51 The liturgy of St John Chrysostom was published separately in the same year, as *Chyn bozhestvennŷa l̈iturg̈ii* (Przemyśl, 1840).

52 *Evkhologïon sïest trebnyk* (Przemyśl, 1844).

53 Ivan Franko, "Rus'ko-ukraïns'kyi teatr: istorychni obrysy," in his *Zibrannia tvoriv u piatdesiaty tomakh*, vol. 29 (Kiev, 1981), pp. 326–328.

54 See Borys, "Z dziejów walk o wyzwolenie narodowe," pp. 223–230.

55 Bolesław Łopuszański, "Przemyśl jako ośrodek ruchów spiskowych w latach 1834–1840," *Rocznik Przemyski*, XII (Przemyśl, 1968), pp. 130–148; idem., "Udział księży diecezji przemyskiej w konspiracjach galicyjskich w latach 1831–1846," *Nasza Przeszłość*, XLIII (Cracow, 1975), pp. 171–199.

56 Bolesław Łopuszański, *Stowarzyszenie Ludu Polskiego* (Cracow, 1975), pp. 184–217; Henryk Barycz, *Wśród gawędziarzy, pamiętnikarzy i uczonych galicyjskich: Studia i sylwetki z życia umysłowego Galicji XIX w.*, vol. 1 (Cracow, 1963), pp. 247–250.

57 Feodosii I. Steblii, ed., *"Rus'ka triitsia" v istorïï suspil'no-istorychnoho rukhu i kul'tury Ukraïny* (Kiev, 1987), p. 23.

58 See Teofil' Kornarynets', *Ideino-estetychni osnovy ukraïns'koho romantyzmu* (L'viv 1983), which attempts to summarize the earlier contributions of Ivan Franko, Kyrylo Studyns'kyi, Mykhailo Vozniak, Ievhen Kyryliuk, Roman Kyrchyv, and Stefan Kozak.

5 Orthodoxy and Autocephaly in Galicia

HARALD H. JEPSEN

Studies of Eastern Christian religious life in Galicia tend to focus on Uniatism. This is largely because the Uniate or Greek Catholic Church and its clergy were instrumental in the formation of the modern Ukrainian nationality. A historical focus on Orthodoxy in Galicia, however, shows that nationality-building was not a straightforward evolution toward the adoption of a pan-Ukrainian identity. In the nineteenth century, there were, indeed, other options for the East Slavic elite in Galicia.[1]

Whereas various pro-Orthodox movements in the nineteenth century arose within the Galician community, Orthodoxy in the twentieth century was mainly imposed from outside. The native Galician pro-Orthodox legacy, the genuine Ukrainian Orthodox traditions of the early 1920s, and Soviet-imposed Russian Orthodoxy all have left a lasting impact on the mind and soul of Ukrainian Galicians, as a glance at recent statistical surveys of the distribution of religious communities in Ukraine confirms.[2]

Before the Soviet Era

Studies of the nationality-building processes in Galicia clearly demonstrate that rite more than any other feature was the primary ethnic marker identifying a person as Polish or Ruthenian (Ukrainian).[3] Even with people who had linguistically, culturally, or politically assimilated to the Polish nationality, a phenomenon common among the educated Ruthenian elite in the first half of the nineteenth century, the Byzantine (Greek Catholic) rite was decisive in determining their ethnic identity. It might be said that the ethnic marker was given at baptism. In this sense, Roman Catholicism played the role of defining the Other during the formation of Ukrainian national identity in Galicia. If Roman Catholicism functioned as a barrier to a Ruthenian or Ukrainian identity in nineteenth-century Galicia, the same cannot be said with certainty of Orthodoxy.

By its very nature, the Greek Catholic Church lacked a spiritual tradition of its own. Thus, it was bound to oscillate between the two traditions that had given birth to Uniatism, that is, Roman Catholicism and Byzantine Orthodoxy. This became obvious by the mid-nineteenth century, when the benefits of the Austrian educational reforms helped to provide the Greek Catholic Church with a well-educated hierarchy and clergy. Polish-Latin influence on the church was strong in 1848 and remained so long afterwards. However, with the defeat of Ruthenian political aspirations after the revolution, this influence became subject to criticism, especially from anti-Polish Galician Russophiles. Within the church criticism took the form of a movement to purify the Byzantine rite in Galicia of its Polish and Latin accretions.[4] As anti-Polish sentiments grew stronger, Greek Catholic purists came very close to Orthodoxy. The purists had been active since the early 1830s. Under the protection and spiritual guidance of Metropolitan Hryhorii Iakhymovych, in the 1860s, they came to occupy a central position in church affairs.[5] This group came to be known as Old Ruthenians (*Starorusyny*), or the St George Circle, after the name of the church complex at the metropolitan see in L'viv. In their anti-Polish political views, the Old Ruthenians resembled the Russophiles, although they cannot be fully identified with the latter, which was mainly a secular movement.[6] The activities of the Old Ruthenians included, but were not limited to, the restoration of the Byzantine character of their church and advocating the use of a local recension of Church Slavonic in secular writing. When expectations associated with a stronger orientation toward Vienna were dashed by the Austro-Hungarian Polish Compromise of 1867, some Old Ruthenians went even further and took their criticism to its logical conclusion: they converted to Orthodoxy and became Russians.[7] In the 1860s and 1870s a number of Greek Catholic canons left Galicia for tsarist Russia to enter imperial service. Former Greek Catholic priests from the St George's Circle had a strong hand in the liquidation of the last surviving Greek Catholic parishes in the Russian Empire – those belonging to the Eparchy of Kholm/Chełm in Congress Poland. Partly as a result of their efforts, the last Greek Catholic Bishop of Kholm converted to Orthodoxy in 1875.[8]

The harsh anti-Uniate politics of the tsarist regime also had the effect that Old Ruthenians in Galicia who were leaning towards Orthodoxy had only a limited impact in their homeland. The easternizing trend seems to have been tolerated as long as it was restricted to the intellectual circles within the church, and as long as it stayed clear of overt Russophilism. But in 1882, when a small Galician village unsuccessfully attempted to convert to Orthodoxy, the spiritual leader of the St George's Circle, Father Ioann Naumovych, and others, were arrested by the Austrian authorities and accused of being tsarist agents. Naumovych and several of his supporters were tried and acquitted. Shortly afterwards Naumovych left for Russia. Because he had failed to curb the spread of Russophilism among leading members of the priesthood. The Greek Catholic Metropolitan Iosyf Sembratovych was made to resign.[9] This incident was a major setback to the Russophile movement in Galicia. Rome and Vienna decided that the metropolitans of the Greek Catholic Church would henceforth be recruited solely from the ranks of clergy educated by Roman Catholics, to ensure that spiritual and political control remained with the Roman church. Yet, as the case of Metropolitan Andrei Sheptyts'kyi shows, this measure did not put an end to the church's easternizing policies.

Sheptyts'kyi entered the metropolitan see in 1900 on the recommendation of Polish conservatives in L'viv and Vienna. But he never lived up to the hopes of his mentors.[10] He continued the easternizing reforms of the rite, but unlike his predecessors never adopted the political program of the Russophiles. In Sheptyts'kyi's view, Byzantine traditions could be restored within the existing structure of the universal Catholic Church. This was the core principle of the reforms that Sheptyts'kyi undertook throughout the more than four decades he occupied the highest office of the Greek Catholic Church in Galicia.

In the years before World War I, tsarist Russia undertook efforts to reduce the growing influence of Galicia on its western provinces.[11] Material support was given to Galician Russophiles and Orthodox writings were sponsored, especially in the borderland area. These efforts had only a limited success in Austrian Galicia. However, among Galician immigrants in the United States, a considerable number of Greek Catholics converted to Orthodoxy as a result of the Russian Orthodox missions abroad.[12] Nevertheless Sheptyts'kyi was on the whole successful in dealing with the Russophiles within the ranks of the church in Galicia.

Galicia and Bukovina were occupied twice by tsarist troops during

World War I. Soon after the first invasion (1914–1915), the Russian Holy Synod appointed Bishop Evlogii (Georgievskii) of Kholm to promote conversion to Orthodoxy. Bishop Evlogii was chosen because he had a record of close contacts with the Galician Russophiles.[13] At the same time, Metropolitan Sheptyts'kyi was arrested after delivering a critical sermon and exiled to a monastery in central Russia. When released from his internment, in March 1917, Sheptyts'kyi undertook the restoration of the Greek Catholic Church in Galicia. At the same time he discreetly examined the possibilities for an expansion of his church into the Russian Empire, including Ukraine. Russia's wartime efforts to convert Galicia to Orthodoxy by force ended in vain. By the end of the war, the Russophile orientation had been discredited in Galicia and some of its most prominent adherents had fled to Russia. Insofar as the Russian occupation and the general turmoil of the war had any long-term impact on Galicia, it was only to contribute to the process of national self-identification among Ruthenians in Galicia in favor of adopting a Ukrainian identity. The forcible introduction of Orthodoxy, in this respect, played a part in paving the way for the nationality-building that crystallized during the Ukrainian Revolution of 1917 to 1920.

The Soviet Era

Galicia's second exposure to Orthodoxy occurred following the Soviet annexation of the region east of the San River in late 1939. As in 1914, the jurisdiction of the Russian Orthodox Church was extended to Galicia, and Soviet authorities placed an Orthodox bishop in L'viv to conduct the planned conversion. Aware that it was too dangerous to remove the extremely popular Metropolitan Sheptyts'kyi, the Soviets tried, instead, to undermine his influence.[14] For this purpose, the Cheka (Soviet security service) approached Father Havriïl Kostel'nyk, well known as an easternizer, in an effort to install him as head of a rival "national" Greek Catholic Church separate from Rome. Kostel'nyk turned them down, and because of the limited duration of that Soviet occupation (1939–1941) these efforts came to nothing. However, they did serve as a prelude to the final liquidation of the Greek Catholic Church in Galicia a year after World War II ended.

Materials recently released from Ukrainian and Russian state and Communist party archives, and from the archives of the Council for Relations with the Russian Orthodox Church, cast new light on the mechanisms behind the so-called Reunification Sobor (Church Council) of L'viv in 1946 and the ensuing forcible conversion of Galician Greek Catholic parishes to Orthodoxy.[15] The abrogation of the 1596 Union of Brest, and the merger of the Greek Catholic Church with the Russian Orthodox Church, were obviously staged by the Soviets, with the reluctant but cooperative acquiescence of the Russian Orthodox Moscow Patriarchal See. Using threats, terror, and disinformation, the Soviet security services forced a number of junior clerics, under the guidance of Father Kostel'nyk, to dissolve the Greek Catholic Church. As the archival record shows, the Kremlin had already taken the decision to eliminate the Greek Catholic Church in the spring of 1945 – shortly after the participants of the Yalta Conference had approved the incorporation of the main part of Eastern Galicia into the Soviet Union. The principal impetus behind Moscow's decision was its determination to break the backbone of the Ukrainian national movement and eliminate the spiritual force behind the Ukrainian partisans' struggle against Soviet power. On the surface, the incorporation of the Greek Catholic Church into the formerly strong but now diminished Russian Orthodox Church was to be seen as a reward for the Orthodox Church's contribution to Soviet patriotism during the crucial war years. It was also a way of creating a single religious body that could be instrumental in the regime's ongoing efforts to control the minds of the faithful.

Why did Kostel'nyk give in to Soviet pressure and undertake the leadership of the movement for (re)unification with the Russian Orthodox Church? Substantial evidence now indicates that he had envisaged himself as a saviour of Greek Catholic traditions in Galicia, at a time when these were being threatened with total annihilation.[16] By April 1945 the entire leadership of the Greek Catholic Church had been arrested and exiled, and Kostel'nyk believed it unlikely they would ever return. Thus, Kostel'nyk used his new position to convince the Moscow see of the necessity to retain as many of the unique traditions of the Greek Catholic Church as possible. This was crucial, he argued, to avoid alienation of the believers and priests and to prevent their defection to what became a Greek Catholic "catacomb" (or underground) church. Both the Moscow patriarchate and the Soviet authorities seem to have accepted these arguments, even though the "imported" Russian Orthodox Bishop Makarii had reported to the Soviet authorities that he feared Kostel'nyk had secret plans to establish an authocephalous Ukrainian Orthodox Church in Galicia.[17]

The "reunited" Orthodox Church in Galicia did in fact manage to preserve some traditions of the Greek Catholic Church, such as the use of Ukrainian pronunciation for Church Slavonic. But these traditions were no longer nurtured in the highly russified Orthodox seminars, and it was difficult to retain them in the long run. It was the "catacomb" church in western Ukraine that preserved the collective memory of the Greek Catholic Church. When it surfaced during the late 1980s, it was this clandestine church and its stalwart supporters in exile who could claim to be the true heirs to the spiritual and institutional legacy of what was now called the Ukrainian Catholic Church in Galicia.[18]

Developments after 1989

Parishes in Galicia began to defect from the Russian Orthodox Church, in 1989, to support the revitalized Ukrainian Greek Catholic Church. To oppose this development, a new Orthodox church emerged in L'viv. This new church was established by priests dissatisfied with the indifference – even hostility – of the Russian Orthodox Moscow Patriarchate, and its Exarchate in Kiev, towards Ukrainian national aspirations.[19] These priests wanted to remain Orthodox but they feared their parishes would defect to the Greek Catholics, who were again asserting their historic role as the standardbearers of the Ukrainian national cause in Galicia. The new Ukrainian Orthodox church was thus designed to attract the nationally minded among believers, especially those who had become fully accustomed to Orthodoxy or who simply did not want to be subject to the Polish pope in Rome. The church came into existence in August 1989: Father Dmitrii Iarema and the parish of Saints Peter and Paul in L'viv announced their decision to leave the Russian Orthodox Church and simultaneously declared their adherence to the Ukrainian Autocephalous Orthodox Church (UAOC).

The roots of the Ukrainian Autocephalous Orthodox Church lay in the Soviet Ukraine in the 1920s.[20] Although dismantled by Soviet authorities, it emerged again for a brief period during World War II in the Nazi-German ruled Reichskommissariat Ukraine; it never managed, however, to attract any significant support on Galician soil.[21] When the Soviet forces returned to Galicia in late 1944, the Autocephalous church was "liquidated" and together with the Greek Catholic Church discredited as a collaborationist church. No UAOC catacomb church seems to have existed in Soviet Ukraine, and only in the late

1980s did a small group for the restoration of Ukrainian Orthodoxy emerge in dissident circles in Kiev and L'viv.[22] Until then, the tradition of the UAOC was kept alive mainly in émigré communities abroad. The Church's overseas leadership welcomed the reborn "Galician" UAOC into its ranks immediately. Within a year, by the end of 1990, some 1,000 UAOC parishes had been formed throughout western Ukraine, mainly in Galicia.[23]

Father Dmitrii Iarema, founder of the restored UAOC in Ukraine, was a former Greek Catholic priest who, in 1946, had followed Kostel'nyk into Orthodoxy. In the initial phase of the UAOC's existence, Iarema explicitly invoked the legacy of Kostel'nyk's "reunited" Orthodox church in the unspoiled form it had allegedly regained in the 1940s.[24] In this way, the Ukrainian Autocephalous Orthodox Church can with some justification be considered heir to both the traditions of the prewar Greek Catholic easternizers as well as to postwar Soviet-imposed Orthodoxy in Galicia.

The last surviving bishop of the wartime, or second, UAOC and spiritual leader of the émigré church, Metropolitan Mstyslav (Skrypnyk), was elected patriarch in May 1990 at a sobor (church council) marking the return of the church to its titular territory. Mstyslav was a nephew of Symon Petliura (hero of Ukraine's first period of independence, 1917–1920) and thus well qualified to link the new church to a positive image of Ukrainian statehood. These features, although essentially non-Galician, gave credibility and popular support to the third, "Galician" UAOC. The very name, Ukrainian Autocephalous Orthodox Church, still attracted respect, and the fact that the first UAOC during the Ukrainian "Golden Age" of the 1920s had mainly served as a national church for eastern, Soviet Ukrainians did not diminish its mobilizing impact on Galician Ukrainians.

As it emerged in Galicia and western Ukraine during the national revival of the late 1980s and early 1990s, the UAOC followed a consistent all-Ukrainian stance. Its priests and bishops attended all major anniversaries in honor of the Zaporozhian Cossacks and the poet Taras Shevchenko, as well as commemorations for victims of the Great Famine of 1933.[25] The UAOC quickly associated itself with the semi-independent Kievan Metropolitanate of the Cossack era (that is, before Kiev was made fully subordinate to the Moscow Patriarchate after 1686) and claimed to be the true church of the Zaporozhians, famed as fierce defenders of Orthodoxy against Catholics.[26] This strategy enabled the UAOC to provide a serious challenge to the Ukrainian Greek Catholic

Church on its traditional territory. More than 90 percent of the UAOC's 1,300 parishes in Ukraine are located in Galicia.[27] In fact, the distribution of UAOC congregations strongly resembles the distribution of Ukrainian Greek Catholic parishes. Both churches face the same problems of how to expand their influence beyond western Ukraine and Kiev and how to attract the support of Ukrainians who are not particularly conscious of their national identity. Conflicts between the two "Galician" churches over property and parishes have occurred, but not to the same degree as conflicts between the Ukrainian Greek Catholic Church and parishes of the Russian Orthodox Church, recently renamed the Ukrainian Orthodox Church-Moscow Patriarchate.

After the death of Mstyslav in 1993, Father Iarema was elevated to the post of patriarch of the UAOC and, claiming Kievan heritage, took up residence in Kiev. The stronghold of the UAOC, however, remains Galicia. By the mid-1990s it was the largest Orthodox church there, claiming some 20 percent of all religious congregations.[28] During its short (renewed) existence the UAOC has proved capable of surviving internal splits, and it has fought off "usurpation" by the Ukrainian Orthodox Church-Kiev Patriarchate. This rival Ukrainian national church is headed by the former Russian Orthodox Church Exarch in Ukraine, Filaret.

In the struggle with the Ukrainian Catholic Church for the mind and soul of Galician Ukrainians, the UAOC stresses that it is independent of foreign control. Neither Rome nor Moscow has any say in its affairs. In pointing out to the Greek Catholics that their church has failed to get permission from Rome to resurrect the Ukrainian Catholic patriarchal see in Kiev, the Autocephalists struck a soft spot among many Greek Catholic priests and bishops, both in Ukraine and abroad, who tend to perceive Rome's reluctance on this matter as a mark of disregard for the national aspirations of Ukrainians and of Ukrainian independence.[29] Irritation with Rome has been strongest among the leaders of the former "catacomb" church, who were further annoyed that many of the highest positions in Ukraine's re-established Greek Catholic Church went to priests from abroad and not to the "martyrs of the underground." Discontent culminated in 1993: a Ukrainian newspaper reported that the former clandestine archbishop of the "catacomb" church, Volodymyr Sterniuk, was imprisoned at the St George Church complex in L'viv. Apparently, he had issued a statement to the Ukrainian people that called upon the Greek Catholic and the Autocephalous Orthodox churches to unite in one Ukrainian Apostolic Orthodox Church.[30] Sterniuk later denied ever being a prisoner and confirmed his loyalty to the pope. But he never withdrew his original statement about the desirability for union of the Greek Catholic and Orthodox churches.

The Ukrainian Autocephalous Orthodox Church has engaged in cross-confessional talks to establish a single church in Ukraine, whether with an Orthodox or an apostolic patriarch of Kiev.[31] Metropolitan-Archbishop of the Ukrainian Greek Catholic Church in L'viv, Lubomyr Cardinal Husar, is in favor of dialogue with the Autocephalous Orthodox Church. Only time will show if these efforts can succeed.

Conclusion

It should be evident from the foregoing that Orthodoxy in the form of *Ukrainian* Orthodoxy has become an integral part of Galicia's confessional life. A new Orthodox Church has emerged, based partly on a Galician legacy of Greek Catholic efforts at easternization and partly on what essentially are non-Galician Orthodox traditions. Orthodoxy is now challenging the position of the re-established Ukrainian Greek Catholic Church, which previously was the dominant church of nationally conscious Ukrainian Galicians. The third Ukrainian Autocephalous Orthodox Church has been able to adjust skilfully to the demands of the present in terms of Ukrainian nationality- and state-building. As far as regional identity is concerned, the success of Ukrainian Orthodoxy in Galicia must be perceived as a sign of Galicia's relatively high level of cultural integration with eastern or Dnieper Ukraine. Pan-Ukrainian spiritual traditions and Cossack mythology, which accompanied the emergence and spread of the Ukrainian Autocephalous Orthodox Church in western Ukraine, have clearly taken roots in the region, although historically the latter are non-Galician in character.

Notes

1 John-Paul Himka, "The Greek Catholic Church and Nation-Building in Galicia, 1772–1918," *Harvard Ukrainian Studies*, VIII, 3–4 (Cambridge, Mass., 1984), pp. 426–452; and his *Religion and Nationality in Western Ukraine* (Montreal and Kingston, Ont., 1999).

2 See Aleksej Krinda, "Kirchenlandschaft Ukraine – Probleme, Kämpfe, Entwicklungen," *Osteuropa*, XLVII, 10–11 (Stuttgart, 1997), pp. 1067–1074. As of January 1, 1996, one-third of all the registered religious congregations

in Galicia (the oblasts of L'viv, Ternopil', and Ivano-Frankivs'k) belonged to the three Orthodox churches active in the area.

3 Himka, "Greek Catholic Church," pp. 446–447.

4 A. Korczok, *Die griechischkatholische Kirche in Galizien* (Leipzig, 1921), p. 121-136.

5 Himka, "Greek Catholic Church," pp. 438-439.

6 See the comments on this subject by Stefan Kieniewicz, "Rudnytsky's *Essays in Modern Ukrainian History* in the Eyes of a Polish Historian," *Harvard Ukrainian Studies*, XI, 3–4, (Cambridge, Mass., 1987), p. 525; and the extensive discussions by Paul Robert Magocsi, "Old Ruthenianism and Russophilism: A New Conceptual Framework for Analyzing National Ideologies in Late 19th Century Eastern Galicia," in Paul Debreczyn, ed., *American Contributions to the Ninth International Congress of Slavists*, vol. 2 (Columbus, Ohio, 1983), pp. 305–324.

7 Ivan L. Rudnytsky, *Essays in Modern Ukrainian History* (Edmonton, 1987), pp. 324-325; and Himka, *Religion and Nationality*, pp. 73–78.

8 Ibid., pp. 57–64.

9 Ibid., pp. 73–98.

10 For a wide-ranging discussion of this prelate's long and variegated career, see Paul Robert Magocsi, ed., *Morality and Reality: The Life and Times of Andrei Sheptyts'kyi* (Edmonton, 1989).

11 Rudnytsky, *Essays*, pp. 343–344.

12 On the impact of the Russian Empire in promoting Russophilism in Galicia and Orthodoxy in the United States, see Anna Veronika Wendland, *Die Russophilen in Galizien* (Vienna, 2001), pp. 427–486; and Keith Dyrud, *The Quest for the Rusyn Soul* (Philadelphia, 1992), pp. 35–57.

13 See the discussion in Mark van Hagen, "War and the Transformation of Loyalties and Identities in the Russian Empire, 1914–1918," paper presented at the 100th International Colloquium, Russia in the Age of Wars (1914–1945): Toward a New Paradigm, Cortona, October 1997, pp. 17-18.

14 Bohdan R. Bociurkiw, "Sheptyts'kyi and the Ukrainian Greek Catholic Church under the Soviet Occupation of 1939–1941," in Magocsi, *Morality and Reality*, pp. 101–123; and O. Ie. Lysenko, "Do pytannia pro stanovyshche tserkvy v Ukraïni u period druhoï svitovoï viiny," *Ukraïns'kyi istorychnyi zhurnal*, XXXIX, 5 (Kiev, 1995), pp. 73–74.

15 Bohdan R. Bociurkiw, *The Ukrainian Greek Catholic Church and the Soviet State, 1939–1950* (Edmonton, 1996).

16 Ibid.

17 Ibid.

18 Serge Keleher, *Passion and Resurrection: The Greek Catholic Church in Soviet Ukraine, 1939–1989* (L'viv, 1993), esp. pp. 83–98.

19 Frank Sysyn, "The Third Rebirth of the Ukrainian Autocephalous Church and the Religious Situation in Ukraine, 1989-91," in Stephen K. Batalden, ed., *Seeking Good: The Rediscovery of Religious Identity in Orthodox Russia, Ukraine, and Georgia* (DeKalb, Ill., 1993), pp. 191–219.

20 Bohdan R. Bociurkiw, "The Rise of the Ukrainian Autocephalous Orthodox Church, 1919–1922," in Geoffrey Hosking, ed., *Church, Nation and State in Russia and Ukraine* (New York, 1991), pp. 228–249; Bohdan Bociurkiw, "The Ukrainian Autocephalous Church, 1920–30: A Case Study in Religious Modernization," Dennis J. Dunn, ed., *Religion and Modernization in the Soviet Union* (Boulder, Colo., 1977), pp. 310–347.

21 Bohdan R. Bociurkiw, "The Soviet Destruction of the Ukrainian Autocephalous Orthodox Church, 1929–36," *Journal of Ukrainian Studies*, XII, I [22] (Edmonton, 1987), pp. 5–7. A similar Autocephalous Orthodox Church had existed briefly during World War II in Nazi-occupied Belarus.

22 Bohdan Nahaylo, "Initiative Group for the Restoration of the Ukrainian Autocephalous Orthodox Church Founded," *Report on the USSR*, no. 10 (Munich, 1989), pp. 24–26. On the earlier defence of the UAOC during the 1960s and 1970s, see Vasyl' Romaniuk, *A Voice in the Wilderness: Letters, Appeals, Essays* (Wheaton, 1980).

23 Sysyn, "Third Rebirth," p. 199.

24 Bohdan Bociurkiw, "Politics and Religion in Ukraine: The Orthodox Church and the Greek Catholics," in Michael Bourdeaux, ed., *The Politics of Religion in Russia and the New States of Eurasia* (New York, 1995), p. 140.

25 Taras Kuzio, "In Search of Unity and Autocephaly: Ukraine's Orthodox Churches," *Religion, State, and Society*, XXV, 4 (Keston, England, 1997), pp. 393–394.

26 Frank Sysyn, "The Reemergence of the Ukrainian Nation and Cossack Mythology," *Social Research*, LVIII, 4 (New York, 1991), pp. 845–864.

27 Krinda, "Kirchenlandschaft Ukraine," p. 1078.

28 Ibid.

29 On the patriarchal movement within the Ukrainian Greek Catholic Church, see Serhii Plokhy, "Between Moscow and Rome: The Struggle for the Greek Catholic Patriarchate in Ukraine," *Journal of Church and State*, XXXVII, 4 (Waco, Tex., 1995), pp. 849–868.

30 See further details in ibid., pp. 854–856.

31 Irina Lukoms'ka, "Pravoslavne ob"iednannia rozpochalosia?," *Vechirnii Kyïv* (Kiev), April 14, 1998.

6 Galician Identity in Ukrainian Historical and Political Thought

VOLODYMYR POTUL'NYTS'KYI

For the purposes of this chapter the term *Galician* means a person of Ukrainian (or Ruthenian) lineage who is from or living in Galicia.[1] The image of Galicia has an important place in the historical development of Ukrainian political thought. Contemporary Ukrainian views on Galician identity largely reflect the positions articulated in Ukrainian political writing in the four or five decades on both sides of the year 1900. An examination of the origins of these positions is therefore pertinent to the understanding of Galicia's regional identity, as well as the continued development of Ukrainian identity more generally.

Historical and political works published after 1860, but especially between 1918 and 1945, provide basic sources for identifying Ukrainian perceptions of Galicia and Galicians in this era. The three major currents promoted in this literature are populism, conservatism, and national statehood. In Galicia, conservatism and aspirations to statehood were dominant. In eastern Ukraine, however, conservatism had strong competition from populism. It becomes important to explore how the image of Galicia and Galicians within Galicia differed from the image of Galicia and Galicians as found in eastern Ukrainian sources. We might ask: Was the problem of Galicia considered to be a separate one from the problem of Ukrainian national identity? Did the idea ever emerge that Galician Ukrainians could perhaps form a nationality in their own right? How far is it accurate to speak of a unified position historically as far as Ukrainian attitudes toward Galicia are concerned? How significant has the Galician theme been in the formulation of Ukrainian identity, and vice versa? Finally, what differences and similarities among eastern Ukrainian and Galician political writers emerge on close examination of what they have to say about nationality, national territory, statehood, and history? These questions will be considered from four perspectives: two images drawn by Ukrainians from outside Galacia, the populists and the conservatives of eastern Ukraine, and another two images from within, the conservatives and national-statists of Galicia.

Images from Outside

The Populists

From the 1840s to the Ukrainian revolutionary era of 1917 to 1920, populism was by far the dominant current in Ukrainian political thought. To populists "the people" (*narod* – strongly identified with the peasantry) was a homogeneous mass. Anything or anyone that arose above the *narod* was condemned as parasitic, morally tainted, and essentially non-Ukrainian. Populist writers focused on the lives of working people, romanticizing their uprisings, revolts, and revolutions, and disregarding the state-authorized depiction of history. Although Mykola Kostomarov was a seminal populist figure, Ukrainian populist ideology is most fully elaborated in the works of historians Volodymyr Antonovych and Mykhailo Hrushevs'kyi. They had many students and disciples, among them Oleksander Lazarevs'kyi, Aleksandra Efimenko, Dmytro Iavornyts'kyi, Mykola Sumtsov, and Dmytro Bahalii. For the most part, these intellectuals discussed Ukrainian culture in relationship to, and in terms of, all-Russian culture, which was, of course, ubiquitous in the life of every Ukrainian living in the tsarist empire. Ukraine and Russia were deemed to be regional societies within a large bicultural (Rus') state. These populists viewed with suspicion the state-building efforts by Ukrainian elites.[2]

Volodymyr Antonovych emphasized the differences between historical developments in western Ukraine (Galicia) and in central Dnieper Ukraine. In the western regions that had been under Polish rule before the Union of Lublin (1569), local Rus' aristocrats and local Lithuanian knights had received the same rights as Polish noblemen; the old communal order was destroyed. In lands that remained under Lithuania, especially southern Podolia and territories east of Volhynia, by contrast, the communes developed into strong organizations. In constant danger from Tatar raids, villagers took up arms and became skilled warriors. In Dnieper Ukraine local princes granted the communes lands and the rights of self-government. According to Antonovych, these free and partially militarized communes grew into the first Ukrainian Cossack communities.[3]

Antonovych lauded the continuity between Old Kievan and Cossack

traditions in Dnieper Ukraine while insisting that in Galicia this continuity had been interrupted. Following the collapse of the old communal
order in Galicia, the villagers borrowed and adapted the ethno-psycho-
logical features of their Polish neighbors. One such feature, acquired
from the Greek Catholic Church, and from Catholicism per se, according
to Antonovych, was intolerance toward alien religions. Another was
doctrinaire methodology in scholarship and a general preference for
philosophy and history. By contrast, Antonovych submitted, the political ideals of eastern Ukrainians were truth, justice, and equality in the
public sphere. These ideals were expressed in the ancient common public meeting or assembly (*viche*), in the Cossack council (*rada*), and in the
"Cossack Stronghold" (Zaporozhian Sich), where all members enjoyed
a certain measure of freedom and equality. As to the religion of the eastern Ukrainians, Antonovych came to the conclusion that this depended
entirely on deep personal feeling, rather than on ritual. Eastern Ukrainians showed a benign intolerance toward the religion of others, an attitude summed up by the saying: "don't touch what is mine, and I won't
touch what is yours."[4] In considering Galician Ukrainians, Antonovych
pointed out that the introduction in 1861 of a constitutional regime
throughout the Austrian Empire gave them the opportunity to fight –
legally – for their national and cultural rights. He predicted that a similar
struggle would develop later among the masses in Russian-ruled eastern Ukraine. Self-interest, he argued, was forcing the great powers to
make concessions to the emerging nationalities as they raised demands
grounded in universally valid and progressive principles.[5]

Mykhailo Hrushevs'kyi stressed that Galicia was part of another
state and that its church was different from that of eastern Ukraine.
Should these different political cultural influences persist, he believed,
the eastern and western parts of Ukraine would each go its own way
and in twenty or thirty years would form two different nationalities –
derived from the same ethnos. Then they will be similar to the Serbs
and Croats: two parts of the Serbian tribe, but, because of political, cultural, and religious circumstances, completely separated from one
another. Hrushevs'kyi remarked that Hungarian Rus' (Subcarpathian
Rus' / Transcarpathia) had already became alienated from Galicia.[6]

Nevertheless, Hrushevs'kyi argued that in its essentials, Ukrainian
society in Galicia was still very similar to Ukrainian society in eastern
Ukraine. This was especially the case when comparing them with
neighboring Poles, Belarusans, or Russians. This perspective reduced
the regional differences among Ukrainians, to a degree. However, Hru-

shevs'kyi did emphasize that among the particularities of Galicia was that western influence which dated back to the period of the medieval principality of Galicia-Volhynia. In stark contrast to eastern Ukraine, Galicia "had completely entered the sphere of western European life." Noting the large number of German colonies in western Ukraine, Hrushevs'kyi explained that from the end of the fourteenth century L'viv, Galicia's main center, had become a typically German town. It remained so during the fifteenth and much of the sixteenth centuries – but at the same time it was also a Rus' cultural center. This part of Ukraine had been fully exposed to both the Italian-German Renaissance and the German Reformation. Galicia had borrowed much from the West, including its architecture and art. Nevertheless, Hrushevs'kyi pointed out that western influences in Galicia "were not borrowed in a slavish manner [nevil'nycho]," but were creatively modified by the peculiarities of the Ukrainian national spirit.[8]

In considering the role of the medieval principality of Galicia-Volhynia in Ukrainian history, Hrushevs'kyi noted that the peripheral location of Galicia had disqualified it from becoming an "all-Ukrainian state." Furthermore, he insisted, this remained the case in the twentieth century. The four centuries of Polish rule had left particularly destructive effects. Indeed, economic and cultural backwardness in Galicia was the main "legacy of historical Poland, which assiduously skimmed everything that could be considered the cream of the nation, leaving it in a state of oppression and helplessness."[8] Polish domination extended beyond the boundaries of Galicia and into the present time. In most of western Ukraine – which for Hrushevs'kyi meant not only Galicia but also Podolia, Volhynia, the lands along the western Bug River / Pobuzhzhia, the Kholm/Chełm region, and Polissia – Poles occupied a privileged position. This he attributed to their extensive landed property holdings and their more favorable historical development. In 1928 he again hurled blame at "historical Poland," which after World War I had reasserted itself in Galicia, as part of a new postwar political entity that Hrushevs'kyi described as Pilsudski-ist.[9]

Whereas Polish and German influences had been decisive in Galicia, Hrushevs'kyi considered eastern Ukrainians to be among the most "orientalized" of Europe's peoples, together with Bulgarians, Serbs, and Spaniards. It was this combination of a western cultural foundation with eastern influences that, in Hrushevs'kyi's mind, made up the very essence of the Ukrainian people. Their eastern heritage was an immutable ethnological and anthropological component of the Ukrainian people. It should not remain silent or be ignored in the future process of nation-building, since it "facilitates relations with our neighbors, who have gone through analogous oriental influences, and helps to form a foundation for cooperation and common moral values."[10]

Hrushevs'kyi spoke of a "lack of culture" (*nekul'turnist'*) among eastern Ukrainians. But he also allowed that national feeling had not been completely extinguished, especially among those who had risen above the level of the popular masses. This "semi-preservation" (*napiv-zberezhenist'*) of the national consciousness "was an incomprehensible racial instinct, which in itself did not promise anything positive."[11] But Galicia, he said, as the western borderland of Ukrainian territory, had never been in a position to unify the Ukrainian lands: "The [medieval] Galician-Volhynian state did not manage to become an all-Ukrainian one in the same way the Kievan state had been. It was confined to western Ukraine, although there were times when it seemed it might take possession of the whole of Ukraine, or at least expand its sphere of influence in the east. Various contingencies stood in the way but, even without them, such an expansion was hampered by the very fact that it was Galicia, the western border of the Ukrainian territory, that had become the basis for the state."[12]

The Conservatives

The conservative position in Ukrainian political thought at this time emphasized the role of the state as the principal organizing factor in society.[13] Conservatives belonged for the most part to the hereditary nobility that used Ukrainian as their native language.[14] They favored the restoration of the eighteenth-century Cossack state, the Hetmanate, and called for recognition of their rights as nobles in Russian society. They also wished to preserve autonomist traditions in the form of a "Little Russian" regional patriotism. In this way, they formed a partial link to the modern Ukrainian national movement.

These conservatives were the descendants of the Cossack Hetmanate's ruling social stratum (*starshyna*), which had been partially co-opted into the Russian nobility. By the nineteenth century many of them had a dual Ukrainian-Russian identity and loyalty, a phenomenon that could also be observed in the largely assimilated nobilities of other nationalities such as the Czechs or Lithuanians.[15] This Ukrainian nobility had preserved the concept of the "noble nation" – that is, a nation, or nationality, defined not by ethnicity but by membership in the Cossack military social stratum. They spoke Russian as well as Ukrainian, and recognized the tsarist government. They also maintained the old traditions of ethnic separateness from Russia and struggled to maintain autonomy for Ukraine.[16] Thus, they cultivated historic traditions, published documents from the Ukrainian past, compiled oral folk literature, and emphasized the importance of bringing together collections of artifacts for the new museums.[17]

From the 1860s until the end of the 1890s the conservative concept of Ukrainian nationality was perhaps best represented by Mykhailo Drahomanov. He lived in the Russian Empire, and so his contacts with Ukrainians in Galicia were limited. Nevertheless, Drahomanov was aware of these evidently prosperous Ukrainians who lived "abroad," in a different country and under a different political system. As he began to treat the Ukrainians of Austria-Hungary as integral to the Ukrainian question, Drahomanov came to realize that the two communities faced somewhat different problems. Ukrainians in Galicia had developed a strong sense of their national identity and cultural distinctness separating them from their surrounding populations, who in the main were Polish and Roman Catholic. By contrast, Ukrainians in Russia found it more difficult to define themselves as a distinct group, even if participation in Russian political and cultural spheres did not preclude the presence of a residual Ukrainian consciousness. Furthermore, in Austrian Galicia, religion and language made the Ukrainians a conspicuously distinct group.[18]

When, in 1873, Drahomanov went to L'viv, he was surprised and dismayed at what he found to be the provincialism of intellectual life there. During the visit he discovered a further feature of Ukrainian society in Galicia which would complicate the introduction of any progressive ideas – an overwhelming deference to the church.[19] Fear of antagonizing the clergy absorbed even the populists (narodovtsi), who otherwise had diverse and often critically liberal views on religion.[20] Drahomanov concluded that in Galicia it would be impossible to encourage independent political development among Ukrainians as long as the influential clergy continued to serve the interests of the dominant Austro-Germans.[21]

A significant barrier to effective literary or political work among Ukrainians in Galicia was the problem of national identity. Drahomanov pinpointed a chronic ambivalence on this issue. On many occasions the Galician-Ukrainian intelligentsia had raised this question: "Who are the Rusyns?" However, they had been unable to reach an answer that would satisfy the population as a whole.[22] Drahomanov made vivid this concern by recalling something from his own experience. On the way by train to the congress of archeologists in Kiev in 1874, he had struck up a conversation with a delegate from Galicia. Unaware of Drahomanov's identity, the man had fumbled rather apologetically in search for how to describe himself in terms of nationality. Aloud, he had discarded, in turn, the ethnonyms *russkyi* (Rusyn) and *Maloros* (Little Russian). Finally, he had settled on *Halychanyn* (Galician).[23]

Drahomanov maintained that Galicia would be able to bring Ukrainians back to the path of European culture only after it rid itself of its own weaknesses. These, he contended, included the low level of education (especially political education), the superficial level of training provided in the region's theological and law schools, and the general unwillingness to apply empirical methodology to scholarly analysis, which was instead dominated by rote repetition of foreign knowledge and of excessive verbiage and emotion.[24] Galician political life he characterized as unstable. Drahomanov argued that Galicia's leaders should abandon vulgar street politics (*vulychnist'*) and their concern with international affairs. Instead, their priority should be supporting the struggle of the Ukrainian people on their own home ground, and they should do this through political education. Nevertheless, as a conservative, Drahomanov called for the complete withdrawal of youth from political life, on the grounds that their involvement would only lead to volatility, sectarianism, and deteriorating standards of national and political thought.[25]

After an extended silence, Drahomanov resumed his work as an activist in Ukrainian political life in the 1890s. In his last two major books, both published in 1915, he elaborated more fully his views on the nationality question. He said that the accumulated experiences of the past decades compelled him to reaffirm the concept of a unified Ukrainian culture but to deny the necessity for political unity, that is, he saw no necessity for a nation-state for all Ukrainians.[26] In the end, Drahomanov considered nationalism to be an outmoded and regressive ideology. Instead, he called for a new universal theory to solve the problem of coexistence between Russians and Ukrainians, one that would supersede nationality. He suggested that Christianity had provided such a theory in the past, but that now a new cosmopolitan principle was needed.[27]

Early in the twentieth century the idea that Ukrainian statehood was the prerequisite for there to be a Ukrainian nationality was revived by the historian and political theorist Viacheslav Lypyns'kyi. He was of the Polish nobility (*szlachta*) from Right Bank Ukraine.[28] Lypyns'kyi insisted that the state, elites, and civil and military institutions, together with specific social groups – but not the undifferentiated popular masses – were the decisive forces in history. This reinvigoration of the conservative position was partly in response to the need, in 1918, to work out a political-legal basis for an independent Ukrainian state. Lypyns'kyi had many followers. The most prominent among them were Stepan Tomashivs'kyi, Vasyl' Kuchabs'kyi, Dmytro Doroshenko, Viacheslav Zaikyn, Ivan Kryp'iakevych, Ivan Krevets'kyi, Ihor Los'kyi, Teofil' Kostruba, and Omeljan Pritsak.[29]

The "Lypyns'kyi school" emphasized the role of the nobility throughout Ukrainian history. Lypyns'kyi himself understood the nobility to include not only the landowning aristocracy but also people in urban occupations.[30] Even during popular movements, such as the insurrection of Hetman Bohdan Khmel'nyts'kyi against Poland in the seventeenth century, the nobility continued to play a constructive role in the government of Cossack Ukraine.[31] The masses might be able to destroy a foreign regime, but they could not by themselves construct a national government. Lypyns'kyi maintained that this work could only be of undertaken by the hereditary nobility. Only the nobility could adapt the state traditions of the Cossack Hetmanate to contemporary efforts towards Ukrainian nationality- and state-building. Lypyns'kyi also believed that only a distinctive Ukrainian monarchy could destroy the superior position of the Great Russian and Polish elites, while preserving Ukrainian culture from the dangers of experimenting with modern democracy.[32]

Lypyns'kyi stressed repeatedly that the basic condition for a Ukrainian state was regional, national, and organizational unity. At the elite level, the first requirement was for an alliance between Ukraine's Left Bank and Right Bank nobility and the Ukrainian elite in Galicia. In his letters to Osyp Nazaruk a lawyer, Lypyns'kyi warned "that emphasizing the Galician and eastern Ukrainian antagonism absolutely interferes with our ideology ... The cause of building the Ukrainian state has always been ruined by the lack of unity among Ukrainians, notably by the regional divide. Regionalism, theoretically, is not harmful, but in practice it brings more chaos into the life of our land, and therefore should be opposed ... Unification of the Ukrainian lands must be the leading idea."[33] Galicians should acquire territorial autonomy. But this would be only the first stage in disseminating the idea of a new state-building monarchy. An alliance or agreement between Ukrainians and Poles in Galicia to oppose domination by Warsaw would be the way forward for the political liberation of western Ukrainian lands – as well as a catalyst for opposition movements in eastern Ukraine.[34]

Images from Within

The Conservatives

According to Galician conservatives, negative influences on Ukrainian spiritual life began with the imposition of Byzantine culture. Stepan Tomashivs'kyi and his followers, including Ivan Kryp'iakevych, Ivan Krevets'kyi, Teofil Kostruba, among others, are the best known of the writers who expounded this view. In this scenario, Orthodoxy played an entirely negative role throughout Ukraine's history – because it brought the Ukrainians closer to the Russians and thereby weakened the national strength of Ukrainians. Tomashivs'kyi looked at occidental (western European) influences much more positively. Indeed, before long he became a vigorous proponent of westernization. Western influences had been strongest in the Galician-Volhynian principality during the rule of the Romanovych dynasty, in the thirteenth and early fourteenth centuries. Tomashivs'kyi believed that this period constituted the first true Ukrainian state.[35] The westernizing trend led to a new movement in Galicia, which aimed to consolidate the influence of the Ukrainian Greek Catholic Church on political life.[36] The first organized manifestation of this was Catholic Action, founded in 1931 with the support of Metropolitan Andrei Sheptyts'kyi. Its goal was to infuse Ukrainian secular life with a Christian spirit. The impetus for the second was purely clerical: the Ukrainian Catholic National party was established in 1930. Although renamed two years later the Ukrainian National Regeneration, it found few adherents outside the ranks of the clergy.

Tomashivs'kyi explained the significance of the Galician-Volhynian state for the history of Ukraine from five perspectives. First, this regime preserved Ukraine as a whole from enslavement and assimilation by Poland. Second, it disrupted dynastic, ecclesiastical, and political ties with Muscovy. Third, it facilitated the introduction of western European culture to the Ukrainian lands and protected the Ukrainian people from further influences from the Asiatic Mongols. Fourth, it gave western Ukraine material and moral support in its struggle against Polish expansion, opening up new spaces in the east for the benefit of the Ukrainian people. Fifth, this state's existence (in the thirteenth and fourteenth centuries) made possible the contemporary national, political, cultural, and, to a certain extent, linguistic distinctiveness of Ukraine.[37]

Tomashivs'kyi was convinced that because of the penetration of Lithuanian, Polish, and Hungarian influences into western Ukrainian lands, which had begun during the period of the Galician-Volhynian state, Ukrainian culture had been preserved in Galicia. The eastern Ukrainian lands, however, sustained the direct impact of the Mongol-Tatar invasion and, sharing the historical fate of the Russian lands, lost their political and cultural independence. In short, Galicia was a unique mixture of economic and cultural influences, both eastern and Western, as symbolized by the Byzantine and Roman branches of the Catholic Church. The synthesis of these influences culminated in 1596 with the Union of Brest, Tomashivs'kyi believed that as a result of the union a new church and also a new cultural type came into being – one that was Byzantine in form and Roman in content.[38]

Vasyl' Kuchabs'kyi was another Galician conservative. He examined the historical and political peculiarities of the short-lived West Ukrainian National Republic. The republic had been but a transitory creation, Kuchab'kyi argued, because the local intellectuals had proved themselves incompetent for the work of state formation. The population as a whole had displayed much common sense, even self-sacrifice, and rejected all tendencies linked to anarchism and radicalism. But the weakness of "mechanical" parliamentarism, which reflected only the ephemeral views of the electorate, as well as the low level of consciousness among the intellectuals had impeded the process of state-building. Furthermore, the corruption of the state apparatus, together with political upheavals and an increase in social-revolutionary movements, facilitated the rise to dominance of two ideologies: nationalism and Bolshevism.[33]

Kuchabs'kyi commented on the role of the armed forces in state-building. He made mention of the initial military victories of the Sich Riflemen and the Galician Ukrainian Army during World War I and its aftermath. These were to be explained, he said, by the initiative of a few officers and soldiers. But their effectiveness could not disguise or compensate for the underlying weaknesses of the Ukrainian military command. The West Ukrainian National Republic was so feeble, and died so quickly, Kuchabs'kyi concluded, because it lacked capable leaders who could coordinate the efforts of the local elites and public organizations. He did not find this dearth of statesmen surprising. Indeed, he accepted it as a natural result of the narrow-mindedness and mean spiritedness of Galicians, who had among them no intellectuals, and their lack of nobility, heroism, and other virtues. Moreover, Kuchabs'kyi pointed out, the local authorities had grown accustomed to getting away with slipshod work. The corruption of bureaucrats in the West Ukrainian National Republic was to be explained, he said, by their material poverty, low salaries, and desire for an aristocratic lifestyle of a kind that the Ukrainian elite of Galicia had otherwise never experienced.[40]

Kuchabs'kyi did concede that such positive features of the Galician population as its industriousness, "obedience," efficient labor management, purposefulness, sober-mindedness, and patriotism, could – under suitable tutelage – provide a solid foundation for an independent state. Another positive feature that he found in Galicia, especially evident in 1918–1919, was the energy, efficiency, and professionalism of the local politicians – as revealed in the organization of their local self-governments. All in all, although Kuchabs'kyi did not believe that Galicia could become Ukraine's political center, he did see Galicia as a very important, indeed necessary, model for eastern Ukraine to study in undertaking its own state-building project.

In contrast to Tomashivs'kyi, Kuchabs'kyi had little respect for Catholicism or western orientation. In his view the Ukrainian people "with the sole exception of Galicia, and that only for less than the last two hundred years, belongs by its spiritual structure to the Eastern Christian world."[41] Galicia had a special role in the formation of a future Ukrainian state, Kuchabs'kyi argued, and that derived from two factors. First, Galicia had the right "psychological" composition to organize the rest of country for the liberation struggle. Second, Galicia had the unique conditions to nurture an elite that would be both anti-Polish and anti-Russian. And this "would create people of a completely new spiritual and political type in Ukraine."[42]

The Nationalist-Statists

In the 1890s young Galician radicals advanced the idea that Ukrainians should form their own nation-state. At the founding congress of the Ukrainian-Ruthenian Radical party, in 1890, Viacheslav Budzynovs'kyi proposed the creation of a separate Ruthenian state in eastern Galicia. He argued that Galicia was being exploited by the western parts of the

Habsburg Empire, particularly by Vienna and the province of Bohemia. The only way to escape poverty and to ensure the development of Galicia's economy was to secede.[43] By 1895 Iuliian Bachyns'kyi had taken up the call for "a free, great, politically independent Ukraine, one and indivisible from the San [River] to the Caucasus."[44]

The nationalist trend in Ukrainian political thought in Galicia was best represented by Stanislav Dnistrians'kyi and his followers, among them Stepan Rudnyts'kyi, and Volodymyr Starosol's'kyi. Ukranian nationalism acquired an increasing number of strong voices. From the beginning of the twentieth century these included scholars from eastern Ukraine and from Galicia. The majority of these people were forced into exile after World War II.[45]

Starosol's'kyi found that the process of "denationalization" among the Ukrainian aristocracy in the early modern period proceeded fastest and furthest in the southern and western Ukrainian territories. In Galicia the Ukrainian nobility made a last stand against Poland early in the sixteenth century. In Volhynia, eastern Podolia, and the Kiev province Ukrainian nobles had participated in the liberation struggles of Bohdan Khmel'nyts'kyi.[46] Starosol's'kyi observed that feudal, aristocratic ideology persisted only on the territories of the former Ukrainian Hetmanate, that is, Left and Right Bank Ukraine, while Galicia underwent a different development. In Galicia the Greek Catholic Church was the most important institution, and its clergy were the only educated Ukrainian social stratum. Starosol's'kyi found that "in their lifestyle they [the clergy] resembled the lesser gentry."[47] They preserved a dual (Ukrainian and Habsburg Austrian) identity and loyalty down to 1918. They followed a conservative, pro-Habsburg policy, opposed Hungarian and Polish insurgents, and called for the formation of a separate Ruthenian crownland within the Austrian Empire. Circumstances had also transformed the clergy into the main leaders of the Ukrainian cultural renaissance – and this inevitably had political repercussions. During the period of eastern Ukraine's Hetmanstate (1918) and the interwar years the dominant conservatives in Galicia were to be found among the Greek Catholic clergy and the Galician intelligentsia.[48]

The Galician intelligentsia had a close relationship with the peasantry. Starosol's'kyi identified this as one of its prime characteristics. This relationship remained important during the interwar decades, when both groups made common cause against Polish rule.[49] In 1918 Ukrainian-inhabited eastern Galicia was incorporated into the Republic of Poland. The result was a general pauperization of the population – and profound changes in the psychology of the Ukrainian people. For one thing, the world war had opened up new contacts with other peoples. As Starosol's'kyi described it:

> Galicia was a military theater, as a result of which thousands of Ukrainian peasants were evacuated from their homes and were forced to seek temporary shelter in the western part of the Austro-Hungarian Empire ... Thousands of Galician-Ukrainian soldiers who served in the Austrian imperial army were captured and found themselves prisoners of war in Italy and Russia ... The wars of national independence, during which more than 100,000 Galician-Ukrainian peasant soldiers crossed into eastern Ukraine and thus came into contact with their cultural and linguistic bretheren, had a considerable impact and deepened the national and political consciousness of the Ukrainian peasantry.[50]

Galicia's incorporation into Poland, was met immediately with an energetic and determined response by Ukrainians. The Ukrainian intelligentsia, now under Polish domination, was deprived of its former status and had to adapt to the new circumstances. Thousands of unemployed officials and the young people, now no longer admitted to Poland's universities, were forced to look elsewhere for ways to support themselves. Driven to find work among their own people, they rose to the challenge. Starosol's'kyi believed that "the experience which the Ukrainian intelligentsia had to endure during the world war and the period of mass political emigration, not to mention the wars of national independence, proved very valuable; the fact that large numbers of emigrants had been at first in Austria, then later in Czechoslovakia, where thousands of Ukrainian youth graduated at various colleges and universities, was especially important."[51] In Bohemia young Ukrainians obtained professional training. They also became familiar with the methods of the Czechs, whose position had until recently been similar to that of Ukrainians in Habsburg Austria. During the 1920s in western Ukrainian lands peasants revived the pre–World War I voluntary, cooperative movement in Habsburg Galicia. Many new Ukrainian educational and cultural organizations were established. From these developments, Starosol's'kyi concluded that during World War I and the interwar decades a "special type of Ukrainian national identity evolved in Galicia, one that was opposed not only to Poles and Russians but also to the traditional conservatism of the nobility."[52]

Geopolitics was the explanatory variable favored by Stepan Rud-nyts'kyi. Twice, he argued, Galicia had played an outstanding role in Ukrainian history: "The first time was in the fourteenth to sixteenth centuries, when Ukrainian statehood, ruined in the Dnieper region, found shelter in the Galician-Volhynian principality; the second time came at the end of the nineteenth century, when the Ukrainian cultural movement found shelter beyond [west] of the Zbruch River from persecution and oppression at the hands of the Russian government."[53] Rudnyts'kyi contended that, although political circumstances had given rise to certain differences between Galician and eastern Ukrainians, both were "anthropologically" and "racially" the same – Ukrainian. He supported this view with "anthropogeographical" data and concluded that western Ukraine was a borderland between eastern Europe and central Europe: "The great spaciousness, vast scale, and monotony of the landscape in eastern Europe become much more gentle in western Ukraine, although central European diversity remains little developed and sporadic. This transitional character is evident not only in geographical position and geomorphological relations, but also in all other geographical features of western Ukraine: its climate, flora, and fauna, as well as in anthropogeographical relations."[54]

Western Ukraine had a mediating position between Germany, Poland, Czechoslovakia, and Hungary, on one side, and central and eastern Ukraine, on the other. The evidence, said Rudnyts'kyi, lay in the historical sources about the ancient Amber Route. The Amber Route passed through western Ukraine, thus linking the Baltic Sea to "the whole south of the eastern European complex of countries, which, for their part, form the threshold of the Middle East."[55] Galicia would be able to rediscover its geographical mission only when it became an inseparable part of Ukraine. At the same time, Rudnyts'kyi insisted that Galicians were a separate group within the Ukrainian nationality: "Just as the Swiss Germans form, from a national and cultural point of view, a separate group of the German nationality, so are the Galician Ukrainians distinct within the Ukrainian nationality."[56] Given their historic differences, Rudnyts'kyi cautioned, a premature unification of Galicia and Greater (Soborna) Ukraine could seriously damage the Ukrainian cause. Independently, Galicia could do nothing in Greater Ukraine, where the level of national consciousness was very substantially lower.[57]

Rudnyts'kyi called special attention to forests. He argued that forests had a far-reaching impact on the political life of western Ukraine, above all because they facilitated resistance against invaders: "The forest made social cohesion difficult; it divided the population into small groups living in natural clearings, or in burned down and grub zones, or on the riverbank meadows, each of them living its own life. These conditions were conducive to political and economic localism, which became a distinctive feature of life in western Ukraine."[58] Rudnyts'kyi's geographical explanation accounted for the differences between Galician individualism and ethic of hard work and the collectivist and egalitarian (*rozmirenist'*) spirit that allegedly typified eastern Ukrainians. In spite of these differences, unity was essential. The road to an independent Ukraine might begin with an independent and neutral Galician-Ukrainian state, but, he advised, this entity should then embrace the rest of Ukraine as rapidly as possible.[59] Rudnyts'kyi was confident that "East Galicia's government would be able, at a decisive moment and at one stroke, to take possession of eastern Ukraine and organize it both politically and militarily with the help of local Ukrainians."[60]

Analyzing Galicia within the framework of the Russian-Ukrainian relations, Rudnyts'kyi graphically demonstrated the imperial character of the Russian state. Rudnyts'kyi explicitly warned that Russia considered possession of all of Ukraine as the precondition for its domination of eastern and central Europe: "For Russia the geopolitical significance of Ukraine lies in the fact that it is a large, populous, and rich country along the [tsarist] empire's southern frontier. Only by conquering Ukraine would it be possible to reach the natural boundaries of the Caucasus, the Black Sea and the Carpathians, which any state would dream of [doing]."[61] At this point Rudnyts'kyi provided his own political forecast: "The first two of these boundaries were reached by Russia in the eighteenth century. The third would be reached in the world war of 1914–1918. The symptomatic gravitation of Russia toward firm natural boundaries in the south would have its natural conclusion in Galicia, Bukovina, and the Transcarpathian region. So far, Russia has not managed to establish itself securely along the Carpathian boundary. But if a unified Russian state is resurrected, the struggle for a Carpathian boundary will be resumed."[62]

Conclusions

In their estimation of the tasks of state- and nationality-building, and of the possibilities and ways both to regenerate the old Ukrainian identity and to create a new one, the various currents in Ukrainian political thought were quite distinct from each other. Their different images of Galicia and the Galicians were clearly related to all these other differences.

Eastern Ukrainian conservatives and populists agreed that Galicia had to preserve its own identity, which could not be transferred to other Ukrainian lands. In the populists' opinion, eastern Ukraine had eastern as well as western cultural values, while in the opinion of the conservatives Right Bank and Left Bank Ukraine had to unite to forge a common identity. Galician conservatives and nationalist-statists both emphasized the special role of Galicia in the history of Ukraine, with its unique identity, and its role in carrying out a certain all-Ukrainian mission. They understood that role differently, however. The conservatives stressed the formation of the armed forces and the Greek Catholic elite in Galicia, while the statists insisted that Ukrainians in the region had developed a modern national consciousness thanks to the model provided by the Czechs and by the general western European environment.

All currents in Ukrainian political and historical thought regarded Galicia as part of a single Ukrainian patrimony, not as anything separate. Therefore, Galician distinctiveness did not pose a danger for a Ukrainian state or the Ukrainian nationality. And if Galicians identified themselves as Galicians, this did not make them any less Ukrainian.

In the twentieth century both the conception of nationality and the vision of a state were more closely related in the thinking of eastern Ukrainian and Galician conservatives than in that of eastern Ukrainian populists and Galician nationalist-statists. The vision of state and nationality was dramatically different in the eyes of the Galician and eastern Ukrainian conservatives, on the one hand, and of eastern Ukrainian populists and the Galician statists, on the other. All four schools of thought considered the role of national territory differently. The various historical traditions and multiple factors in identity formation resulted in ideological – but not regional – coherence in terms of the main currents of Ukrainian historical and political thought.

The foregoing analysis of the attitudes toward Galician identity of representatives of four Ukrainian historiographical and political trends in the past also provides a basis for understanding the attitudes of various groups of intellectuals toward the problems of identity in contemporary Ukraine, but that is a subject for another study.

Notes

1 For background on the research methodology used in this chapter, see Volodymyr Potul'nyts'kyi, *Ukraïna i vsesvitnia istoriia* (Kiev, 2002), pp. 3–480. For additional critical discussion of the works examined here, of the terms *Galicians, Russians, Germans, Poles, Jews,* and *Ukrainians* as meaningful categories, and of attitudes to the conceptions of statehood and federation as developed by Ukrainian political thinkers, see three studies by Volodymyr Potul'nyts'kyi: "Das ukrainische historische Denken im 19. und 20. Jahrhundert: Konzeptionen und Periodisierung," *Jahrbücher für Geschichte Osteuropas,* XLV, 1 (Stuttgart, 1997), pp. 2–30; "The Image of Ukraine and Ukrainians in Russian Political Thought, 1860–1945," *Acta Slavica Japonica,* XVI (Sapporo, 1998), pp. 1-29; and "Ukraïns'ka i svitova istorychna nauka," *Ukraïn'skyi istorychnyi zhurnal,* XLIV, 1,2,3, and 4 (Kiev, 2000), pp. 1–24, pp. 27–43, pp. 22–44, and pp. 20–37.

2 On the development of Ukrainian political thought in the nineteenth and twentieth centuries, see Ivan Rudnytsky, *Essays in Modern Ukrainian History* (Edmonton, 1987); and V. Potul'nyts'kyi, "Main Directions of Ukrainian Historical and Political Science in Emigration" (Ph.D. thesis, Harvard University, 1990).

3 Volodymyr Antonovych recognized the emergence of the Cossacks as a new social estate and not as the continuation of the communal order associated with proto-Slavic and early Slavic history. See his *Korotka istoriia kozachchyny* (Chernivtsi, 1897), pp. 17–18. Elsewhere Antonovych concluded that by the end of the fifteenth century a new military landed estate was being formed on the basis of the equality of its members and according to the old assembly traditions of the Grand Duchy of Lithuania, see "Kiev, ego sud'ba i znachenie s XIV po XVI stolietie (1362–1569)," in V.B. Antonovich, *Monografii po istorii Zapadnoi i Iugo-zapadnoi Rossii,* vol. I (Kiev, 1885), pp. 251–252.

4 For fuller details, see Volodymyr Antonovych, "Try natsional'ni typy narodni (first published in 1888 under the pseudonym Nyzenko)," in his *Tvory,* vol. 1 (Kiev, 1932), pp. 196–210.

5 Antonovych, *Korotka istoriia kozachchyny,* pp. 230–231. See also his "Istorychni baiky p. Mariiana Dubetskoho (pryvodu pratsi pro pochatok Zaporizhzhia)," in *Tvory,* p. 212.

6 Mykhailo Hrushevs'kyi, *Z bizhuchoï khvyli: statti i zamitky na temy dnia, 1905–1906 rr.* (Kiev, 1907), p. 123.

7 Mykhailo Hrushevs'kyi, *Na porozi novoï Ukraïny: hadky i mrii* (Kiev, 1918), p. 14.

8 M. Grushevskii, *Ukraintsi: formy natsional'nogo dvizheniia v sovremennykh gos-udarstvakh – Avstro-Vengriia, Rossiia, Germaniia* (St Petersburg, 1910), p. 170.

9 M. Hrushevs'kyi, "Z sotsial'no-natsional'nykh kontseptsiï Antonovycha," in *Ukraïna*, 5 (Kiev, 1928), p. 7.

10 Hrushevs'kyi, *Na porozi novoï Ukraïny*, p. 22.

11 M. Hrushevs'kyi, "Na porozi stolittia: prysviacheno peremys'kii ukraïns'ko-rus'kii hromadi," in his *Tvory v 50 tomakh*, vol. 1 (L'viv, 2002), p. 209.

12 M. Hrushevs'kyi, *Istoriia Ukraïny-Rusy*, vol. 3 (Kiev, 1913), p. 1.

13 The older, Little Russian conservative concept of Ukrainian nationality persisted into the nineteenth century, when it was developed mainly in the works of Mykhailo Maksymovych and Mykhailo Drahomanov. See V. Potul'nyts'kyi: "Das ukrainische historische Denken," pp. 5–7 and 16–20; his "Deutsche Einflüsse auf die Entwicklung des historischen Denkens in der Ukraine im 19. Jahrhundert," *Zeitschrift für Ostmitteleuropa-Forschung*, XLVI, 4 (Marburg, 1997), pp. 475–499; and his "The Image of Russia and the Russians in Ukrainian Political Thought (1860–1945)," in K. Inoue and T. Uyama, eds., *Quest for Models of Coexistence: National and Ethnic Dimensions of Changes in the Slavic Eurasian World* (Sapporo, 1998), pp. 163–195.

14 On the political views and identity of the hereditary Ukrainian nobility in the eighteenth and first half of the nineteenth centuries, see Zenon E. Kohut, *Russian Centralism and Ukrainian Autonomy: Imperial Absorption of the Hetmanate 1760–1830* (Cambridge, Mass., 1988). For the second half of the nineteenth and the beginning of the twentieth centuries, see V. Potul'nyts'kyi: "Das ukrainische historische Denken," p. 14–28; *Ukraïna i vsesvitnia istoriia*, pp. 181–410; and Taïsa Sydorchuk-Potulnyts'ka, "Het'mans'kyi rukh naperedodni druhoï svitovoï viiny ta Osyp Nazaruk," in *Zapysky Naukovoho tovarystvo im. Shevchenka: pratsi Istoryko-filolohichnoï sektsiï*, CCXXXVII (L'viv, 1999), pp. 236–254.

15 Andreas Kappeler, "A Small People of Twenty-Five Million: the Ukrainians circa 1900," *Journal of Ukrainian Studies*, XVIII, 1–2 (Toronto, 1993), pp. 85–92; and his "Ein Kleines Volk von 25 Millionen: Die Ukrainer um 1900," in Manfred Alexander, Frank Kämpfer, and Andreas Kappeler, eds., *Kleine Völker in der Geschichte Osteuropas: Festschrift für Günther Stökl zum 75. Geburstag* (Stuttgart, 1991), pp. 33–42.

16 Oleksander Ohloblyn, *Liudy staroï Ukraïny* (Munich, 1959); Nataliia Polons'ka-Vasylenko, "Do istoriï Het'mans'koï Ukraïny XVII–XX vv.," in *Zbirnyk na poshanu Ivana Mirchuka (1891–1961)* (Munich, 1974), pp. 121–139; John-Paul Himka and Frances Swyripa, *Researching Ukrainian Family History* (Edmonton, 1984).

17 Omeljan Pritsak and John Reshetar, "The Ukraine and the Dialectics of Nation-Building," *Slavic Review*, XXII (Seattle, 1963), pp. 224–255; Oleksander Ohloblyn, "Mykola Vasylenko i Vadym Modzalevs'kyi," *Ukraïns'kyi istoryk*, III, 3–4 (New York and Munich, 1966), pp. 5–25; M. Dmytriienko, ed., *Ukraïns'ka genealohiia: teoriia, metodolohiia, istoriia ta praktyka* (Kiev, 1996), pp. 3–165.

18 In the words of Drahomanov, "without ceasing to be Ukrainians, we will not lose the strength which the Russian state and culture has given us, the strength to be of use to our nation, to the Slavic world, and to the world as a whole." Cited from his essay, "Literatura rossiis'ka, velykorus'ka, ukraïns'ka i halyts'ka," in O.I. Dei, ed., *Mykhailo Petrovych Drahomanov: literaturno-publitsystychni pratsi*, vol. 1 (Kiev, 1970), p. 186. This view presupposed that culture would not be an instrument of state policy, and that Ukrainian literature and culture would have the internal vitality to enter into such a role on equal terms with the culture of "Great Russia."

19 M. Drahomanov, "Russkie v Galitsii," *Vestnik Evropy*, nos. 1–2 (St Petersburg, 1873). See also M. Grevs and B. Kistiakovskii, eds., *Politicheskie sochineniia M. P. Dragomanova*, vol. 1, *Tsentr i okrainy* (Moscow, 1908), pp. 268–342.

20 Drahomanov discovered this trait through his own experience. The L'viv newspaper *Pravda* had agreed to accept an article in the first edition of its renewed run. Drahomanov awaited its publication impatiently, only to discover that the editor had vetoed his article on the grounds that it was too provocative toward the church. M. Drahomanov, "Avstro-rus'ki spomyny (1889–1892)," in Ia. Lysenko, ed., *M.P. Drahomanov: literaturno-publitsystychni pratsi*, vol. 2 (Kiev, 1970), p. 181.

21 Ibid., p. 196.

22 Drahomanov, "Russkie v Galitsii," p. 318.

23 Drahomanov, "Avstro-rus'ki spomyny," p. 236.

24 Stepan Tomashivs'kyi, "Tragediia Drahomanova," *Polityka*, nos. 1–6 (L'viv, 1925), nos. 1–6, pp. 27–30.

25 Stepan Tomashivs'kyi, "Drahomanov i Halychyna," ibid., pp. 78–84; idem "Drahomanov i molod'," ibid., pp. 44–46.

26 M.P. Drahomanov, *Lysty na Naddniprians'ku Ukraïnu* (L'viv, 1915), pp. 42–43.

27 M.P. Drahomanov, *Chudats'ki dumky pro ukraïns'ku natsional'nu spravu* (L'viv, 1915), p. 3.

28 On Lypyns'kyi and his heritage in the field of Ukrainian historiography and political thought, see Jaroslaw Pelenski, "Geschichtliches Denken und politische Ideen V. Lypyns'kyjs," *Jahrbücher für Geschichte Osteuropas*, IX, 2 (Stuttgart, 1961), pp. 223–246; Jaroslaw Pelenski, ed., *Political and Social Ideas of Vjaèeslav Lypyns'kyj*, Special Issue of *Harvard Ukrainian Studies*, IX,

3–4 (Cambridge, Mass., 1985), pp. 237–508. See V. Potul'nyts'kyi: "Politychna doktryna V. Lypyns'koho," *Ukraïns'kyi istorychnyi zhurnal*, XXXVI, 9 (Kiev, 1992), pp. 37–45; "Viacheslav Lypyns'kyi i problema politychnoï kul'tury," in O. Lupanov, ed., *Ostannii Hetman: zbirnyk pamiati Pavla Skoropads'koho* (Kiev, 1993), pp. 123–137; and idem, "Vjacheslav Lypyns'kyi – politoloh," in Y. Pelens'kyi, ed. *V. Lypyns'kyi: Historical and Political Heritage and Contemporary Ukraine* (Kiev and Philadelphia, 1994), pp. 103–114.

29 More generally on the representatives of the conservative trend, see Potul'nyts'kyi, *Teoriia ukraïns'koï politolohiï*, pp. 76–78 and 82–85; and his *Narysy z ukrains'koï politolohiï: 1819–1991* (Kiev, 1994), pp. 151–226.

30 In this sense Lypyns'kyi included not only the Ukrainian-speaking nobles of Left Bank Ukraine (the territory of the former Hetmanate) but also the former East Slavic nobility of the Right Bank Ukraine, who had long since been polonized but who preserved a regional consciousness that could be activated in individual cases. On the Ukrainian nobility of the Right Bank, which had a dual (Ukrainian and Polish) or even triple (Ukrainian, Polish, and Russian) identity and loyalty, see Rudnytsky, *Essays*; and Potul'nyts'kyi, *Ukraïna i vsesvitnia istoriia* (Kiev, 2002), pp. 335–410.

31 W. Lipinski, *Szlachta na Ukrainie* (Kiev and Cracow, 1909); idem, *Z dziejów Ukrainy* (Kiev and Cracow, 1911–1912).

32 Viacheslav Lypyns'kyi, *Lysty do brativ-khliborobiv* (Vienna, 1926), pp. 375–376, 387–388, and 391.

33 Tsentral'nyi derzhavnyi istorychnyi arkhiv u L'vovi (hereafter: TsDIAL), folio 359, opys 1, sprava 266, ark. 67–90.

34 TsDIAL, ark. 84, 91.

35 Stepan Tomashivs'kyi: *Halychyna* (L'viv, 1915); *Ukraïns'ka istoriia*, (L'viv, 1919), pp. 1–2, 6–8, 28, 89–91, 111–112; and *Pid kolesamy istoriï* (Berlin, 1922), pp. 26, 30, 42–45, 74–76.

36 See Potul'nytskyi, *Narysy z ukraïns'koï politolohiï*, pp. 204–205; TsDIAL, folio 359, opus l, sprava 18, ark. 2–6.

37 Tomashivs'kyi, *Ukraïns'ka istoriia*, pp. 111–112.

38 Ibid., pp. 89–110.

39 V. Kuchabs'kyi, "Vaha i zavdannia zakhidno-ukraïns'koï derzhavy sered syl skhidnoï Ievropy na perelomi 1918/1919 roku," *Dzvony*, I (L'viv, 1932), pp. 112–120.

40 Ibid., p. 118.

41 TsDIAL, folio 359, opys 1, sprava 266, ark. 18.

42 V. Kuchabs'kyi, "Ukraïns'ka derzhavna put'," *Dzvony*, IV (L'viv, 1934), p. 68.

43 Budzynovs'kyi's program was eventually published by the Russophile

newspaper, *Halytska Rus'*. It also appeared as a separate two-part pamphlet, *Kul' turnaia nuzhda* (L'viv, 1891).

44 Iuliian Bachyns'kyi, *Ukraina irredenta* (L'viv, 1895), p. 74.

45 The theoretical background of the nation-state orientation was reflected in Stanyslav Dnistrians'kyi, "Zvychaieve pravo ta sotsial'ni zviazky," *Chasopys pravnychyi ta ekonomichnyi*, IV–V (L'viv, 1902); *Natsional'na statystyka: mova iak kryterii narodnosti* (L'viv, 1910); "Das Gewohnheitsrecht und die sozialen Verbände," in *Festschrift zur Jahrhundertfeier des Allgemeinen Bürgerlichen Gesetzbuches* (Berlin and Vienna, 1911), pp. 23–57. See also V. Starosol's'kyi, "Prychynky do teorii sotsiologii," *Chasopys pravnychyi ta ekonomichnyi*, 7 (L'viv, 1904) and Stefan Rudnyts'kyi, *Ukraina und die Ukrainer*, 2nd ed. (Berlin, 1915); *Die Geographie der Ukraine* (Vienna, 1916).

46 V. Starosol's'kyi, "Suspil'no-politychni rukhy ta ïkh nosiï," in TsDIAL, folio 360, opys 1, sprava 466, ark. l.

47 Ibid., pp. 5–6.

48 Starosol's'kyi, "Suspil'no-politychni rukhy v Ukraïni," in Tsentral'nyi arkhiv vyshchykh orhaniv vlady I upravlinnia, folio 4186, opys 2, sprava 10, ark. 12.

49 Ibid., pp. 18–19.

50 Ibid., pp. 7–8.

51 Ibid., p. 9.

52 Ibid., p. 18.

53 Stepan Rudnyts'kyi, *Chomu my khochemo samostiinoï Ukraïny* (Vienna, 1923; repr. L'viv, 1994), p. 220.

54 S. Rudnyts'kyi, "Zakhidna Ukraïna: heohrafichnyi narys," in Tsentral'na naukova biblioteka AN Ukraïny, Viddil rukopysiv, folio 10, sprava 4744, ark. 2, 3.

55 Ibid., ark. 4.

56 Rudnyts'kyi, *Chomu*, p. 410.

57 Ibid., pp. 381–383.

58 Rudnyts'kyi, "Zakhidna Ukraïna," ark. 49 and 50.

59 Stepan Rudnyts'kyi, *Ukraïns'ka sprava zi stanovyshha politychnoï heohrafiï* (Berlin, 1923), p. 113.

60 Rudnyts'kyi, *Chomu*, p. 384.

61 Rudnyts'kyi, *Ukraïns'ka sprava*, p. 142.

62 Ibid., pp. 142–143. On Rudnyts'kyi's conception of Ukrainian identity, see V. Potul'nyts'kyi, "Jews and the Jewish Theme in Ukrainian Historical Thought," in *Jews in Eastern Europe*, III [43] (Jerusalem, 2000), pp. 5–36.

7 Peasants and Patriotic Celebrations in Habsburg Galicia

KAI STRUVE

Public festivals are an important means for presenting and communicating models of national identity. As such they contribute to the development of the nation as an "imagined community," to quote the title of the well-known book by Benedict Anderson. An analysis of such festivals demonstrates the extent to which a population can be mobilized on behalf of the nation, as well as the precise forms of communication and motivations that shape national identification.[1]

Since Galicia had a predominantly agrarian economy until well into the twentieth century and had no developed middle and working classes, the emergence of modern nations depended primarily on the integration of the peasant population. That social stratum is the focus of this chapter, which explores the participation of peasants in Polish and Ruthenian (Ukrainian) patriotic celebrations. For the Polish nation, which in the early modern period had been restricted to the nobility (*szlachta*), modern nation-building meant transcending the limits of feudal social estates to include previously excluded groups. In the Ruthenian case, however, it essentially meant the creation of a new nation. Traditionally, those individuals who belonged to the Greek Catholic Church and observed its rite, (*rus'ka vira*), were considered Ruthenian (Ukrainian: *Rusyn*; Polish: *Rusin*).

Among the Ruthenian intelligentsia of the second half of the nineteenth century there existed three distinct positions on the question of national identity. One of them, the Polonophile interpretation of Ruthenian identity, asserted that the Ruthenians were a specific branch of the Polish nation. The other two positions both maintained that the Ruthenians were separate from Poles, although they held differing views of the Ruthenians' relationship to Russia and the Russians. The Ukraino-

philes considered Ruthenians to be part of a distinct Ukrainian nation
that also included the population of the Russian Ukraine. For the Russophiles, however, the Ruthenians were a branch of the Russian nation.[2]
These currents took different views of the cultural project of Ruthenian
nation-building. The Russophiles emphasized the association with the
Church Slavonic and Russian languages and culture. The medieval
principality of Galicia-Volhynia and the more powerful contemporary
Russian state were the main sources of inspiration for their nation-
building projects. The Ukrainophiles, on the other hand, placed greater
emphasis on the peasants (*narod*),[3] and their folk language and culture.
For many of these populists (*narodovtsi*), the seventeenth-century Cossack rebellions and the incipient Cossack state or Hetmanate were the
most important historical events.

After initial efforts during the revolution of 1848–1849, more intensive attempts were undertaken by the Ruthenian and Polish intelligen-
tsias to end the isolation of the villages and to incorporate the peasants
into larger communicational and organizational structures following
the Austrian constitutional reforms of the 1860s. It was relatively easy
to persuade the Greek Catholic peasants that their Ruthenian identity
constituted a foundation for a new national community, since such a
status implied equality with the Poles and an end to discrimination.
Since Polish landowners were their prime social and political antago-
nists, the struggle for the national movement effectively coincided
with their struggle for social emancipation.

In the Polish case the process was much more complicated because,
from the peasants' point of view, Polish identity was tied to that of the
landowners.[4] Whatever differences may have existed among Ruthenian intellectuals, when it came to political mobilization they pursued
a common strategy. They urged the peasants not to follow the lead of
the traditional local elite, the landowners, but instead to vote for the
Ruthenian candidates at elections. In contrast, Polish intellectuals
restricted themselves for quite a long time to issues concerned with
agrarian and economic matters, all the while encouraging the peasants
to accept existing social relationships and the political domination of
the traditional elites.

Among the Poles, the Roman Catholic priest Stanisław Stojałowski,
from 1875 the publisher of *Wieniec* and *Pszczółka* (two newspapers
directed at the peasant population), was the first to adopt a new course.
Initially, he acted very cautiously, but gradually he became outspoken in
his criticism of the Polish nobility and their indifference to the interests

of the peasants. Stojałowski believed that the political mobilization of the Roman Catholic peasants would not damage but, on the contrary, strengthen Polish national interests.[5] In the provincial elections of 1889, Stojałowski called for the establishment of independent peasant election committees, which would choose their own candidates to run against the conservatives. The latter were mostly landowners, who until then had dominated rural politics. This priest, who was strongly influenced by the new Christian-social ideas, reached the same conclusion as a group of leftist Polish democrats assembled around Bolesław Wysłouch, co-publisher of *Kurjer Lwowski* in L'viv. Wysłouch went on to found the newspaper *Przyjaciel Ludu* in support of the independent political organization of the peasants in the elections of 1889.[6]

In the 1890s newly established peasant parties presented themselves both as representatives of peasant interests and as Polish nationalist parties. The strength of peasant parties was not only the result of the work of the intelligentsia, but also of the improved levels of education and the civic experience peasants were acquiring at the local level, notably in village councils and in social organizations such as the Society of Agrarian Circles (Towarzystwo Kółek Rolniczych). The most important of these new political organizations was the Peasant party (Stronnictwo Ludowe, after 1903 the Polish Peasant party / Polskie Stronnictwo Ludowe or PSL), which came about as a result of the cooperation between the democrats working with Wysłouch and several peasant election committees during the elections to the Galician diet in 1895.

While the Polish peasants were organized in separate peasant parties, the Ruthenian peasants were integrated into overarching national political organizations.[7] Popular enlightenment organizations were of vital importance for breaching the isolation of the villages and integrating the rural population into a nationwide political arena. The Prosvita Society was created by the Ukrainophiles in 1868. For nearly a decade its activities developed relatively slowly, but then took off rapidly. In the 1870s the Russophile Greek Catholic priest Ivan Naumovych was even more successful in educational work. He started to publish the peasant newspapers *Russkaia rada* (1871) and *Nauka* (1872), which quickly became popular in the villages. In 1874 Naumovych initiated the establishment of another Ruthenian popular enlightenment organization, the Mykhailo Kachkovs'kyi Society (Obshchestvo im. Mykhaila Kachkovs'koho), which for a time enjoyed much greater success than the Prosvita Society.[8] As in Ruthenian political life generally, during the 1870s Russophiles dominated the work of public enlightenment and the emerging public sphere in rural areas. Only from the 1880s did they give way to the populists (*narodovtsi*), whose ranks were strengthened by a new generation of the Ruthenian intelligentsia, including for the first time many who were not priests.

In 1879 the *narodovtsi* founded the peasant newspaper, *Bat'kôvshchyna*. From the 1880s onward, more and more village reading rooms were established. These subscribed to newspapers and other publications that in turn helped fashion the Ruthenian national movement in rural areas.[9] Agrarian circles (*kółka rolnicze*) among Poles had a similar function. They developed in villages from the end of the 1870s following the model of organizations in the Poznań region, although in contrast to their Ruthenian counterparts they focused more on agricultural progress and the cooperative organization of retail trade. In the early 1880s, alongside the Society of Agrarian Circles, Polish popular enlightenment societies were founded and they established small libraries and reading rooms in villages.[10]

Such initiatives on both the Polish and the Ruthenian sides were intended to strengthen the national identification of the peasants. They provided the organizational and communication structures upon which the nationality could be constructed. National festivals played a key role in promoting the new identities. A more detailed examination of these festivals will help us understand the strategies pursued by the intelligentsia as well as the response of peasants to these nation-building efforts.

Ruthenian Festivals Commemorating the Abolition of Serfdom

One festival with national coloring regularly celebrated in many Ruthenian villages from 1849 on was the so-called Liberation Festival. This festival, which commemorated the peasant emancipation of 1848, was celebrated on May 3 according to the Julian calendar and on May 15 according to the Gregorian calendar. Although peasant emancipation equally affected the Roman Catholic peasants, it was only celebrated by the Greek Catholic Church. Wawrzyniec Dayczak described in his memoirs the sequence of the festival in the roughly half Roman Catholic, half Greek Catholic village of Reniv (Polish: Reniów) in the district of Brody: "In memory [of the decree of emancipation] the peasants carved a large oak wayside cross and planted it on the square in front of the manorial estate along the main road in the Nove Khaty quarter of the village. Every year since then a 'liberation festival' has been celebrated in May, but only by the Greek Catholic community. After the Divine Liturgy in church, a procession with the Ruthenian priest and banners went to the wayside cross, and after the prayer of thanksgiving the fields and the people were blessed. Then the procession returned to the church. The whole population took part, even the Poles, but there was no Polish priest."[11]

The Supreme Ruthenian Council (Holovna rus'ka rada) decided immediately after the revolution in 1848 to hold an annual ceremony to commemorate the liberation of the peasants to demonstrate its gratitude toward the Habsburg emperor. The intention was to highlight the loyalty of the Ruthenians, which contrasted with Polish aspirations to independence. Unlike the case with Polish landowners, the emperor was depicted as a benefactor of the peasants. Over time, these commemorations lost much of their political character and were incorporated into the general calendar of religious holidays. During the 1870s the Rus' Council (Russkaia Rada), a Russophile political organization,[12] tried to tie these celebrations more strongly to the ideals of the Ruthenian national movement and to introduce them in areas where the tradition had not yet developed or had even disappeared. At its annual general meeting of 1873, the council called for an extensive celebration to mark the twenty-fifth anniversary of the 1848 decree.[13] *Russkaia Rada*, the newspaper for the peasants, stressed that it was important to celebrate such occasions, since many people no longer had any direct memory of the age of serfdom. The newspaper also wanted to link the celebrations to a program of reforms in the villages, and it was critical of many communities that had not used the opportunities provided by the emancipation to improve their situation. They were urged in connection with the celebrations of May 3 (Julian calendar) to establish credit unions, temperance societies, and reading rooms – activities which came to be viewed as patriotic endeavours. The May 3 celebrations also provided an opportunity to hold meetings with broader agendas, notably on how to improve the general situation of the Ruthenian populace.[14]

In this period the festivities connected with the Liberation Festival often failed to conform to the virtues of abstinence and frugality or to the social discipline espoused by the Ruthenian national movement. In 1872 *Russkaia Rada* described quite contrasting celebrations in two fictitious villages, one in a model community, the other in a village where poor morals prevailed. The festival began in both villages with a mass and a ceremony at the memorial cross. In the model village the citizens met afterwards for communal readings and the narration of newspaper articles, as well as "light-hearted conversation and respectable pranks." In the other village the citizens were said to have moved on quickly to a tavern run by a Jew and then become completely drunk.[15]

There were, however, even then some villages where commemorative celebrations followed the model recommended by the newspaper. In 1873 in the village of Beleluia (Sniatyn district), where the long-time parliamentary deputy Ivan Ozarkevych was a priest, a credit association was founded and a collection taken up for the Ruthenian boarding school in Kolomyia. In the village of Korostno a new reading association was created. Besides the usual church services and processions, the reports from both villages mentioned, in particular, older peasants who recalled the period of serfdom. But even these "model" celebrations ended with a raucous dance, probably held in the tavern.[16]

Pledges of loyalty to the Habsburg emperor remained a conspicuous part of the celebrations. *Bat'kôvshchyna* suggested in 1882 that the May 3 celebrations be tied to a centenary commemoration of the restrictions on the power of landlords that were introduced in 1782 by Emperor Joseph II.[17] But the newspaper also called for "urban" forms of celebration, in addition to masses, processions, and dancing in taverns: "In every Ruthenian church there should be held the Divine Liturgy, in every Ruthenian reading circle there should be a cultural evening (*vechernytsi*), with music, singing, speeches, presentations, and declamations of beautiful poetry."[18]

At that time, relatively few villages were able to hold celebrations with proper decorum. At Serafyntsi near Horodenka there was singing in the early evening on the village square, where local musicians presented "wonderful Ruthenian arias." This was followed by a social evening in the reading room, which began with a long speech by the local priest, who was also the chairman of the reading room association. He emphasized "what a good deed the abolition of the *corvée* had been, and what benefits had been gained from the laws against usury and drunkenness. He concluded by counselling all present to engage in honest work and warned that neither the guardianship of the best of monarchs nor the best of laws could protect people from a fall, if they did not first try to save themselves."[19] There were attempts to organize "cultural evenings" in other villages, although at the time the educational level of the peasants was still low and the necessary commitment was generally lacking.[20]

In a few places, however, peasants were already acting in a manner consistent with the goals of the national movement. For example, in the village of Zheldtsi near Zhovkva, the peasant Demko Iatsura, as he later testified in court, read to fellow peasants from *Bat'kôvshchyna*, spoke about the abolition of serfdom, about a coming solar eclipse, and about the persecution of Jews in the Russian Empire. As a result, the local bailiff charged him with having called for the expulsion from Galicia of Poles, Jews, and *shvaby* (Germans).[21] The charge of agitation against other nationalities could not be proven, however, and Iatsura was acquitted.[22]

In 1898, the Ruthenian national movement transformed the fiftieth anniversary celebrations of peasant emancipation into a great national event that was supported by both the Russophiles and the populist Ukrainophiles (*narodovtsi*). Veneration of the Habsburg emperor and pledges of loyalty to him by now played only a minor role, while Ruthenian demands for genuine equality stood in the foreground. In 1896 an appeal from the National Council (Narodna rada) – a Ukrainophile political association founded in 1885 as rival to the Russophile- oriented Rus' Council – to commemorate May 3 was still filled with pledges of loyalty to the Habsburgs.[23] In 1898, however, the emperor and the monarchy were not even mentioned in a joint declaration issued by the populist Ukrainophiles and the Russophiles. The improvement of the status of Ruthenians after 1848 was no longer presented as the result of the compassionate policies of the emperor, but rather as the achievement of the Ruthenians themselves, who were urged to continue their efforts in the future.[24] Commemorative church services with the appropriate sermons and processions to wayside memorial crosses were to be held in all Greek Catholic churches. Villages without such a cross were to erect one for the occasion. In the afternoon, following religious ceremonies, meetings were to be held at the local reading room. These were to include "presentations and talks as well as declamations and songs accompanied by music appropriate to the occasion." Where there was no reading room, people were to gather in the houses of respected peasants, the elders were to tell younger people about the period of serfdom, and the literate were to read about the period from newspapers and books. The establishment of new reading rooms, shops, credit associations, warehouses, and other socially useful institutions was to be discussed "so that this memorable day does not pass without benefit for the Ruthenian people."[25]

A particularly important event took place in L'viv on May 19, 1898, attended by an estimated 5,000 participants "from all parts of Galician

Rus', including several hundred from L'viv."[26] This gathering was sponsored jointly by the Russophiles and the Ukrainophile populists. It began with a Divine Liturgy at the Church of the Ascension, after which everyone proceeded to the Castle Hill and what turned out to be the first open-air Ruthenian political gathering in L'viv. The speeches lacked the traditional pledges of loyalty to the emperor or the Habsburg monarchy.[27] Even the priest, Vasyl' Davydiak, who belonged to the moderate wing of the Russophiles, showed no sign of veneration for the emperor. Instead, having lamented the decline of the Ruthenian people under Polish rule, Davydiak effectively described the Austrian emperor as a successor to the Polish rulers, a less than flattering association from the Ruthenian point of view.[28]

The populist Ukrainophiles highlighted the meaning of the year 1848 for the national awakening and the importance of the peasants for the Ruthenian nationality as a whole. Their leading political spokesperson, Iuliian Romanchuk, stressed that "for us the peasantry is not only the basis for the whole nationality, [the peasantry] is our very nationality."[29] Nevertheless, the Ruthenian nationality was one that still needed to be developed, one that still had to struggle for equality with others. The year 1848, when serfdom was abolished, was considered to be the beginning of that struggle, since it allowed the most important part of the nation, the peasants, to begin to develop. The year 1848 was, therefore, the starting point for further efforts to transform the Ruthenian people into an independent nationality (*narodnost'*).[30]

If, for the Ukrainophile populists, the peasants symbolized the "real" nation, the Russophile Davydiak placed more emphasis on the decline of the Ruthenians under Polish rule. The Polish period was represented as one in which the peasants were forced into servitude, and the Russophile account on this occasion also paid close attention to the peasantry's historical fate.[31] The newspaper *Svoboda* formulated the basic position of Ukrainophiles regarding national identity in the form of an "all-national oath" (*vsenarodna prysiaha*), which was to be read at the gathering in L'viv.[32] The oath stated: "We are as worthy a people (*narod*) as the Poles, the Czechs, the Germans, or any other of the Austria's nationalities. We have a right to the same rights and no one has a right to have greater priority than us."[33] The declaration then explained how this statement meant real equality for the peasants: "We will invest all our strength, in order that our people [*liud*],[34] as the basis of the whole Ruthenian nationality (*narod*), can stand educationally, materially, and morally as high as possible and enjoy the same respect as other social strata and peoples."[35] The equality of the peasants was thus to be achieved not through simple recognition as equal citizens of Austria, but as members of the Ruthenian nationality. Only through equality with other nationalities could the emancipatory ambitions of the peasants be realized.

The increased politicization of the Ruthenians that occurred in the 1890s, epitomized by the 1898 meeting in L'viv, is also evident in numerous gatherings elsewhere throughout eastern Galicia. In that year, church services, public meetings, and other commemorative events took place in at least half of eastern Galicia's district capitals. In many villages the program extended well beyond the traditional church liturgies and processions to memorial crosses.[36] The response was greatest in Stryi, where 4,000 people were reported to have taken part, and in Rava Rus'ka where 1,000 gathered. Generally, however, the celebrations attracted only a few hundred participants.[37]

Most events began with the Divine Liturgy, followed by a procession to the roadside cross, where the priest delivered a patriotic sermon. In the afternoon, there was usually a general assembly with speeches devoted to historical and political themes, accompanied by patriotic songs and poetry. The celebrations in the neighboring villages of Romaniv and Pidhorodyshchi in the Bibrka district were especially elaborate. After bell ringing and cannon fire, a procession of sixty horsemen decked out with blue and yellow sashes rode into the village carrying flags. They accompanied a decorated wagon carrying the priest, who had celebrated a mass first at a memorial cross in Pidhorodyshchi. Over 1,000 people took part. This was followed by a procession to the cross in Romaniv, where a commemorative service was held for Emperor Ferdinand. The entire congregation then moved on to the cemetery, where another commemorative service was held, this time for the serfs. In the afternoon the villagers gathered again. The procession included six decorated wagons carrying older peasants who had lived under serfdom. A second group of horsemen then arrived from neighboring Pidhorodyshchi. The group's leader held a hetman's mace, which was clearly understood as a national symbol. Then, with the horsemen from Romaniv in the lead, the village youth, elders, and a choir sang patriotic songs on their way to the village square for the May 3 celebration. The last wagon in the procession, which "had not a single piece of metal, showed how a peasant in the older days went off to do serf labor and transport dung." After a speech by the mayor, the elders who had personally experienced serfdom sat down in places of honor.[38]

Many peasants from the surrounding villages also participated in this celebration, the course of which clearly demonstrates how the commemoration of the emancipation from serfdom had acquired an increasingly national profile. Those peasants who themselves had experienced serfdom became in essence "martyrs" of a community that now understood itself as a nation equal to other nations. The celebrations were simultaneously a reminder that the Ruthenians, even at the end of the nineteenth century, still lived under Polish rule. Poles were classified as the "other" within the framework of Ruthenian nation-building, which was founded on the peasantry's collective memory of oppressive, exploitative Polish landlords.

In numerous other villages too, celebrations went well beyond traditional, religious forms and sometimes provided an opportunity for the realization of concrete organizational goals.[39] New oak wooden memorial crosses to commemorate the liberation from serfdom were erected in almost every village in the district of Kaluzh.[40] At Khomyntsi in the Iavoriv district, the peasants invited a high school student to hold "a popular talk based on books from Prosvita." Before he could do so, however, he had to undergo questioning by the district administrator, because the village mayor had reported that this student intended to agitate the peasants "against the Jews and the landlords [pany] etc."[41] In some villages amateur theater groups gave performances.

The increasing politicization of the celebrations transformed them into settings of conflict between the reform-oriented peasants, who were increasingly organized in reading rooms, and community officials, who opposed any kind of change which they perceived as a threat to their authority.[42] Such polarization is described in a report from the village of Ul'vovok (Sokal' district). The local reading room prepared intensively for the commemorative celebrations by rehearsing a play and learning songs and poetry. Meanwhile the opposing party was in the tavern, where it attempted to win support for the upcoming community elections by offering gratis generous portions of beer and vodka. It turned out, however, that even those who drank with the incumbent mayor voted for the candidates proposed by the reading room, so that no one from the "old" party was re-elected.[43]

A planned commemorative ceremony with an open-air lecture, singing, and political speeches in the village of Horodnytsia in the Husiatyn district could not take place, because the district administrator would only agree to allow the program on condition that the priest also participated. The priest, however, who was apparently well connected to the local landlord, refused to support the event.[44] This example shows that peasants were by now ready to organize "modern" forms of commemoration independently and even against the will of their clergymen. In effect, it became a matter of honor and esteem for villages to organize such festivals, and those that failed to do so could expect to be rebuked in the columns of the peasant newspapers. Such civic engagement became part of the "new order," which included the establishment of reading rooms, credit unions, and other mutual aid societies, as well as organized support for Ruthenian candidates at district, provincial, and Reichstag elections and for reformers at community council elections. Aware of such activity in many places, one correspondent complained in the following terms about the apathy shown by some villages towards the commemorative celebrations in the district capital of Husiatyn: "How unfortunate it is that the people of Chabarivka, Horodnytsia, Trybukhivtsi, and Tovsten'ko have not participated as have other communities! We are ashamed and sorry, but it is your own fault. My esteemed communities (*panove hromada*), why don't you care about your honor and your reputation? See, the citizens of Husiatyn would have welcomed you just like the others. Why did you not come? Where were you?"[45]

The "traditional" way of celebrating May 3 was, with the exception of the religious ceremonies, increasingly less respected, even if it was still widespread. Thus, it was reported in 1897 for the Sokal' district village of Vytkiv: "Most of the peasants (*hospodari*) went to mass in the morning, met thereafter for breakfast, and then went home. Nevertheless, the village mayor, together with other *khruni*,[46] ate, drank, and celebrated the whole day. Those who were no longer able to go home even stayed overnight."[47] The celebrations had become part of an all-encompassing reform and temperance project of the Ruthenian national movement in the villages, so that behavior like that of the mayor of Vytkiv was only to be expected from the *khruni*.

In summary, celebrations to honor the emancipation of peasants in 1848, which initially were observed in villages with religious and traditional forms of social interaction, acquired in the course of time an increasingly patriotic profile. Influences from larger towns transmitted the contents and political goals of the national movement into the villages, complementing or replacing older forms of celebration and remembering. Villages became increasingly politicized and nationalized during the agrarian strikes of 1902 and 1906, during the campaigns for election reform in the middle of that decade, and through the introduction of universal suffrage for the 1907 elections to the imperial parliament. This can be seen not only in the strong increase of Ruthenian organizational and communication structures after the turn of the century, but also in the increased engagement of villagers in the planning and observance of national celebrations.

Ruthenian National Festivals in Honor of Taras Shevchenko

Other national holidays also began to find a greater response in the villages in the last years of the empire. Among populist Ukrainophiles, the poet Taras Shevchenko was the foremost national icon. As early as the 1860s Ukrainophiles were organizing regular events in his memory in L'viv and, to a lesser extent, in other towns. For the most part these occurred on the anniversaries of his birth (March 9) and death (March 10).[48]

Shevchenko was the son of serfs in Russian-ruled Ukraine. With these peasant origins he ideally qualified as a figure with whom Galician peasants could identify. Nonetheless, the Shevchenko celebrations met with greater support in rural areas only after the turn of the century, in particular the large celebrations commemorating the fiftieth anniversary of his death, in 1911, and the centenary of his birth, in 1914. For instance, in 1897 *Svoboda* could still lament: "The Poles not only in their own country [that is, western Galicia] but also here in Rus' [that is, eastern Galicia] have in nearly every city a celebration to honor their poet Adam Mickiewicz. Is it not a disgrace for us Ruthenians that we, in our own land, pay less honor to our own prophet? We should celebrate the anniversary of the death of Shevchenko in every city and in every village reading room."[49] For earlier years we have only a few reports of villagers who travelled to town to participate in celebrations of the great poet. For example, in 1884 *Bat'kôvshchyna* described a Shevchenko evening in Ternopil', which was attended not only by the urban intelligentsia but by large numbers of peasants. The peasant choir from the town of Denysiv performed for the event.[50]

As on the Polish side, large-scale participation by peasants in such commemorations occurred only on the eve of World War I. The celebrations of the fiftieth anniversary of Shevchenko's death were preceded by a successful campaign begun two years earlier to raise funds for the construction of a monument to the poet in L'viv.[51] The commemorative acts that took place in 1911 were held not only in cities but in a large number of villages as well.[52] Many small monuments commemorating the national poet were erected and streets and places were named after him.[53]

The story was similar in 1914. An extended program of events was organized in L'viv between March and June to mark the centenary of Shevchenko's birth.[54] This time there was more interest in rural areas than ever before. Reports in the Vienna journal *Ukrainische Rundschau* may have been exaggerated when claiming that the anniversary was celebrated "in all the Ukrainian towns and villages in Galicia."[55] Yet few of Prosvita's 2,000 or so active reading rooms failed to honor Shevchenko in one way or another.[56] The society's executive instructed its reading rooms on how to mark the occasion: there should be lectures, concerts, processions, and the erection of permanent monuments, such as busts or portraits of Shevchenko, an oak tree or an elaborate garden planted in his name, or even the renaming of streets and squares after him.[57]

One of the first Shevchenko celebrations that year took place in Kasperivtsi, Zalishchyky district. It was planned, for the most part, by the local Sich Association.[58] The central event was a parade in which 2,000 people participated. At its head marched a Sich orchestra under the direction of the association's district chairman (*ataman*), followed by various other Sich organizations, including women's branches, each under its own standard. A bust of Shevchenko was unveiled at the entrance to the village and a street was renamed after him. This ceremony was followed by a concert given by the Sich orchestra and combined choirs, interspersed with declamations of patriotic poetry. All this was accompanied by the presentation of a "living image" (*żywy obraz*) appropriate to the occasion. The event concluded with the singing of the national hymns, *Shche ne vmerla Ukraïna*, *Ne pora*, and *My haidamaky*, with everyone apparently leaving for home in high spirits.[59]

Not all celebrations were as extensive. Nevertheless the one in Kasperivtsi was far from atypical. It is important to note the appearance of new elements: an orchestra, a choir, and recitation of the great man's poetry. All this suggested that "urban" forms now dominated national festivals, even in rural areas, where many participants were obviously familiar with and able to sing national songs. It is also important to note what had gone missing: the religious element. This was probably because the entire event was organized by the anti-clerical Sich Association. The Prosvita Society executive also did not explicitly recommend that its members attend religious services as part of the celebrations. In many villages, however, the priests continued to play a central role.[60]

Even if the number of celebrations honoring Ukrainian national poets remained low in the villages before the turn of the century, knowledge about them as representative symbols of the Ruthenian nationality was widespread.[61] The declamation of patriotic poems was an element in many celebrations commemorating the fiftieth anniversary of the emancipation from serfdom, and an increasingly regular feature at the opening of reading rooms and other village institutions. It is reasonable to assume that the works presented at these events, if not poems written by the peasants themselves, were drawn from the emerging national canon, with Shevchenko's verse at the top of the list. On the walls of Ruthenian reading rooms, images of Shevchenko and other national heroes hung alongside pictures of the Habsburg emperor and of local bishops and saints.[62] Even the Russophiles could not avoid the influence of such symbolic figures. Consequently, they too recognized both Shevchenko and the Galician poet Markiian Shashkevych as important vernacular writers, although they argued against appropriating them in support of a national Ukrainian political program.[63] The Russophiles tried instead to promote Mykhailo Kachkovs'kyi, Ivan Naumovych, and Nikolai Gogol' as figureheads for the nation, but with only limited success.[64]

National Celebrations among the Poles

The peasant liberation of May 1848 was not commemorated by the Roman Catholic Church or by the Polish intelligentsia. It made no sense from a Polish nationalist point of view to celebrate an event that was remembered by the peasants primarily as a "Gift of the Emperor." The emancipation was an event perfectly suited to strengthening not only peasant loyalty to the emperor, but also the historic antagonism between peasants and landlords. Nevertheless, during the post-1868 phase of increasing Polish autonomy in Galicia, a multifaceted national festival culture developed among the Polish educated classes.[65] At first the celebrations in Galician were largely confined to the intelligentsia in the cities. The participation of the peasants developed only slowly and was a part of a political process wrought with conflict, which reflected the difficulties in integrating the peasants into the Polish nation. As in the Ruthenian case, so too among the Poles religion played an important role in promoting national identity throughout the countryside.

Father Stanisław Stojałowski exerted considerable effort at attracting the peasants and making them feel themselves part of the Polish nation by appealing primarily to their religious identification as Roman Catholics. Early in his years of activism, Stojałowski organized several peasant pilgrimages which featured some national elements. In effect, he took religious forms with which villagers were familiar and filled them with highly patriotic content. Information about such national-religious syntheses spread well beyond the participants through extensive reports in the newspapers *Wieniec* and *Pszczółka*.

The first larger pilgrimage that Stojałowski organized, one which he described as a "national-religious" endeavor, took place in 1879 from May 6 to 9.[66] It led from L'viv to Cracow, where the pilgrims visited the grave of Saint Stanislaus in Wawel Cathedral. This pilgrimage began with the blessing in the Cathedral in L'viv of a banner on which was written: "Saint Stanislaus, patron of Poland, pray for us!" After mass, and a visit to the Roman Catholic Archbishop of L'viv for a blessing, around 160 participants left the city by train. More pilgrims joined en route so that, as Stojałowski reported, as many as 1,300 people reached the station in Słotwina. The journey was interrupted here to allow the pilgrims to join a procession to Szczepanów, the birthplace of Saint Stanislaus.

An incident which occurred at this point makes it clear how poorly developed national consciousness was among the rural population. A rumour had spread in Szczepanów that a group of "insurrectionists and Poles" (*powstańcy i Polacy*) was approaching. Years earlier, in 1846, when peasants were confronted with the news of a Polish national uprising, they in turn revolted – attacking and slaughtering hundreds of Polish insurrectionists, landlords, and estate officials. On this occasion in 1879, however, there was no panic or violent encounter with the pilgrims because community leaders managed to counter the rumours.[67] A mass was celebrated at the birthplace of the saint, and then the pilgrims continued their journey to Cracow, with more pilgrims joining them along the way. After their arrival in the city, they walked from the train station through the Floriańska Gate across the market square down the "Royal Way," eventually reaching the Wawel Cathedral and the grave of Saint Stanislaus. Here – in this most holy shrine of Polish history – Stojałowski celebrated another mass. The next day all went to confession in various churches across the city, and after that a common mass was celebrated.

The primary aim of this pilgrimage was to strengthen the national identification of the peasants. Their negative opinion of all things Polish was to be overcome by making Polishness correlate with Catholicism. In addition to this national-religious synthesis, Stojałowski combined the pilgrimage with attempts to establish peasant self-help organizations in the villages. Therefore, in the program of the pilgrims' stay in Cracow he included a large assembly in the garden of the Sokół building. Three thousand people attended. During the gathering several speeches were devoted to possibilities for improving rural and agricultural conditions.

Stojałowski had yet another motive in mind. The large-scale participation of peasants in national holidays was intended to demonstrate that they, too, were an integral part of the Polish nation and that indeed they were patriotic, not anti-Polish. This was to form the basis of the peasants' claims to greater social and political equality. This feature became more clearly discernible when Stajałowski called on peasants to participate in the bicentennial celebrations of the lifting of the Ottoman siege of Vienna by a Polish army led by King Jan Sobieski. The celebrations were to take place in Cracow on September 12, 1883. Stojałowski combined the participation in the Sobieski celebrations with attendance at another event. A few days before the bicentennial festivities, religious ceremonies to mark the crowning of a miraculous painting of the Virgin Mary were to be held in the town of Piasek, which was not far from Cracow. In his newspapers, Stojałowski invited peasants to participate in both events, and he proclaimed the journey to Cracow a pilgrimage. In all probability, only the inclusion of this great religious event would have ensured a large peasant turnout. The response was overwhelming, and far stronger than had been expected. Around 8,000 peasants joined Stojałowski's pilgrimage. This large number of participants caused severe problems, however, since accommodation had only been prepared for about 2,000 people.[68] Stojałowski later wrote, "The news that several thousand peasants would come to Cracow [caused] panic in the minds of townspeople unfamiliar with the rural folk (*lud*), and the Jews asked for protection."[69] In fact, everything went smoothly, even if numerous peasants had to sleep in the open. Nevertheless, the "panic" in Cracow before the festivities is indicative of the fears that Stojałowski had to allay, which also resulted in the withdrawal of previously agreed offers of accommodation.[70]

Through their participation in national festivities, Stojałowski hoped to demonstrate the validity of peasant demands for equality with other social strata. This was particularly evident on the solemn occasion in 1890, when the body of Adam Mickiewicz was transferred to Cracow's Wawel Cathedral. Calling for a large peasant turnout, Stojałowski published a brochure, in which he argued: "It can be proven that you are no 'uneducated mass' (*ciemną masą*) but rather a living nation, a nation full of power and spirit, not yet born but just beginning to come to life ... The peasants will be there in Cracow, not merely as an unformed mass but together as a distinct and meaningful class that, in fact, already has its place in the nation as its most numerous class, but which has not as yet enjoyed the honor and respect that they – as Poles and citizens – deserve."[71]

The conservative-oriented organizational committee in Cracow was anxious to prevent the celebrations from becoming a political demonstration, under the leadership of the radical priest, and had Stojałowski arrested the day before the event.[72] In the end, only 150 peasants organized by a People's Committee (Komitet ludowy), which had been founded by Stojałowski in Wadowice, were permitted to take part in the procession carrying Mickiewicz's remains from the Cracow train station to the Wawel Cathedral. A public meeting after the funeral was not permitted. The peasants brought forty-four huge wreaths woven out of cereal sheaves from all parts of Poland. The sheaves were decorated with letters that together formed the message: *Adamowi Mickiewiczowi lud wszystkich ziem Polski* (For Adam Mickiewicz from the people of all regions of Poland).[73] The number 44 had a symbolic meaning in Mickiewicz's writings about the future resurrection of Poland. This message, emblazoned on gifts from peasants from all parts of Poland, was a clear declaration of peasant patriotism and its importance for the nation.

Tadeusz Kościuszko and the Uprising of 1794 (in reaction to the second partition at 1792) held special interest for the Polish peasant movement (*ruch ludowy*). At the Battle of Racławice, in 1794, Polish victory was assured when a unit of peasants, armed with scythes (*kosynierzy*, from *kosa*, scythe), launched the decisive attack on a Russian artillery emplacement. Over the course of the nineteenth century, the *kosynierzy* became a symbol, especially for the left, of the patriotism of Polish peasants, embodying the hope that one day peasants would rise again in a war for the restoration of the Poland. Kościuszko, who had undertaken some preliminary steps in 1794 toward greater equality for the peasants and for the reduction and regulation of the *corvée*, was systematically presented as a positive figure with whom peasants could identify. A cult also began to develop around Wojciech Bartosz Głowacki, one of the few *kosynierzy* known by name to posterity because he was decorated by Kościuszko for his valour at the Battle of Racławice.[74]

The centenary of the Uprising of 1794 was observed throughout Galicia. These celebrations contributed significantly to the founding of the Peasant party (Stronnictwo Ludowe) the following year. This party united politically active peasants with leftist elements among the Polish intelligentsia. A large public commemoration was held in Cracow on April 1, 1894. Despite repeated public announcements in *Pryjaciel Ludu*, peasant participation was apparently not very high.[75] The Cracow newspaper *Czas* reported that only a few hundred peasants took part in the celebrations on the market square and the parade to the Wawel that followed, all the while carrying wreaths decorated with the emblems of Polish cities.[76]

This would suggest that unless the events were presented in a religious context, like the Sobieski celebrations of 1883, it was difficult to mobilize the peasants for national celebrations. Historian Magdalena Micińska has counted eighty celebrations of the Kościuszko Uprising in provincial cities and villages in which local peasants usually participated. In most cases, however, they did so only passively as spectators.[77] The general peasant mistrust of organized national rituals at this time is confirmed in the memoirs of a later peasant leader Wincenty Witos:

> The peasants had a strange aversion toward the national celebrations that took place from time to time in the district capitals. It took much work and energy to get at least some of them to attend. Normally they were sick, or did not have a clean shirt, or found one of a dozen other reasons not to go. This suspicion arose not only out of fear of a meeting with the *panowie* but also for reasons unknown to others. The peasant never forgot that the Polish *szlachta* had for centuries held him as a serf, and that it was the emperor who had abolished this practice and granted him his rights and his freedom. He was also convinced that, had Poland not disintegrated, serfdom would have existed forever. The most important hurdle was the unwillingness to meet with the *panowie* and the fear that they would somehow deceive him. So the peasant, in order to avoid such eventualities, preferred to stay away.[78]

Peasant attitudes changed only slowly. Compared with the opening rituals of the Kościuszko centennial in Cracow, a peasants' assembly on August 26–27, 1894, organized by *Przyjaciel Ludu* and political democrats in L'viv, was much more successful. L'viv police spoke of "over 1,000 peasants," while the organizers claimed that there were between

2,000 and 3,000 peasants in attendance.[79] Elections to the Galician diet were to be held in the following year. The major task of the L'viv assembly, therefore, was to develop an independent political program in preparation for them. The peasants were also attracted by the large commercial and agricultural exhibition that was to be held in L'viv at the same time. The major attraction was the Battle of Racławice panorama, a large-scale painting contracted especially for this occasion, that showed Kościuszko (not Głowacki) at the head of scythe-waving peasant units (*kosynierzy*) storming the Russian cannons. Peasants were able to view the panorama when they visited the exhibition, with students from L'viv and Maria, wife of Bolesław Wysłouch, as guides.[80] The choice of this particular painting to highlight the exhibition, together with the wide resonance of the Kościuszko centennial throughout Galicia, made it obvious that by 1894 something had changed. The idea that the *lud* was the basis of Polish national existence, and that any hope for the nation's future lay not with the *szlachta* but rather with the *lud*, had become predominant in the Polish public sphere. Now peasants themselves could appreciate their national role when seeing themselves represented in this painting.

The birthday centennial of the national poet Adam Mickiewicz was celebrated in 1898. The highlight was the unveiling of a monument to him on the market square in Cracow. Peasants participation was greater than for the Kościuszko celebrations a few years earlier.[81] Jakób Bojko, representing the Polish peasantry at Cracow, claimed that by now the name Mickiewicz was known to at least a few peasants in every village. In his youth it had been different, however: "In 1868, when I brought the pamphlet *Opiekun polskich dzieci* containing a portrait and a short résumé of Mickiewicz's life home from school to show it to my father, and even though he could read ... he had never heard of 'such a *pan*.'[82] After I discovered that Mickiewicz had written a wonderful book called *Pan Tadeusz*, I looked for it for a long time but I could not get it anywhere. The local teacher did not have it and the priest said that it was an expensive book and not for a peasant ... In my thirtieth year [1887] a village teacher finally gave me a copy of the book, which I devoured immediately."[83]

Nevertheless, it was Kościuszko and the Battle of Racławice that remained the central historical image for Galicia's Polish populists (*ludowcy*). In 1903 the executive of the Polish Peasant party resolved to celebrate the anniversary of the battle every year – as the People's Holiday (Święto Ludowe), either on April 4 or the Sunday following.[84]

Thus, the populists appropriated these historical symbols for their political party even more than before, and the celebrations themselves took on the character of Polish Peasant party conventions. By now, the festivities were very often planned and organized by peasants themselves. This is evidence of not only their heightened national identification but also the improving levels of education among the peasantry, especially the younger generation.[85]

Usually, the celebrations began with a mass, followed by lectures, patriotic songs, and poetry recitation by peasants. The number of amateur peasant theater groups increased significantly in the years before World War I, Władysław Ludwik Anczyc's patriotic play, *Kościuszko pod Racławicami* (Kościuszko at Racławice), was especially popular. In some villages memorial trees were planted and the festivities were often taken as an opportunity to discuss plans for new educational initiatives or cooperative organizations.[86]

A statue in honor of Bartosz Głowacki was unveiled in the west Galician town of Tarnobrzeg in 1904, and in L'viv another such statue was unveiled in 1906. In Tarnobrzeg, a fundraising committee had been created for this purpose in September 1901. The chairmen of this committee were the local mayor and the peasant publicist Jan Słomka. Other driving forces behind this committee were Wojciech Wiącek, a peasant from the village of Machów and a leading peasant politician among Galicia's National Democrats, as well as the local lawyer Antoni Surowiecki.[87] Wiącek had already made an impact in 1895, when under his direction the villagers in Machów had re-enacted the Battle of Racławice, probably the first such re-enactment. He claimed that the production drew some 5,000 spectators from surrounding villages.[88] Encouraged by this success, the peasants of Machów re-enacted the 1831 Battle of Grochów a year later, on the occasion of the sixty-fifth anniversary of the November Insurrection, and two years after that, in May 1898, they repeated their performance of the Battle of Racławice.[89]

Racławice was re-enacted yet again by the peasants of Machów on the occasion of the unveiling of the Głowacki monument in Tarnobrzeg. Among the peasants who participated in the event were 300 from the district of Mielec. They had been organized by the local parliamentary deputy Franciszek Krempa of the Polish Peasant party. They were dressed as *kosynierzy*.[90] The peasants had adopted national symbols originally created by the intelligentsia. In this way they demonstrated the national importance of the peasantry and implicitly staked their claim for equality or even priority vis-à-vis the traditional ruling elites. They made themselves part of the Polish nation and hoped to occupy a leading position in national life. Peasants utilized the national discourse and the resources of symbolic politics to make their case and gain support among the Galician public. The erection of the statue in Tarnobrzeg could be interpreted as a demonstration of peasant demands for further emancipation. More importantly, that the citizens of L'viv erected a monument to the leader of the *kosynierzy* deserves to be seen as a symbolic recognition of the peasantry as an important part of the nation by the Polish urban population.[91]

The substantial degree of political and national mobilization reached among the peasantry by the eve of World War I is evident in the large number of Polish national celebrations in the villages. For instance, in 1910 only a very few Polish villages remained untouched by commemorations of the 500th anniversary of the Battle of Grunwald,[92] in which a Polish-Lithuanian army had defeated the Teutonic Knights. In many instances, peasants from several villages took part in joint celebrations, and as a result the number of participants sometimes reached several hundred or even a thousand. The celebrations nearly always began with a mass and a procession accompanied by music, hymns, and in the majority of cases, patriotic songs as well. The program usually included speeches about the battle and the relationship between Poland and Prussia. Often these conveyed a strong social and political message. The processions were frequently accompanied by horsemen led by politically active and particularly respected peasants. In many places the events concluded with performances of patriotic plays.[93]

Village youth were especially active, in choirs, theater groups, and other cultural institutions, and also in the actual organization of the celebrations. The erection of stone monuments, crosses, and plaques, and the planting of memorial trees for the Battle of Grunwald all called for serious civic commitment on the part of the village communities, which had to invest money and labor.[94] The central public ritual took place in mid-July in Cracow. With an estimated 150,000 participants, many from the peasantry, it was the largest of all patriotic celebrations to take place in that city up to that point. Together with the patriotic spectacle, Cracow itself left a deep impression on many peasants. Wincenty Witos had come to the city with a group of peasants from his home region of Tarnów. As he later recalled, many were in Cracow for the first time: "They could not even for a moment tear their eyes away from the festive decorations of the city and the colourful masses ... While I was returning home with my neighbors that evening, we talked the whole time about the experiences of this great day. One of them, Franciszek Stawarz, was sunk deep in thought, and when I asked him why he was so contemplative he answered: 'Do you know what, friends? It's good that we came to Cracow today, because we have seen much, and that makes a man light of heart, but I think that we shall never be finished with the Prussians, and that is where my sorrow comes from.'"[95]

In the Grunwald celebrations, the peasant movement was not simply subsumed into the Polish nation. The conflict with Prussia and later Germany still provided ample opportunity to emphasize that the peasantry (*lud*) was to be considered the leading element within the Polish nation. In this way, references to national identity served an important function in the demands to improve the position of the peasantry. As early as 1886, in his *Szkice programowe*, which contained the political program for the activities of the democratic intelligentsia, and led later to the founding of the Peasant party in 1895, Bolesław Wysłouch had insisted on placing the peasantry at the center of national politics. He believed that the future of the nation was to be found among peasants. Wysłouch based his argument on the resistance that the peasantry, as opposed to the nobility (*szlachta*), had offered to the pressures for germanization in Prussia.[96] The newspaper *Przyjaciel Ludu* argued in a similar vein during the celebrations of 1910, emphasizing the national qualities of the peasantry when compared with the nobility, who had sold their estates to the Prussian settlement commission against the interests of the Polish nation:

On whom, if not on the peasantry, is thrust the weight of our national resistance against the Prussians? Who, if not they, stand strong and brave against impertinent attacks and the denationalizing Prussian politics? Who preserve the earth and do not squander it? ... Who unite and organize themselves, and who know no other thought than loyally holding out for the Fatherland? Who is looking forward to change and not dishonoring the Polish name through the sale of estates to the settlement commission for Judas's shining silver? ... Who is it, if not the Polish peasants, if not our brothers, who there under the Prussians, always emerge victorious in quarrels with the Hakatists![97] The peasants are a secure base on which to build the national spirit. They will surely be among the first to carry it to the peaks, when our nation is reborn.[98]

Conclusions

The comparison of patriotic celebrations among Poles and Ruthenians in rural areas shows significant differences, but also commonalities in the way the peasantry was included into the nation. The Liberation Festival commemorating the emancipation of serfs in 1848, which was observed primarily in a religious mode, functioned for a long time as the most important Ruthenian national celebration. It was a strong point of reference in the "traditional" understanding of Ruthenian identity, primarily defined through religion. Increasingly, however, these festivals took on a secular and national profile. Other ritual occasions were disseminated from the cities relatively late, although they were then adopted very quickly. The Shevchenko celebrations of 1914 found probably an even greater resonance among the rural population than did the Polish Grunwald rituals of 1910.

The first national celebrations among the Poles in which peasants participated en masse were the pilgrimages organized by Father Stojałowski. Religious identity was over time infused with more and more national content. Polish national celebrations drew on the experience of the established form of the pilgrimage, but they could not, in contrast to the Ruthenian Liberation Festival, be integrated into the traditional ritual calendar of the villages. Hence, their impact was comparatively limited. The Poles did, however, even before the turn of the century manage to develop an intensive culture of public rituals that, although primarily the work of the intelligentsia, also percolated down to rural communities. Eventually, peasant mistrust of events organized by "gentlemen" (*panowie*) weakened. The Polish intelligentsia busied itself trying to find individuals and events in Polish history with which the peasantry could identify. Tadeusz Kościuszko and the scythe-bearing peasant units (*kosynierzy*) associated with the Battle of Racławice served as most the important symbols tying the peasants to the Polish nation.

National celebrations were propagated intensively by the Polish peasant movement. This was not only a question of strengthening the peasantry's national identification, but also of demonstrating via the massive presence of villagers in the public sphere that the peasantry was an important part of the Polish nation. Reference to peasant national identity was a strategy for the peasant movement in pursuing its demands in Galician politics. The national discourse to which the new public rituals belonged served to underscore the importance of the peasantry for the Polish nation at the same time that it revealed the deficient patriotism of the nobility. As well, it showed that the continuing political domination of the peasants by the nobility lacked legitimacy. The patriotic celebrations thus became part of the movement for imroving the lot of the peasant, with the result that the traditional gulf between the peasant and Polish identity was reduced.

In both the Ruthenian and the Polish cases, peasant emancipation was connected to national identity. National identity offered a basis for asserting calls for equality with and even primacy over traditional elites. The legitimacy of their privileges and their political dominance was challenged in the first case by reference to the identity of the Ruthenians as a different nationality. In the second, Polish case, the privileged position of the traditional elites was destabilized by the peasant movement, which argued that the real guarantor of Polish national existence was the peasantry, the *lud*, and not the *szlachta*.

Notes

1 The study of national rituals has become an important field of research within studies of modern nation-building. It has been strongly influenced by Eric Hobsbawm, "The Invention of Tradition," in Eric Hobsbaum and Terence Ranger, eds., *The Invention of Tradition* (Cambridge, 1983), pp. 1–14, and by Benedict Anderson, *Imagined Communities: Reflections on the Origin and Spread of Nationalism* (London, 1983). For eastern and central Europe, see Maria Bucur and Nancy M. Wingfield, eds., *Staging the Past. The Politics of Commemoration in Habsburg Central Europe, 1848 to the Present* (West Lafayette, Ind., 2001); and Emil Brix and Hannes Stekl, eds., *Der Kampf um das Gedächtnis: Öffentliche Gedenktage in Mitteleuropa* (Vienna, 1997), which includes a survey of the latest research by Hannes Stekl, "Öffentliche Gedenktage und gesellschaftliche Identitäten," pp. 91–116.

2 Here I distinguish only two competing orientations among Galicia's Ruthenians: the Ukrainophile populists (*narodovtsi*) and the Russophiles. This distinction follows the framework outlined in Anna Veronika Wendland, *Die Russophilen in Galizien: Ukrainische Konservative zwischen Österreich und Rußland 1848–1915* (Vienna, 2001).

Alternatively, Paul Robert Magocsi lays much more emphasis on the breach that developed within the group referred to here as Russophiles at the turn of the twentieth century. At that time a more radical trend among them emerged which used literary Russian and hoped to transform Ruthenians into a Russian national group within Austria While these more radical "followers of a new trend" (*novokursnyky*) strove openly for unification with the Russian Empire, the more moderate Russophiles (or Old Ruthenians in Magocsi's terminology) continued to emphasize their loyalty to the Habsburg emperor and to Austria. Magocsi reserves the term *Russophiles* for the radical *novokursnyky*. In the period prior to this break he contrasts the Old Ruthenians to the Ukrainophile "Young Ruthenians." See the discussion in three works by Magocsi: "Old Ruthenianism and Russophilism: A New Conceptual Framework for Analyzing National Ideologies in Late 19th Century Eastern Galicia," in Paul Debreczeny, ed., *American Contributions to the Ninth International Congress of Slavists*, vol. II (Columbus, Ohio, 1983), pp. 305–324; "The Language Question as a Factor in the National Movement," in Andrei S. Markovits and Frank E. Sysyn, eds., *Nationbuilding and the Politics of Nationalism: Essays on Austrian Galicia* (Cambridge, Mass., 1989), pp. 220–238; and *A History of Ukraine* (Seattle, 1997), pp. 436–452. For the various options open to the Galician Ruthenians in the process of modern nationality-building, see also John-Paul Himka, "The Construction of Nationality in Galician Rus': Icarian Flights in Almost All Directions," in Ronald Grigor Suny and Michael D. Kennedy, eds., *Intellectuals and the Articulation of the Nation* (Ann Arbor, Mich., 1999), pp. 109–164.

3 In the political language of the Ruthenians in the second half of the nineteenth century the term *narod* (in Ukrainian sometimes also *narid*) had the double meaning of "nation/nationality/people" or the "common (peasant) folk," that is, the mainly peasant population that did not belong to the intelligentsia (in this respect the second meaning of *narod* is largely identical with the Polish term *lud*). The range of meaning for *narod* is therefore very similar to that of the German *Volk*.

4 See Keely Stauter-Halsted, *The Nation in the Village: The Genesis of Peasant National Identity in Austrian Poland, 1848–1914* (Ithaca, NY, 2001); Jan Molenda, *Chłopi, naród, niepodległość: kształtowanie się postaw narodowych i obywatelskich chłopów w Galicji i Królestwie Polskim w przededniu odrodzenia Polski* (Warsaw, 1999). For a comparison of the Polish and the Ruthenian cases, see Kai Struve, *Bauern und Nation in Galizien: über Zugehörigkeit und soziale Emanzipation im 19. Jahrhundert* (Göttingen, 2005).

5 On Stojałowski, see Franciszek Kącki, *Ks. Stanisław Stojałowski i jego działalność społeczno-polityczna*, vol. I, *1845–1890* (L'viv, 1937); and Andrzej Kudłaszyk, *Ksiądz Stanisław Stojałowski: studium historyczno-prawne* (Wrocław, 1998). These studies either conceal his anti-Semitism or they play it down. On this point, see Frank Golczewski, *Polnisch-jüdische Beziehungen 1881–1922* (Wiesbaden, 1981), pp. 60–84; Claudia Kraft, "Die

jüdische Frage im Spiegel der Presseorgane und Parteiprogramme der galizischen Bauernbewegung im letzten Viertel des 19. Jahrhunderts," *Zeitschrift für Ostmitteleuropaforschung,* XLV (Marburg, 1996), pp. 381–409; and Kai Struve, "Gentry, Jews, and Peasants: Jews as the 'Others' in the Formation of the Modern Polish Nation in Rural Galicia during the Second Half of the 19th Century," in Nancy Wingfield, ed., *Creating the Other: Ethnic Conflict and Nationalism in Habsburg Central Europe* (New York, 2003), pp. 103–126.

6 On Wysłouch, see Peter Brock, "Bolesław Wysłouch, Pioneer of Polish Populism," in his *Nationalism and Populism in Partitioned Poland: Selected Essays* (London, 1973), pp. 181–211; and Andrzej Kudłaszyk, *Myśl społeczno-polityczna Bolesława Wysłoucha 1855–1937* (Warsaw, 1978).

7 For an overview of Ruthenian politics in Galicia, see Kost' Levyts'kyi, *Istoriia politychnoï dumky halyts'kykh ukraïntsiv, 1848–1914* (L'viv, 1926); and Ivan L. Rudnytsky, "The Ukrainians in Galicia Under Austrian Rule," in Markovits and Sysyn, *Nationbuilding,* pp. 23–67. On the development of the Ruthenian political groupings and the social composition of the Ruthenian parliamentarians in the provincial diet and the Austrian imperial parliament, see Harald Binder, "Parteiwesen und Parteibegriff bei den Ruthenen der Habsburgermonarchie," *Österreichische Osthefte,* XLII, 3–4 (Vienna, 2000), pp. 211–240.

8 On these two organizations, see Paul Robert Magocsi, "The Kachkovs'kyi Society and the National Revival in Nineteenth-Century East Galicia," *Harvard Ukrainian Studies* XV, 1–2 (Cambridge, Mass., 1991), pp. 48–87; Wendland, *Die Russophilen,* pp. 262–321; and Roman Ivanychuk et al., *Narys istoriï "Prosvity"* (L'viv, 1993). An in-depth history of these organizations remains to be written.

9 For details, see John-Paul Himka, *Galician Villagers and the Ukrainian National Movement in the Nineteenth Century* (Edmonton, 1988), pp. 59–104. A first wave of Ruthenian reading circles had been established as early as the 1870s, but these were quickly dissolved; see the detailed account by Mykhailo Pavlyk, "Pro rus'ko-ukraïns'ki narodni chytal'ni," in his *Tvory* (Kiev, 1985), pp. 159–283. For changes in the rural society before the turn of the century, see also Stella Hryniuk, *Peasants with Promise: Ukrainians in Southwestern Galicia 1880–1900* (Edmonton, 1991).

10 On Galician agrarian circles, see Antoni Gurnicz, *Kółka rolnicze w Galicji: studium społeczno-ekonomiczne* (Warsaw, 1967). For a good overview of adult education initiatives among Poles in Galicia, see Ryszard Terlecki, *Oświata dorosłych i popularyzacja nauki w Galicji w okresie autonomii* (Wrocław, 1990).

11 Wawrzyniec Dayczak, "Z dni wielkich przemian: wspomnienia architekta," manuscript in the Biblioteka Zakładu Narodowego im. Ossolińskich, Wrocław 140931/II, p. 66.

12 On the Rus' Council, established in 1870, see Wendland, *Die Russophilen*, pp. 243–261.

13 *Russkaia Rada*, no. 9, May 1/13, 1873, pp. 68f.

14 Ibid., pp. 65f; "Mityng," *Russkaia Rada*, no. 7, April 1/13, 1873, pp. 52f.

15 "Svoboda," ibid., no. 10, May 15/27, 1872, p. 74. In this account, the lack of freedom and economic dependence on the Jews caused by the consumption of alcohol substituted for the lack of freedom under the rule of the Polish landlords (*pany*). The next national goal was to free Ruthenians of this vice. On the relationship between Ruthenian peasants, the national movement, and Jews, see John-Paul Himka, "Ukrainian-Jewish Antagonism in the Galician Countryside during the Late Nineteenth Century," in Peter J. Potichnyj and Howard Aster, eds., *Ukrainian-Jewish Relations in Historical Perspective* (Edmonton, 1988), pp. 111–158.

16 The newspaper accounts do not mention, however, where the dancing took place. See "Pys'mo z Belelui," *Russkaia Rada*, no. 10, May 15/27, 1873, pp. 77f; Andrej Pavliuk, "Pys'mo yz Korostna," ibid., no. 13, July 1/13, 1873, pp. 102f.

17 "Velyka rôchnytsia," *Bat'kôvshchyna*, no. 7, April 1, 1882, p. 49; "Do nashykh hospodarîv," ibid., no. 9, May 1, 1882, p. 65.

18 "Velyka rôchnytsia," p. 49.

19 "Pys'mo z-pôd Horodenky," *Bat'kôvshchyna*, no. 11, June 1, 1882, p. 86.

20 This, at least, is how a correspondent from the village of Kaminobrid near Horodok interpreted the situation, ibid., pp. 85f.

21 A term sometimes used pejoratively for Germans.

22 "Pys'mo z Zhovkôvskoho," *Bat'kôvshchyna*, no. 15, Aug. 1, 1882, p. 120.

23 "Pamiatnŷi den'," ibid., no. 9, May 1/13, 1896, p. 65.

24 "Rusynŷ halytskoi zemlî!" *Svoboda*, no. 14, April 2/14, 1898, p. 106. In 1897 *Svoboda* replaced *Bat'kôvshchyna* as the leading Ukrainophile paper for the peasants.

25 Ibid. For further appeals to commemorate the anniversary of 1848, see "Pered piat'desiat'my rokamy," ibid., no. 6, Feb. 5/17, 1898, p. 41; the anonymously published memoirs of a peasant about serfdom, "Spomynky panshchyny," ibid., pp. 42f; and "Lad'te sia, panove hromada!," ibid., no. 15, April 9/21, 1898, p. 113. For a reprint of the imperial patent which abolished serfdom, see *ibid.*, No. 18, April 30/ May 12, 1898, pp. 137–139. For calls to commemorate the anniversary in the villages, see also the articles in the Russophile paper for peasants: "50-lîtniaia rôchnytsia," *Russkoe slovo*,

no. 12, March 20 / April 1, 1898, pp. 1f; and "Rusynŷ halytskoi zemlî!" ibid., no. 14, April 2/14, 1898, pp. 1f.

26 "Sviatkovanie narodnoho iuvyleiu," *Svoboda*, no. 20, May 14/26, 1898, p. 154. For this meeting, see also "50-lîtniaia rôchnytsia snesen'ia panshchyny i ôtrozhdeniia russkoho naroda," *Russkoe slovo*, no. 19, May 8/20, 1898, p. 1.

27 It was only Iuliian Romanchuk who spoke briefly about the circumstances surrounding the abolition of serfdom in 1848. First, however, he mentioned the Vienna revolutionaries as deserving of respect, followed by Galicia's governor Count Stadion, and only then did he mention the emperors Ferdinand and Franz Josef. "Sviatkovanie narodnoho iuvyleiu," *Svoboda*, no. 20, May 14/26, 1898, p. 154.

28 Ibid., p. 157. What contributed decisively to Ruthenian alienation from Vienna were the massive election manipulations of the 1890s, which were not only tolerated but indeed approved by the emperor. This was apparently confirmed by the emperor's appointment of Kazimierz Badeni, the viceroy of Galicia primarily responsible for these manipulations, as Austria's prime minister in the autumn of 1895.

29 Ibid., p. 154.

30 Ibid.

31 Ibid., pp. 156f.

32 The report on the meeting, however, does not mention this oath. The Russophiles, who co-sponsored this event, would in any case hardly have given their agreement.

33 "Vsenarodna prysiaha," *Svoboda*, no. 19, May 7/19, 1898, p. 145.

34 Ibid. The term *liud* was rarely used in the political language of the Ruthenians. It was more common to use the word *narod*, which in this sentence is also invoked in the sense of people, or nationality. The term *natsiia* (nation), which in the twentieth century became more widespread, was hardly used in this sense at the end of the nineteenth century. See also above, note 3.

35 Ibid.

36 Cf. the reports in *Svoboda*, no. 20, May 14/26 1898, pp. 158f; no. 21, May 21 / June 2 1898, pp. 162–164; no. 22, May 28 / June 9, 1898, pp. 170–172; and no. 23, June 4/16, 1898, pp. 178–180.

37 Ibid., no. 20, May 14/26, 1898, pp. 158f.

38 Ibid., No. 21, May 21 / June 2, 1898, p. 162.

39 For example, the celebrations in the villages of Zalavia (Terebovlia district) and Krasnyi (Turka district) were connected to the founding of a Prosvita Society reading room. Ibid., no. 22, May 28 / June 9, 1898, p. 171; and no. 25, June 18/30 1898, p. 197.

40 Ibid., no. 22, May 28 / June 9, 1898, p. 170.

41 Ibid., No. 21, May 21 / June 2, 1898, p. 163.

42 On conflicts between the "old" authorities and "reformers" in the villages, see Himka, *Galician Villagers*, pp. 175f; Hryniuk, *Peasants with Promise*, pp. 104f.

43 Chlop z-nad Buha, "Z Sokal'shchynŷ," *Svoboda*, no. 23, June 4/16, 1898, pp. 180f.

44 S-a, "Z Husiatynshchynŷ," ibid., no. 26, June 25 / July 7, 1898, pp. 204f.

45 Ivanyshyn, "Z Husiatynshchynŷ," ibid., no. 21, May 21 / June 2, 1898, p. 165. Later correspondence cast doubt on the claim that no one from these communities was present at the celebrations. It seems there was no procession with banners to Husiatyn because it was a long way to travel; consequently, the members of these communities who attended were not noticed. S-a, "Z Husiatynshchynŷ," ibid., no. 26, June 25 / July 7, 1898, p. 205.

46 Ibid. The custom of calling those who actively supported the Polish side against the Ruthenian national movement *khruni* began as early as the 1880s. *Khrun'* is another term for pig; it is perhaps best translated as someone who grunts.

47 Y. Sokolyn, "Z Husiatynshchynŷ," ibid., no. 21, May 22 / June 3, 1897, p. 165.

48 On Shevchenko's reception and cult in Galicia, see Mykola Dubyna: *Shevchenko i Zakhidna Ukraïna* (Kiev, 1969).

49 "Dva narodni sviata," *Svoboda*, no. 16, April 17/29, 1897, p. 121. In the following year *Svoboda* repeated the call to celebrate the Shevchenko anniversary and encouraged its readers by printing a talk about the poet that had been given in a local reading circle. "Borets' za svobodu chlopôv," ibid., no. 8, Feb. 19 / March 3, 1898, p. 58.

50 M. Seliukh, "Pys'mo z-pôd Zborova," *Bat'kôvshchyna*, no. 7, Feb. 15 / March 3, 1884, p. 41. For an account of the participation of peasants in a Shevchenko festival at the Prosvita Society office in Stryi, see ibid., no. 19, Oct. 1/13, 1894, p. 147. Apparently only people from the city were present at an evening in honor of Shevchenko in the Ruthenian reading room in Terebovlia, the first Shevchenko commemoration in this town, ibid., July 4, 1890; Hryniuk, *Peasants with Promise*, p. 106.

51 Dubyna, *Shevchenko*, pp. 114f.

52 Ibid., pp. 115f; Levyts'kyi, *Istoriia*, pp. 569f. On the Shevchenko celebrations in 1911, see the detailed accounts in *Dilo*, no. 55, Feb. 26 / March 11, 1911, no. 56, Feb. 28 / March 13, 1911, and the following issues, and *Svoboda*, no. 10, March 9, 1911, and the following issues. The annual report of Prosvita for the year 1911 spoke of "hundreds, thousands of concerts in honor of

T. Shevchenko in cities, towns, and villages." *Zvit tovarystva "Prosvita" z diial'nosti za chas vid 1 sichnia 1910 do 31 hrudnia 1912 r.* (L'viv 1913), p. 34.

53 The poor artistic quality of many of these monuments was a source of concern for Prosvita's "Commission for Arts and Crafts" (*komisyia artystychno-promyslova*); see *Zvit tovarystva "Prosvita" z dijal'nosti za chas vid 1 sichnia 1910 do 31 hrudnia 1912 r.*, p. 47. On the occasion of the Shevchenko anniversary, Prosvita produced 210,000 copies of a portrait of Shevchenko and called upon Ruthenians to fix it to the windows of their houses as a "demonstrative illumination." "S'viatkuite pamiat' Tarasa Shevchenko," *Svoboda* no. 8, Feb. 23, 1911, p. 1 and no. 9, March 2, 1911, p. 4.

54 Dubyna, *Shevchenko*, pp. 118f. For more detail on the celebrations, see the special issue of the Austrian journal on Ukrainian affairs, which appeared on the occasion of the Shevchenko anniversary, *Ukrainische Rundschau*, 3–4 (Vienna, 1914), pp. 202f.

55 *Ibid.*, p. 204. In the district of Sniatyn, for example, out of 42 communes there were 36 celebrations to honor Shevchenko. *Pys'mo z Pros'vity*, no. 2 (L'viv, 1914), p. 38.

56 About 3,000 communities in Galicia had a Ruthenian majority. *Podręcznik Statystyki Galicyi* 9.1, 1913, pp. 22–25. The number of 2,944 Prosvita reading rooms usually mentioned in the literature is not the number of actually existing and working reading rooms, but the sum of all Prosvita reading rooms ever established; in other words, it includes as well dissolved and inactive reading rooms. See Struve, *Bauern und Nation in Galizien*, pp. 178–180.

57 "1914 rik – Shevchenkovym rokom," *Svoboda*, no. 6, Feb. 12, 1914, "Pered Shevchenkoym iuvylei," ibid., no. 8, Feb. 26, 1914, p. 1; "Iak sviatkuvaty Shevchenkovyi iuvylei?" ibid. no. 11, March 19, 1914, p. 5.

58 On the Sich Association, see Petro Tryl'ovs'kyi, ed., *"Hej, tam na hori 'Sich' ide!": propam'iatnaia knyha "Sichei"* (Kiev, 1993).

59 *Dilo*, no. 53, Feb. 25 / March 10, 1914, p. 6.

60 The festival in the village Uhertsi Vyniavs'ki (Rudky district) was organized primarily by priests and the headmistress and pupils of a local girls' school for home economics as well as by the Sich Association. A Divine Liturgy was not, however, part of the program. The Ukrainian weekly for the rural population, *Svoboda*, introduced a new column with reports of Shevchenko commemorations in the provincial towns and villages: *Svoboda*, no. 11, March 19, 1914, and the following issues. Commemorations took place not only close to the actual anniversary date in March but also in later months. See, for example, *Svoboda*, no.17, April 30, 1914, p. 5.

61 Aside from Shevchenko, Markiian Shashkevych was the most important poet who functioned as a Ukrainian national symbol. In 1897, for example, a celebration was held to honor him in the Prosvita reading room at Zhuriv (Rohatyn district) organized by the local priest who seems to have been especially sympathetic to the peasants. *Svoboda* reported how "the priest Sozans'kyi and his wife appeared in traditional dress; this impressed the villagers who appreciated seeing their attire worn by a woman of the intelligentsia." The evening continued with talks, the declamation of poetry by Shashkevych, Shevchenko, and peasant writers, and the performance of songs. Terentii Borys, "Z Zhurova," *Svoboda*, No. 11, March 13/25, 1897, p. 84.

62 In 1882, the reading room in Pidberizhtsi put up pictures of Emperor Franz Josef, Shevchenko, and Bishop Hryhorii Iakhymovych (a Ruthenian leader of national significance in 1848, who was propagated in this role even more emphatically after his death in 1863). Hryniuk, *Peasants with Promise*, p. 103.

63 For a Russophile reaction to the Shevchenko and Shashkevych cults, see "Taras Hryhor'evych Shevchenko: vospomynanie v 50-uiu hodovshchyny smerty," in *Iliustrovannyi kalendar OMK na hod 1912* (L'viv, 1911), pp. 189–196; and "Markiian Shashkevych (v 100-litnuiu hodovshchynu ieho rozhdeniia)," ibid., pp. 196–204. For a critique of Shevchenko as a national Ukrainian symbol, see "T.H. Shevchenko," *Russkoe slovo*, no. 9, Feb. 28 / March 13, 1914, p. 4. The Russophiles also planned to have their own Shevchenko celebration in L'viv in 1914; these included a memorial service in an Orthodox church. *Dilo*, no. 52, Feb. 24 / March 9, 1914, p. 5.

64 Kachkovs'kyi himself never adopted a clearly Russophile stance. On Russophile attempts to create national symbolic figures, see Wendland, *Die Russophilen*, pp. 318–321.

65 For a discussion of Polish national holidays and anniversaries in Galicia, see Christoph Freiherr Marschall von Bieberstein, *Freiheit in der Unfreiheit: Die nationale Autonomie der Polen in Galizien nach dem österreichisch-ungarischen Ausgleich von 1867* (Wiesbaden, 1993), pp. 314–323; and Stanisław Grodziski, "Nationalfeiertage und öffentliche Gedenktage Polens im 19. und 20. Jahrhundert," in Brix and Stekl, *Der Kampf um das Gedächtnis*, pp. 207–211.

66 Already in the spring of 1877, Stojałowski led a pilgrimage of 100 peasants to Rome for the 50th anniversary of the episcopal consecration of Pius IX. This, too, was marked by a mixture of religious and national elements, as reflected in the reports in Stojałowski's newspapers. The pilgrims carried a red flag to symbolize "Polish blood shed for God and the fatherland." On one side there

was a picture of "our Queen," the Madonna of Częstochowa and on the other side, the symbol of the Heart-of-Jesus Movement. The flag carried the inscription: "Polish peasants, pilgrims in the year 1877, ask in the Eternal City for the victory of the church and the resurrection of the fatherland." "Odezwa do włościań polskich w sprawie pielgrzymki narodowej," *Pszczółka*, no. 3, January 25, 1877, p. 1, and no. 5, March 8, 1877, p. 3. On the pilgrimage to Rome, see also Kącki, *Ks. Stanisław Stojałowski*, pp. 46–49.

67   "Pielgrzymka do grobu św. Stanisława i wiec ludowy w Krakowie," *Wieniec*, no. 10, May 16, 1879, p. 77. On the events of 1846, see Thomas W. Simons, Jr, "The Peasant Revolt of 1846 in Galicia: Recent Polish Historiography," *Slavic Review*, XXX, 4 (Columbus, Ohio, 1971), pp. 795–817; and Arnon Gill, *Die Polnische Revolution 1846: Zwischen nationalem Befreiungskampf des Landadels und antifeudaler Bauernerhebung* (Munich, 1974).

68   "Obchód rocznicy dwusetnego jubileuszu wyprawy wiedeńskiej króla Jana III," *Pszczółka*, no. 15, July 26, 1883, p. 113, and no. 17, Aug. 23,1883, p. 129; *Wieniec*, no. 18, Aug. 30, 1883, p. 137; Kącki, *Ks. Stanisław Stojałowski*, p. 113. On the Sobieski celebrations, see Patrice Dabrowski, "Folk, Faith, and Fatherland: Defining the Polish Nation in 1883," *Nationalities Papers*, XXVIII, 3 (2000), pp. 397–416; Wiesław Bieńkowski, "Rok 1883 w Krakowie Uroczystości 200-lecia odsieczy wiedeńskiej w Galicji w 1883 r.," *Rocznik Krakowski*, LI (Cracow, 1987), pp. 97–118; Adam Galos, "Obchody rocznicy odsieczy wiedeńskiej w Galicji w 1883 r.," *Acta Universitatis Wratislaviensis*, no. 1108, *Historia* 75 (Wrocław, 1990), pp. 123–143.

69   "Do towarzyszów pielgrzymki ludowej do Krakowa," *Wieniec*, no. 19, Sept. 20, 1883, p. 145.

70   Kącki, *Ks. Stanisław Stojałowski*, p. 113. The peasant pilgrimage was met by criticism in the conservative and the liberal press, see Helena Hempel, *Wspomnienia z życia ś. p. ks. Stanisława Stojałowskiego* (Cracow, 1921), pp. 40f.

71   Stanisław Stojałowski, *Hołd ludu polskiego* (1890), cited in Kącki, *Ks. Stanisław Stojałowski*, p. 153.

72   On the celebrations, see Stefan Kawyn, *Ideologia stronnictw politycznych w Polsce wobec Mickiewicza 1890–1898* (L'viv, 1937), pp. 35–54. It should be noted that Kawyn interpretes Stojałowski's political aims as too conservative.

73   "Uroczystości pogrzebowe nieśmiertelnej pamięci wieszcza narodu naszego Adama Mickiewicza w Krakowie," *Pszczółka Ilustrowana*, no. 13, July 13, 1890, p. 210, and *Złożenie zwłok Adama Mickiewicza na Wawelu dnia 4go Lipca 1890 roku: książka pamiątkowa z 22 ilustracyami* (Cracow, 1890), pp. 48f. See also the description in Jan Stapiński, *Pamiętnik* (Warsaw, 1959), pp. 227–230.

74 On the elevation of Wojciech Bartosz Głowacki and the *kosynierzy* to the rank of national symbols, see Franciszek Ziejka, *Złota legenda chłopów polskich* (Warsaw, 1984), pp. 151–198. On the Battle of Racławice and the historical figure of Głowacki, see Jan Lubicz-Pachoński, *Wojciech Bartosz Głowacki: Chłopski bohater spod Racławic i Szczekocin* (Warsaw, 1987). On the memory of Kościuszko and the uprising of 1794, see Krystyna Śreniowska, *Kościuszko – bohater narodowy: opinie współczesnych i potomnych 1794–1946* (Warsaw, 1973), and the anthology compiled by Jerzy Kowecki, ed., *Kościuszko – powstanie 1794 r. – tradycja* (Warsaw, 1997).

75 "Uroczystość Kościuszkowska w Krakowie," *Przyjaciel Ludu*, no. 8, April 15, 1894, p. 113.

76 See the discussion in Magdalena Micińska, *Gołąb i Orzeł: obchody rocznic kościuszkowskich w latach 1894 i 1917* (Warsaw, 1997), p. 21.

77 Ibid., p. 31.

78 Wincenty Witos, *Moje Wspomnienia*, vol. I (Warsaw, 1988), p. 104. Stauter-Halsted assumes on the basis of reports in peasant newspapers a massive engagement of peasants in the national celebrations of 1894. These, however, described very few celebrations in the villages, and they were for the most part organized by the intelligentsia. See Keely Stauter-Halsted, "Patriotic Celebrations in Austrian Poland: The Kościuszko Centennial and the Formation of Peasant Nationalism," *Austrian History Yearbook*, XXV (1994), pp. 83f. On the Polish national celebrations and the peasants, see also Stauter-Halsted, "Rural Myth and the Modern Nation: Peasant Commemorations of Polish National Holidays, 1879–1910," in Bucur and Wingfield, *Staging the Past*, pp. 153–177. This article contains good observations on national holidays as part of the peasant movement's strategies for pursuing the peasants' emancipation, but it does not distinguish clearly enough between the changing roles of the intelligentsia and peasants in the celebrations and attributes too active a role to the peasants in this period.

79 Report of the L'viv police directorate, Aug. 28, 1894, Tsentral'nyi derzhavnyi istorychnyi arkhiv u L'vovi, fond 146, opys 7, od. zb. 4485, pp. 142f; "Historja Wiecu we Lwowie," *Przyjaciel Ludu*, no. 17, Sept. 9, 1894, pp. 258–260.

80 The guided tours led by Maria Wysłouchowa are said to have made a particularly strong impression on the peasants; see Dioniza Wawrzykowska-Wierciocha, *Wysłouchowa: opowieść biograficzna* (Warsaw, 1975), pp. 241–245. For his part, Wawrzyniec Dayczak emphasized the impression the exhibition had made on his father, a peasant and for some time mayor of the village of Reniv in the eastern Galician district of Brody: "My father went to the Galician exhibition in L'viv in 1894. He came back enthralled, particu-

larly by the Battle of Racławice panorama." Dayczak, "Z dni wielkich przemian," p. 102.

81   See the reports in "Jak lud święcił rocznię urodzin Mickiewicza?" *Przyjaciel Ludu*, no. 16, June 1, 1898, pp. 246–249, and no. 17, June 10, 1898, pp. 261–263.

82   The term *pan*, which may be rendered in current English usage as *Sir*, was traditionally used to refer to the lord of the manor. By the end of the nineteenth century peasants used this term for all educated males.

83   Jakób Bojko, "Z chłopskiej chałupy w setną rocznię urodzin Mickiewicza," *Przyjaciel Ludu*, no. 15, May 20, 1898, p. 226. On Bojko, see Bogusław Kasperek, *Jakub Bojko 1857–1943* (Lublin, 1998).

84   "Zebranie Rady Naczelnej," *Przyjaciel Ludu*, no. 23, June 7, 1903, p. 2. See also the extensive advertisements in this paper for the organization of the People's Holiday in the first year of these celebrations in 1904, which was also the 110th anniversary of the Kościuszko Uprising.

85   *Przyjaciel Ludu* reported proudly that "almost everywhere the celebrations were organized by locals ... there are enough intelligent activists among the peasants, even without university degrees." "Budźmy śpiących," *Przyjaciel Ludu*, no. 15, April 10, 1904, p. 1.

86   On the People's Holiday celebrations, see Józef Bińczak, *Święto ludowe 1904–1964* (Warsaw, 1965), pp. 9–22; and Jolanta Kur, "Tradycja kościuszkowska w publicystyce i działalności ruchu ludowego w okresie zaborów," in *Roczniki dziejów ruchu ludowego*, XXVIII (Warsaw, 1994), pp. 30–33.

87   Jan Słomka, *Pamiętniki włościanina: od pańszczyzny do dni dzisiejszych* (Warsaw, 1983), pp. 195f.

88   W. Wiącek, "Jak to Polacy nazywani ciemną masę przeżyli i obchodzili najboleśniejszą setną rocznicę ostatniego rozdarcia Polski," *Przyjaciel Ludu*, no. 3, Jan. 20, 1896. Wiącek himself played the part of Kościuszko.

89   W. Wiącek, "Nie spijcie, bracia Polacy!," ibid., no. 2, Jan. 10, 1897, p. 21.

90   On the course of the celebrations, see "Bartoszowi Głowackiemu Naród polski," ibid., no. 38, Sept. 18, 1904, pp. 1–5; Józef Ryszard Szaflik, *O rząd chłopskich dusz* (Warsaw, 1976), pp. 38f; and Ziejka, *Złota legenda chłopów*, pp. 173–175.

91   This is also how the deputy to the Galician diet from the Polish People's party, Michał Olszewski, interpreted the erection of this statue. See his article, "Przy pomniku Bartosza Głowackiego," *Przyjaciel Ludu*, No. 27, July 8, 1906, p. 1.

92   On the position of the peasant movement and of the peasant population toward these celebrations of the 500th anniversary of the Battle of Grunwald, see Stefan Józef Pastuszka, Józef Ryszard Szaflik, and Romuald

Turkowski, "Chłopi i ruch ludowy w obchodach grunwaldzkich przed 1914 r.," in Tadeusz Maternicki, ed., *Tradycja grunwaldzka*, vol. V (Warsaw, 1989–1990), pp. 114–163. This study analyzes 77 celebrations in villages and small towns on the basis of reports in peasant newspapers. In fact, the total number of such celebrations was much higher. For example, in the district of Ropczyce there were at least five other villages, not listed by these authors, where larger celebrations took place. See Jerzy Fierich, *Przeszłość wsi powiatu ropczyckiego* (Ropczyce, 1936), p. 69. The Ternopil' branch of the Polish Society of Elementary Schools (Towarzystwo Szkoły Ludowej) listed in its annual report 22 further Grunwald celebrations which took place in the course of that year in rural reading rooms and libraries run by this association. There were, additionally, many lectures about the battle and a large celebration in Ternopil' itself. See the list of reading room activities in *Sprawozdanie Zarządu Koła Towarzystwa "Szkoły Ludowej" w Tarnopolu za rok 1910* (Ternopil', 1911), pp. 31 and 43–51. The celebrations of the 50th anniversary of the 1863 January Insurrection in 1913 also found much resonance in the countryside. They are discussed extensively in Molenda, *Chłopi*, pp. 172–185; and idem, "Wpływ obchodów rocznicy powstania styczniowego na kształtowanie się świadomości narodowej chłopów od lat dziewięćdziesiątych XIX w. do 1918 r.," in Janusz Wojtasik, ed., *Powstanie styczniowe 1863–1864: aspekty militarne i polityczne* (Warsaw, 1994), pp. 78–107.

93 Pastuszka et al., "Chłopi i ruch ludowy," pp. 131–145.

94 "The great shock [of the Grunwald celebrations] did not leave the Polish village untouched, as witnessed not only by the unusually numerous and festive celebrations, but also by the stone monuments that were put up in almost every village at the people's own expense." Witos, *Moje Wspomnienia*, vol. 1, p. 237. In the village of Borek Wielki (Ropczyce district), the rock which was to become the memorial stone was rolled after "two weeks of hard night labor out of the river onto the bank. On the following morning peasants gathered to drag the rock pulled on planks by 20 pairs of horses and 8 pairs of oxen" with the full support of the population. See Fierich, *Przeszłość*, p. 69. On the Grunwald monuments of 1910, see also Sven Ekdahl, "Die Grunwald-Denkmäler in Polen: politischer Kontext und nationale Funktion," *Nordost-Archiv*, VI, 1 (Lüneburg, 1997), pp. 76–83, with some photographs; and idem, "Tannenberg – Grunwald – Žalgiris: Eine mittelalterliche Schlacht im Spiegel deutscher, polnischer und litauischer Denkmäler," *Zeitschrift für Geschichtswissenschaft*, L, 2 (Berlin, 2002), pp. 104–107.

95 Witos, *Moje Wspomnienia*, vol. I, p. 238.

96 The *Szkice programowe* are reprinted in Stanisław Lato and Witold Stankie-

wicz, eds., *Programy stronnictw ludowych: zbiór dokumentów* (Warsaw, 1969), p. 39.

97 Hakatists referred to the German Eastmark Association. The term was derived from HKT, the initials of its leading officials: Hansemann, Kennemann, and Tiedemann.

98 "W wielką rocznicę," *Przyjaciel Ludu*, no. 30, July 12, 1910.

8 Neighbors as Betrayers: Nationalization, Remembrance Policy, and the Urban Public Sphere in L'viv

ANNA VERONIKA WENDLAND

Historians investigating the urban public sphere have always to grapple with the problem of sources. Ordinarily, the researcher must be content with journalistic documentation – that is, products of the mass media stored in libraries for posterity – which allow the so-called wider public sphere, or at least its "highest" level, to come into view.[1] In Poland between the two world wars, the urban public sphere was already a highly developed world unto itself. Professional journalists produced local news for the municipal market, while an older variety of the mass press and the party press persisted. The party press was oriented not only to news and sensationalism but also to the transmission of political messages and the mobilization of supporters. It is true that what the city press printed was not "the talk of the town," that is, the direct communication of citizens with one another. Nevertheless, this medium could certainly generate such talk, steer and manipulate it, and eventually assist it to die.[2]

The historian also needs access to another realm, in which association records or news reports on mundane, everyday events supply information about "average" communities. The two realms combine to reveal the urban public sphere in interwar L'viv. Closer observation, however, shows that rather than one public sphere, several different ones existed side by side and delimited by the constructs of ethnic identity and religion. The "national" discourse of the mass media and the senior, respected shapers of public opinion was transported to more intimate levels such as the neighborhood, talk between colleagues, and also the gray area of gossip and rumors. This gray area is neither public nor private, but derives its (often very considerable) influence precisely from its diffuse middle position. Before turning to an examinination of the discourses involved in the case of L'viv between the two world wars, we turn our attention to a brief look at the city's history in order to understand the emergence of its "nationalized" communities.

The City and the Public Sphere

In 1914 L'viv (German: Lemberg; Polish: Lwów) was the capital of the Austrian province of Galicia, a rapidly growing city that attracted many Jews and Ukrainians from the *shtetl* and villages of the surrounding countryside.[3] Alexander Granach, the son of Jewish parents from a village near Kolomyia who later made a career in Berlin as an actor in the theater founded by Max Reinhardt, remembers his first impression of the city:

> We entered the large train station of Lemberg-L'viv, the capital of Galicia. There was a lot of noise and shouting. Hundreds of people were getting on and off, pushing and shoving each other, calling for porters with carts and suitcases, all the while as locomotives were breathing, puffing, blowing, screeching, and whistling. People were busy rushing around in every direction. And there, in the middle of this confusion, a group was approaching, laughing and waving, and coming to meet us. It was my older brother Abrum, elegantly dressed, with his wife and grown-up children ... [We] would get together so that I could move to live with a different brother every other month ... The next day, Schimele Ruskin came and took me with him to Tabaczynski's electric bakery. I was hired for a salary of two gulden fifty a week, plus a loaf of bread and twelve rolls daily.[4]

This was the typical arrival experienced by thousands of migrants to L'viv. Most of them found work as artisans in small-scale industrial enterprises and shops, or in the case of young Ukrainian women, almost invariably as low-wage household servants. The rapid increase in population had predictable consequences. Living conditions in the growing suburbs were often catastrophic, and the infrastructure (water, gas, electricity supplies, and the urban transport system) lagged well behind the rapidly rising demand.

Immigration influenced the multiethnic and multidenominational character of the city, which dated back to the Middle Ages. Around 1914 about half of L'viv's inhabitants were Roman Catholic Poles. Next in size were a large Jewish community and a partly polonized group of Greek Catholic Ukrainians. There were also small groups of Protestant and Roman Catholic German-Austrians, as well as Armenians, who spoke Polish but were distinguished by their affiliation with the Armenian Catholic denomination.[5] Polish was the dominant language used widely by all groups. With the introduction of partial autonomy for Galicia in 1867, it was made the province's official and legal language. The highest positions in the civil service were held by Poles, and Polish families owned a high proportion of the city's real estate.

Polish domination in L'viv contrasted with the predominantly Ukrainian character of the city's rural hinterland, where farmers confronted Polish landowners in terms of both culture and class. This context had considerable bearing on the development of separate partially public spheres in the city. For Poles, Ukrainians, and Jews alike, L'viv had enormous practical and symbolic significance. Next to Cracow, L'viv was from the Polish perspective one of the "two capitals" of Galicia, a region which had been an integral part of pre-partitioned Poland. L'viv was a major center of Polish culture and science, home to the Ossolineum (Ossoliński National Foundation / Zakład narodowy im. Ossolińskich), which held one of the most important Polish libraries and manuscript collections. The city was a venue for many Polish artistic exhibitions and social events. The Municipal Theater, constructed at the beginning of the twentieth century in the Viennese style, was a center of Polish high culture. The Polytechnical Institute and the Jan Kazimierz University, although originally Austrian institutions, became in the later Habsburg period predominantly Polish in character and capable of competing even with the time-honored Jagiellonian University in Cracow. L'viv before World War I was the center of the movement for the liberation of Poland. Thus, the city's higher educational institutions, state administration, and dynamically growing service sector (banks, insurance companies, and private businesses) produced a host of talented people who later would have key roles in the re-establishment of the Polish state.[6]

These institutions and the business sector were also significant for Galician Jews, who after 1867 became increasingly acculturated to Polish rather than German culture. The Polish-language daily *Chwila* was the most important Jewish newspaper, and it continued to be after Galicia became part of the new Polish Republic. L'viv's large Jewish community had a dense network of religious, cultural, social, and medical facilities, some of them differentiated according to their more specific orientation: reformed-liberal, orthodox, or Hasidic. Jewish institutions were located mainly in the neighborhoods of L'viv's third district,

Żółkiewski (Ukrainian: Zhovkivs'kyi), from which Jewish social climbers could escape by moving into the Polish-dominated middle-class neighborhoods. L'viv's Jewish theater life was acclaimed both within and far beyond the city's limits. Alexander Granach, who first worked as a baker's assistant, discovered his talent in L'viv's legendary Yiddish theater. The theater provided a crucial link between the myths and stories of the provincial *shtetl* and the world of the big city.[7]

Not primarily a Ukrainian-inhabited city, L'viv was nonetheless also the mainspring for Ukrainian social mobilization. Into the middle of the nineteenth century, the Ukrainian elite still consisted almost exclusively of Greek Catholic clerics. With the development of Galician educational institutions, however, several generations of priest's sons were trained in the secular professions. Many of them settled permanently in L'viv. Others returned to their small towns in eastern Galicia, where with their experience from the capital they bolstered the local Ukrainian elite. The first generation of well-educated children of peasants followed a similar pattern. Almost all Ukrainian educational associations, cultural organizations, press organs, and political parties had their headquarters in L'viv. However, in terms of the urban topography, they remained virtual islands in a Polish city. The best example was the National Center (Narodnyi dim) and its surrounding neighborhood adjacent to the Ruthenian Street (*vulytsia Rus'ka*). The neighborhood also contained the Ruthenian city parish church, a printshop, the Stauropegial Institute (which had emerged from a secular church brotherhood), various educational associations, and the first Ukrainian insurance company (located in one of L'viv's finest art nouveau buildings). Above all, L'viv was the seat of the Greek Catholic Church of Galicia. From 1900 to 1944 it was headed by Metropolitan Andrei Sheptyts'kyi, a national figure well respected also by non-Ukrainians.[8]

These distinct public spheres in L'viv developed against the backdrop of a general process of transformation that overtook the entire Habsburg monarchy from the middle of the nineteenth century onward. The revolution of 1848 was followed by a neo-absolutist setback. Then, in the 1860s, a constitutional process began, which provided an institutional and legal framework that facilitated reciprocal communication between the elites and the lower classes and between each of the empire's national communities.[9] The cities of Galicia, and especially the provincial capital L'viv, exemplified the new forms of the public sphere that emerged under the recently implemented legal guarantees of freedom of the press, freedom of association, and freedom of assembly. These new

forms of the public sphere were often based on earlier stages of community formation, such as church structures in the case of the Ukrainians
and the salons of the nobility in the case of the Poles.

The new public spheres strengthened communication inside a
national group without necessarily leading to monolithic identities and
mutual exclusion between groups. Meanwhile, general loyalty to the
Habsburgs came under considerable pressure from the new national
and social movements as the nineteenth century neared its end. In comparison with Cracow, the bastion of Polish traditionalists and conservatives, L'viv initially was regarded as more progressive and liberal. This
applied not only to politics but also to the cosmopolitan world of the
theater, coffeehouses, and later, the movie theaters and dance halls of
which the people of the city were so proud.[10]

Increasing Polish-Ukrainian conflicts, however, gradually poisoned
the atmosphere. Given the population ratios, the sharpest tensions
were in the countryside. Landlords manipulated votes, while citizens
who felt betrayed responded with demonstrations. The police used terror against peasants, who in turn organized agrarian strikes. Struggles
grew over the language of instruction in state schools or that used on
town signposts. The social mobilization of the Ukrainians eventually
brought these various conflicts into the very center of L'viv's urban life.
Poles opposed to the establishment of a Ukrainian-language university.
There were outbreaks of student unrest, and in 1908, a disaffected
Ukrainian assassinated the governor of Galicia, the Polish Count
Andrzej Potocki. A compromise settlement between Poles and Ukrainians was finally reached in 1914, but it came too late to reconcile Galicia's two largest national communities.[11]

War as a Nationalizing Factor

World War I acted as a catalyst in helping the competing national
movements to concretize their programs and goals, as well as their
choice of means to achieve them. Violence had been the exception
before 1914. The everyday experiences of the war, however, brought to
the people of L'viv a brutalization that degenerated inevitably into further armed conflict after the armistice of 1918. The civilian population
came under attack not only from enemies but also from "their own."
During the tsarist Russian occupation of 1914–1915, numerous Ukrainian institutions were suppressed and people suspected of being anti-
Russian were deported, among them Jews caught up in battle zones by

chance. Deportations and arbitrary executions were also common from the Austrian side, which accused many Ukrainians of being "Russian spies." When Austria-Hungary collapsed at the end of the war, L'viv was filled with demobilized soldiers and officers – skilled in handling weapons and with access to large stores of ammunition.

The ensuing Ukrainian-Polish civil war left deep and lasting injuries on the city's public sphere. The Poles had reclaimed all of Galicia as an integral part of their newly independent Polish state. The Ukrainians continued to envision L'viv as the natural capital of an independent Western Ukraine. The struggle for Galicia was essentially decided in L'viv, where after three weeks of street battles in November 1918 the Poles maintained the upper hand.

Ukrainian forces had been largely dependent on support from out-side the city. But the Polish side was able to count on widespread civil participation in what came to be known as the Defense of L'viv (*Obrona Lwowa*). Recollections of the military valor of underage schoolboys and young university students who fought "for the Polish city" became extremely important to the Poles of L'viv in the interwar years. Poles preferred not to remember how merciless much of the fighting was, or the violence done to civilian Ukrainians after the Ukrainian troops were expelled, or the pogrom during which seventy-four Jews were killed by Polish soldiers and civilians.[12] Instead, Poles glorified their young "eaglet" (*orlę*), who barely had the strength to carry his own rifle. This symbol was reproduced everywhere in shaping the image of Polish Lwów as the "city of heroes."[13] Polish poets also took to this theme, for example, Henryk Zbierzchowski in his sentimental poem, "L'viv November":

And then this little soldier appeared again in my memories
He who defended Lwów for the glory of Poland
With a cap bigger than his head, under which a lock of hair peeked out
And his face rosy, holding a rifle longer than the soldier
How is it that this child is defending the Polish city?
And in this child lives a spirit which is enough for two.
In this child alone there is a hunger to receive the baptism of battle fire.[14]

The official commemorative culture of 1920s and 1930s L'viv was dedicated to *polskość* – to the Polish character of the city. Non-Polish people in the city were not treated as equals. This was in stark contrast to L'viv of the Habsburg Empire. Then the symbols on display during major ritual occasions corresponded to the numerical size of the different national groups in the city.[15] Public memory of the L'viv November (*lwowski listopad*) provided self-confirmation of Polish patriotism. Public memory reinforced national divisions by excluding or snubbing both Jews, who perceived themselves as neutral and as victims of the pogroms, and Ukrainians – perceived by themselves to be the underdog and by Poles as the former enemy.

The central memory was of the "eaglet" or, in more general terms, the "children of L'viv" (*dzieci Lwowa*)[16] – children who had given their lives for Polishness (*polskość*). The Roman Catholic Church took part in the festivities by integrating the newly adopted Defense (*Obrona*) commemoration into the services on All Saints' Day and All Souls' Day (November 1 and 2). L'viv's *Obrona* celebrations, thus, had a permanent place in the popular culture of the city. They also included secular elements. The celebrations made extensive use of the city's public spaces and were strongly militarized. Parades, paramilitary sporting events, street illumination, religious retreats, ceremonies at the graves of the dead, and commemorations at particular streets where the battles had been especially violent were all novel appropriations of public space. A vast memorial monument was erected, in the 1930s, in that part of the Lychakiv/Łyczakow cemetery where the "defenders" were buried. All this was organized with close cooperation among the city administration, the military, and the veteran's organization *Związek Obrońców Lwowa* (Association of the Defenders of L'viv). This multifunctional association collected Polish sources about the civil war, organized lectures, published brochures and books, and, not least, served as a lobby organization for Obrona participants and their families, for whom it arranged subsidies and even jobs in the public sector.[17]

In patriotic Polish discourse, L'viv was an "island" in a Ukrainian "sea," a stronghold of the Polish state in the hostile environment of the eastern "borderlands" (*kresy*), an image that was historicized through a revival of the old motto *Leopolis semper fidelis*. This evoked memories of the seventeenth and eighteenth centuries, a time when L'viv, "always true [to the Polish crown]," withstood various sieges – including those of the Zaporozhian Cossacks and Ukrainian peasant armies, led by Bohdan Khmel'nyts'kyi. The Obrona remembrances fitted seamlessly into this historical picture, with its images of a flood-threatened, island-like outpost whose city walls were under attack by eastern "hordes."[18]

Such images reflected currents of Polish national thought as they had developed since the nineteenth century. They also reflected deep-seated fears that one day L'viv would be lost to the Ukrainians. The demographic situation in eastern Galicia, and the movement of Ukrainians into the city (although census data show that this was hardly as threatening as believed), fed these fears. Contemporary talk about "the right to self-determination," which implied that legitimate political borders must correspond to "ethnic" criteria, only reinforced them. The establishment, just after World War I, of a Soviet Ukraine along the old eastern borders of Galicia did not serve to dampen Polish worries.

Galicia's Ukrainians also worked hard to keep alive memories of the L'viv November. Like their Polish countrymen, in celebrations and memorial services they stylized their "own" victims as martyrs for the national cause. By contrast, the Jews of L'viv had no reason to memorialize the November events. Once again they found themselves poised between the two conflicting parties and always liable to be blamed if they were thought by either side to be favoring the enemy.[19]

Is L'viv of the interwar period, to use the words of Alfred Döblin, an outstanding example of "the tyranny of the national principle"? Caution is advised in attempting an answer to this question. Media articles and organized commemorations do not tell us how ordinary people reacted to such events in their everyday conversations within their neighborhood or among friends and colleagues. Other sources, for example, autobiographical literature and also statistical materials, would indicate that everyday life in interwar L'viv proceeded relatively free of conflict. Friendships and marriages were still contracted across denominational and ethnic lines. Furthermore, the cohesive mobilization of the separate national groups in their long-established neighborhoods gradually dissolved during this period.[20]

The nation-builders confronted other agents, who rejected exclusionary strategies as out of date. A number of significant recollections of L'viv were written along these lines after World War II, although even earlier Joseph Roth had called L'viv the "city of blurred borders."[21] Many citizens saw the civil war as a tragic conflict between brothers (bratobójstwo). Those engaged in the socialist movement opposed the creation of any national pathos.[22] A great many ordinary people basically had no interest in politics. They just wanted to forget the war and enjoy the new forms of big city entertainment – movie theaters, jazz clubs, soccer games, and car racing. For them, the identity of the city was not embodied in the sad spirit of sacrifice epitomized by the Defense of L'viv. Rather, it was to be found in L'viv's distinctive popular culture, already immortalized before the war in countless street songs, ballads, and satirical verses in the local dialect (an eastern variety of Polish mixed with Ukrainian, German, and Yiddish). Even the middle social strata flirted playfully with this "light-hearted L'viv," which became very popular through film and radio in the 1920s and 1930s. Here was a genuine alternative for urban identification, as well as the illusion of a healing environment beyond national boundaries. But patriotism was not entirely absent even from this "light-hearted" world. For example, the contribution of street urchins to the defense of L'viv was frequently adopted as thematic material by popular artists.[23]

Still, other sources, private as well as institutional, confirm that the population of L'viv was divided. The November 1918 events were commemorated separately, and the tendency to form parallel associations according to nationality persisted. Public space was correspondingly segregated. Polish, Jewish, and Ukrainian sports, fraternal, and philanthropic organizations acted independently of one another, as did the two Catholic churches and the synagogue communities with their associated networks.[24]

The Public Sphere at the Micro-Level: The Case of Two Sisters

The "lower" reaches of the public sphere are difficult to access because casual communication seldom leaves written traces. It is in any case extraordinarily difficult to evaluate the interaction of various levels in both the public and the private spheres.[25] No contemporary witnesses are available for interviews, witnesses who might be capable of probing and criticizing written sources. Historians are instead left to approach this level through "classical" archival sources, such as court records. Lawsuits and inheritance disputes, for example, if used carefully, can reveal important information about everyday social interaction at the micro level of the public sphere. The archives of the magistrate's court in L'viv include files describing citizens' complaints against "unlawful acts by magistrate's clerks" and the proceedings in which these charges were heard. One such case centres around a character assassination campaign dating from the mid-1930s, involving two sisters of Ukrainian descent who were employed by the city. In an anonymous letter addressed to the city, they were accused of having betrayed the Polish side during the L'viv November. An enquiry was set up to examine their trustworthiness, and by the time the case was settled, two years had passed.[26]

The discourse of higher levels (the press and the commemorative policy already described) had a discernible impact on discourse at the level of the neighborhood and workplace. Events that had allegedly taken place some twenty years previously in the L'viv neighborhood of Klepariv (Polish: Kleparów) were now cast in a new frame, so that people who had hitherto been perceived only as neighbors and colleagues suddenly became representatives of the "other" nationality.[27] This micro-historical development occurred in the years between 1936 and 1938, a difficult time for L'viv not only because of an economic and social crisis but also because of increasing political insecurity.

A dozen people had lost their lives in the spring of 1936 in a succession of clashes between striking workers, the jobless, and the police. The Nazi regime in neighboring Germany was troubling for all of Poland's citizens, and when Marshal Jósef Piłsudski, the great champion of the second Polish republic, died, military regimes seized power in Warsaw. Both anti-Semitic and anti-Ukrainian sentiments had become widespread throughout the Polish community. Outside the city, in the regional hinterland of L'viv, in an undertaking that euphemistically was called pacification (*pacyfikacja*), the military and the police had been brutally repressing the Ukrainian population since 1930. Ukrainian ultra-nationalists were aggravating the situation further. They directed their terrorist actions not only against the Polish state, but also against anyone who wanted a peaceful settlement of Ukrainian-Polish differences.[28]

Klepariv, was one of the "classical" suburbs of L'viv, just beyond its northern city walls. The aristocratic Klopper family from Germany had developed the area when it was a medieval domain of the Polish crown. By the early twentieth century, with the help of settlers who came from the countryside, it had become a typical L'viv suburb, with its own characteristic dialect. Klepariv was thus a neighborhood of "little people." Mainly artisans and lower income white-collar workers lived in Klepariv, although the military (with its barracks and an infirmary) was also a major employer. The people involved in the character assassination case described here were Polish and Ukrainian residents of the neighborhood, employees of the district and city administration, and some members of the Association of the Defenders of L'viv. Many of these "veterans" were only in their late thirties, which meant they were old enough in 1918 to have participated in the fighting as the city's "young defenders" (*orlęta / dzieci Lwowa*) and, therefore, to be honored throughout Poland as national heroes.

Events unfolded as follows. In December 1936 the city administration received an anonymous letter in which Julia Pikas, née Lechka, forty-three-years old, of Roman Catholic faith, and working as a city employee in District Office II, was described as having participated in the 1918–1919 fighting on the Ukrainian side. "Trustworthy people," claimed the letter, could testify that she, "together with her sister Janina Jeziorska, née Lechka, likewise employed by the city in Administrative District V, had betrayed a Polish defender of the city during clashes at the Podzamcze train station in the north of the city. This Polish defender was subsequently murdered by Ukrainians."[29] The informer named a witness, Karolina Zimmermann, who would be able to confirm the story of the events at the train station. Furthermore, the Association of the Defenders of L'viv could also supply witnesses. The informer, who was apparently personally acquainted with the accused, pointed out that she was financially well off and able to travel on vacation every summer. Therefore, her dismissal could not be objected to on humanitarian grounds. It was further claimed that Julia Pikas had only recently converted from the Greek Catholic (Ukrainian) to the Roman Catholic (Polish) faith, no doubt in order to promote her career. This anonymous letter prompted the city administration to undertake a thorough investigation, in the course of which many people were questioned. After a year and a half of anguished inquiry – which imperiled the livelihood of the two sisters – the accusations proved to be unfounded. It is, however, worth tracing the course of events in some detail, for the information they reveal about the public sphere at the micro-level, the powerful effect of rumors, and the response of government agencies in 1930s L'viv.

The denounced sisters were excellent examples of how people from Ukrainian families that had been living in L'viv for a long time, perhaps generations, had become attached to Poland through marriage and a far-reaching process of acculturation. That these people could nevertheless fall victim to such arbitrary denunciation says much about the atmosphere of the time. The sisters' family was Polish-speaking, and although in the years before World War I years they were all still Greek Catholic, by the postwar period they were Ukrainian in name only. The family ran a saddlery business on St Martin Street (ulica Świętego Marcina) and was not committed to the Ukrainian side.[30] The younger sister, Janina, testified that her family had never been involved in politics. Her older brother was said to have been in the Polish Legion. During the Defense of L'viv he did not participate on the Polish side because he did not want to fight against his Greek Catholic brothers in faith.[31] The elder sister, Julia, confirmed her sister's testimony: "In spite of our Greek Catholic religion, our family was Polish. My sister and I were raised in the Polish way of thinking, and my brother Karol Lechki joined the Legion in 1914 and fought as a defender of Poland. My grandmother was Polish."[32] Suddenly, relatively banal incidents and inter-personal conflicts turned colleagues and neighbors into representatives of an entire people. According to the testimony of Janina Jeziorska, the denunciation probably originated from a regional office manager who bore a grudge against the sisters: they had secretly informed his wife, their colleague in the city administration, that he was having an affair with someone in his office. The anonymous letter followed shortly afterwards.[33]

The city administration pursued the matter very seriously, despite the obvious flimsiness of the case. No effort was spared to find witnesses for the prosecution, while the accused women were heard only months later. Meanwhile, the Association of the Defenders of L'viv, a far from unbiased source, as it was explicitly dedicated to commemorating the Polish heroes of November 1918, produced three of its members as "witnesses for the prosecution" – the city employees Marjan Fischbach and Józef Gradowski, and the master mason Józef Walter. Their testimonies, in which rumors picked up from Klepariv were represented as facts, seriously incriminated the sisters.[34]

It is also fascinating to see how rumors and gossip concerning the two "Ukrainian women" circulated. The witnesses from the Association of the Defenders of L'viv, though former combatants, knew the story of the alleged events only from hearsay. In master mason Walter's version, the Lechki house, rather than the "railway station," was at the very center of the events.

As I heard, both of the Lechki sisters – now [Julia] Pikas and [Janina] Jeziorska – handed over some defenders of L'viv to the Ukrainians in 1918. For a while some Ukrainians were hidden in the Lechki house and there, in the basement, the Polish defenders were tortured. *This is commonly known all over Kleparów.* In 1919, the current Mrs Jeziorska was held in jail in the garrison prison on Zamarstynowska Street, in connection with the delivery of the city's defenders to the Ukrainians. She sat for one month in prison. How the matter ended, I don't know [emphasis added by the author].[35]

Janina Jeziorska was thirteen years old in 1918. She had never been in prison, a fact confirmed by the prison administration.[36] She actually thought that she might be the victim of an error, and that a different Lechki family in the neighborhood had perhaps had something to do with the matter.[37] The only witness who was explicitly named in the accusatory letter was Karolina Zimmermann, an employee of the emergency services in the second municipal district. She claimed to have heard "rumors" that the elder sister, Julia Pikas, had participated in the fighting on the Ukrainian side by handing over some Polish combatants.[38]

As witnesses were being questioned it gradually became clear that popular knowledge about the Lechki family in the Klepariv neighborhood was a more or less a arbitrary combination of time, location, persons, and events. Rumors spoke about other events that had taken place in a "railway station" (presumably at Podzamcze, a local station nearby). Although Podzamcze was not in Klepariv, the events were now situated in Klepariv. The story was circulated about a "Ukrainian post in a private house." Józef Chrzymeda, who participated in the Defense of L'viv as a nineteen-year-old, testified that the "railway station" episode had indeed taken place. During the alleged battle at the station, the Ukrainian Muliarchuk family living at 109 Żółkiewska Street was said to have turned over the Poles Milian, Stroński, and Lisowski, who were then shot by Ukrainians. After the recapture of L'viv by the Poles, Muliarchuk father and son were executed, and the mother and daughter were thrown into prison. Chrzymeda knew the Lechkis as neighbors and declared that he considered them a "decent" family.[39]

The testimony of Julia Pikas, the elder sister, also revealed how local topographical structures were incorrectly reconstructed in the memory of neighbors and colleagues:

I categorically deny turning over a defender of L'viv to the Ukrainians with my sister in 1918 or 1919 or assisting the Ukrainians in whatever manner ... In 1918, we lived at 45 St Martin Street, and from the spring of 1919, sometime from May, at 48 Graniczna Street, which is Kresowa Street today. As far as Mr Walter's statements are concerned, they are completely incorrect. No Ukrainians nor any Ukrainian armed sentinels have ever been in our house, and no Poles were detained in the basement of our house. During all of the year 1919, when we were living on Kresowa Street, no Ukrainians were ever in our house or in the vicinity ... That part

of the city was always in the hands of the Poles. I suspect that Mr Mik-
szyński is behind the libel against me and my sister, for the reasons my
sister has already put on record.[40]

Ultimately, the testimony of other neighbors demonstrated that the
neighborhood gossip was little more than a web of lies. Michał Wenk
confirmed the integrity and Polish mentality of the Lechki family.[41]
Franciszek Witeusz, a butcher, showed how memories can become distorted, when he demonstrated conclusively that there never had been
any Ukrainian occupation of the neighborhood, despite the belief
based on rumor that a military front had run straight through it.
According to Witeusz, and contrary to the gossip about the alleged
existence of a Ukrainian armed post, the Lechkis' house, had in fact
been a *Polish* armed outpost before the Lechkis had even moved there,
which happened only in the spring of 1919. This evidence, coming
from a man who was active in the immediate vicinity throughout the
fighting in 1918, had the result that the case against Julia Pikas was
dropped on the following day.[42]

Conclusions

The case of the Lechki sisters must be handled with caution, since it
may not be representative. Some conjectures are more plausible than
others, however. The episode certainly shows how a particular combination of circumstances could lead easily to the attribution of personal
actions based solely on the individuals' ethnicity. These circumstances
included traumatic historical experiences and a propaganda campaign
deriving from them; a tense political situation; a personal conflict,
which became an effective trigger; a marker, in this case the construct of
"origin," linked to religion, to allow for stigmatization of the "other";
officials who reacted to defamation charges because they seemed cred-
ible (perhaps on the basis of their own political disposition) until eye-
witnesses could prove the opposite; and, finally, a neighborhood
context in which rumors spread like wildfire, providing the background for "reliable" denunciations.

The final result turned out better than perhaps might have been
expected, since control mechanisms, including the acceptance of testimony from counter-witnesses, functioned properly. Nevertheless, the
favorable outcome still seems conditional on a vehement self-definition
by the accused that she was a "good Pole," albeit of Ukrainian origin.

The cult surrounding the Defense of L'viv was produced by Polish media, city officials, and special interest groups such as the Association of the Defenders of L'viv. As a result, for the nationally oriented Polish (lower) middle class, facts and imagination blended together, and memories of the events of the war were selectively perceived and even newly fabricated. The notion that a Polish-Ukrainian front line existed in Klepariv was the result of unfounded rumor. This belief seemed plausible, however, because at the annual November Defense of L'viv celebration – with its large-scale social mobilization in the public sphere – the entire city was presented as a Polish-Ukrainian front.

We know from witnesses and the memories of victims of subsequent Nazi persecution during World War II that identifying and murdering Jews in the cities of eastern Galicia was made easy because their non-Jewish neighbors (frequently Ukrainians but also Poles) were ready to show the murderers the way. They denounced their fellow citizens voluntarily or disclosed hiding places in which Jews were concealed.[43] It is important to consider the preconditions that were necessary for such a course of events to occur on a massive scale. Did the tremendous brutalization that took place under German military occupation simply facilitate behavior that was dependent on conditions already existing during the interwar period?

No straightforward parallel should be drawn between interwar Polish-Ukrainian conflicts in L'viv and the World War II Holocaust. Nevertheless, it is clear that "national" boundaries between neighbors were solidified long before the German invasion, and that traumatic "national" memories had the desired effects. In other words, the seeds of distrust and hate had obviously been sown much earlier. The disintegration of multinational Galicia was probably already sealed with the outbreak of the World War I, which provided the initial spark for later "national" or "ethnic" conflicts. Nationalized urban communities played a significant role in the consolidation of segregation by nationality, ethnicity, and religion.

The public sphere does not always mean transparent and open discourse. Attempted character defamation can also be a feature, along with the control of public space to bring about the social exclusion of individuals or even entire groups, and the abuse of information. It would be worth examining further the extent to which these negative forms of the public sphere pushed the marketplace and the coffeehouse into the shadows of central Europe's cities during conflict-ridden times such as the 1930s.

Notes

This chapter is a condensed translation by Tanya Kaye Novak from the German original: "Nachbarn als Verräter: Nationalisierungsprozesse, Erinnerungs-politik und städtische Öffentlichkeiten in Lemberg (1914–1939)," in Andreas R. Hofmann and Anna Veronika Wendland, eds., *Stadt und Öffentlichkeit in Ostmit-teleuropa, 1900–1939: Beiträge zur Entstehung moderner Urbanität zwischen Berlin, Charkiv, Tallinn und Triest* (Stuttgart, 2002), pp. 149–169. See also Anna Veronika Wendland, "Post-Austrian Lemberg: War Comensuration, Interethnic Rela-tions, and Urban Identity in L'viv 1918–1939, *Austrian History Yearbook* 34 (2003) pp. 83–102.

1 On the terminology for the public sphere and its various levels, see Jürgen Gerhards and Friedhelm Neidhardt, *Strukturen und Funktionen moderner Öffentlichkeit: Fragestellungen und Ansätze* (Berlin, 1990); Jürgen Gerhards, "Politische Öffentlichkeit: Ein system- und akteurstheoretischer Bestim-mungsversuch," in Friedhelm Neidhardt, ed., *Öffentlichkeit, öffentliche Meinung, soziale Bewegungen*, special issue of *Kölner Zeitschrift für Soziologie und Sozialpsychologie*, XXXIV (Opladen, 1994), pp. 77–105; Jörg Requate, "Öffentlichkeit und Medien als Gegenstände historischer Analyse," *Geschichte und Gesellschaft*, XXV (Göttingen, 1999), pp. 5–32; Elisabeth Klaus, "Öffentlichkeit als gesellschaftlicher Selbstverständigungsprozeß," in Kurt Imhof und Peter Schulz, eds., *Kommunikation und Revolution* (Zurich, 1998), pp. 131–149.
2 On the wide range of press organs in L'viv, see Jerzy Jarowiecki and Bar-bara Góra, *Prasa lwowska w dwudziestoleciu międzywojennym: próba bibliografii* (Cracow, 1994).
3 Between 1869 and 1910, the population of L'viv grew from 87,109 to 195,796 inhabitants; 68 percent of this increase was attributable to immigration. See Stanisław Hoszowski, *Ekonomiczny rozwój Lwowa w latach 1772–1914* (L'viv, 1935), pp. 64–65. Of L'viv's 154,481 inhabitants in the year 1900, only 68,414 were born in the city; the rest were born elsewhere, mainly (81,059) in other parts of Galicia. See "Die ortsansässige Bevölkerung der Großstädte nach der Gebürtigkeit," in *Österreichische Statistik*, no. 6312 (Vienna, 1903), pp. 48–52, Table IV. Between 1900 and 1910, L'viv's population grew by 28.9 percent; of this 17.2 percent was immigration and 11.7 percent was natural growth. See "Zunahme und Abnahme der anwesenden Bevölkerung," in *Österreichische Statistik*, N.F., vol. 1 (Vienna, 1917), Table II, pp. 35–36.
4 Alexander Granach, *Da geht ein Mensch: Roman eines Lebens*, 4th ed. (Munich and Berlin, 1987), pp. 174–175.

5 According to the last Austrian census (1910), of L'viv's 206,113 inhabitants, 51 percent were Roman Catholic, 19 percent Greek Catholic, and 28 percent "Israelite." Almost 86 percent of L'viv's inhabitants with Austrian citizenship spoke Polish as their everyday language, 11 percent Ruthenian, and 3 percent German. *Österreichische Statistik*, N.F., vol. 1 (Vienna, 1917), pp. 43, 63, and 80. The first Polish census (1921) recorded 219,392 inhabitants in L'viv, of whom 51 percent were Roman Catholic, 12 percent Greek Catholic, and 35 percent "Mosaic." Derzhavnyi arkhiv L'vivs'koï oblasti (hereafter DALO), fond 2/opys 26/sprava 2048/arkush 5. On L'viv's social and infrastructural problems during the interwar period, see Anna Veronika Wendland, "Stadt zwischen zwei Kriegen: Lemberg in der Zweiten Republik, 1918–1939," in Thomas Held, ed., *Lemberg*, 2nd ed. (forthcoming).

6 On the significance of L'viv for the Poles, see Kazimierz Karolczak and Henryk W. Żaliński, eds., *Lwów: miasto, społeczeństwo, kultura*, 4 vols. (Cracow, 1995–2002); and Rudolf Mark, "'Polnische Bastion und ukrainisches Piemont' Lemberg 1772–1921,'" in Peter Fässler, Thomas Held, and Dirk Sawitzki, eds., *Lemberg – Lwów – L'viv: Eine Stadt im Schnittpunkt europäischer Kulturen* (Cologne, Weimar, and Vienna, 1993), pp. 75–91.

7 For further details on the significance of L'viv for Jews, see Vladimir Melamed, *Evrei vo L'vove: sobytiia – obshchestvo – liudi* (L'viv, 1994), pp. 134–135; and Granach, *Da geht ein Mensch*, pp. 177–189.

8 For further details on the significance of L'viv for Galician Ukrainians, see Mark, "Polnische Bastion," pp. 63–65; Ivan Krypiakevych, *Istorychni pokhody po L'vovi* [1935] (L'viv, 1991); Anna Veronika Wendland, *Die Russophilen in Galizien: ukrainische Konservative zwischen Österreich und Rußland, 1848–1915* (Vienna, 2001). On nationalization processes in L'viv before 1918 in general, see Christoph Mick, "Nationalisierung in einer multiethnischen Stadt: Interethnische Konflikte in Lemberg 1890–1920," in *Archiv für Sozialgeschichte*, XL (Bonn, 2000), pp. 113–146.

9 See Karl Deutsch, *Nationalism and Social Communication: An Inquiry into the Foundations of Nationality* (Cambridge, Mass., 1969).

10 On the urban development of the two "Galician capitals" and competition between L'viv and Cracow, see Jan Małecki, "Lwów i Kraków – dwie stolice Galicji," *Roczniki dziejów społecznych i gospodarczych*, L (Cracow, 1989), pp. 119–131; Lawrence D. Orton, "The Foundation of Modern Cracow (1866–1914)," *Austrian History Yearbook*, XIX–XX, pt. 1 (Minneapolis, 1983–1984), pp. 105–117; Jacek Purchla, *Matecznik Polski* (Cracow, 1992); and Hoszowski, *Ekonomiczny rozwój*, pp. 55–64.

11 On the Ukrainian-Polish conflict in Galicia, see Kost' Levyts'kyi, *Istoriia politychnoï dumky halyts'kykh ukraïntsiv 1848–1914 r. na pidstavi spomyniv* (L'viv,

1926); Wilhelm Feldman, *Geschichte der politischen Ideen in Polen seit dessen Teilungen, 1795–1914* (Osnabrück, 1964), pp. 123–422 passim; Marian Mudryi, "Vid Avstrïi do Pol'shchi: problema ukraïns'koho universytetu u L'vovi v pershii chverti XX st.," in Karolczak and Żaliński, *Lwów: miasto, społeczeństwo, kultura*, vol. V (Cracow, 2001).

12 For a history of the Polish defense of L'viv, see Ludwik Mroczka, *Spór o Galicję wschodnią 1914–1923* (Cracow, 1998), pp. 90–125; Melamed, *Evrei vo L'vove*, pp. 134–135; Waclaw Wierzbieniec, "Związek Żydów Uczęstników Walk o Niepodległość Polski we Lwowie (1932–1939)," in Karolczak and Żaliński, *Lwów: Miasto, społeczeństwo, kultura*, vol. 2, pp. 287–288; Jerzy Tomaszewski, "Lwów, 22. listopada 1918 r.," *Przegląd Historyczny*, LXXV, 2 (Warsaw, 1984), pp. 279–285; Henryka Kramarz, "Ze sceny walk polsko-ukraińskich o Lwów: życie mieszkańców w warunkach wojny polsk-oukraińskiej," in Kazimierz Karolczak, ed., *Galicja i jej dziedzictwo*, vol. 1 (Rzeszów, 1994), pp. 99–115; and *Obrona Lwowa: źrodła do dziejów walk o Lwów i województwa południowo-wschodnie 1918–1920, relacje uczęstników*, 2 vols. (Warsaw, 1991).

13 See, for example, Wojciech Kossak's paintings *Młody obrońca* (The Young Defender [of L'viv]) and *Orlęta – obrona cmentarza* (Eaglet – the Defense of the Cemetery), both frontispieces in *Obrana Lwowa*.

14 Cited in Janina Augustyn-Puziewicz, *Lwów: wspomnienie lat szczęśliwych* (Wrocław, 1994), pp. 119–120.

15 See, for example, the Program podroży Najjaśniejszego Pana do Galicyi w sierpniu 1892 (Travel program of the Most Serene Lord to Galicia in August 1892); and Program przyjazdu i pobytu we Lwowie Jego Ces. I Król. Apostolskiej Mości Franciska Józefa w wrześniu 1894 (Program of the arrival and stops in L'viv of his Imperial and Royal Apostolic Majesty Franz Josef in September 1894), in contrast to the Program for the Visit of [Polish] President Stanisław Wojciechowski in L'viv, September 5–7, 1924. These and other such programs are held in DALO, fond 3, opus 1, sprava 3903 and 21–37; fond 2, opys 26/6/19, sprava 22–27.

16 This phrase is derived from *Marsz lwowskich dzieci* (March of the Children of L'viv), a popular song from before the World War I describing L'viv recruits dispatched to Bosnia. See Jerzy Habela and Sofja Kurzowa, *Lwowskie piosenki uliczne, kabaretowe i okolicznościowe do roku 1939* (Cracow, 1989), p. 239.

17 The State Archive of L'viv Oblast (DALO) contains several examples of celebratory programs from this period. In 1920 the city was decorated with a high military medal "for the defense of Polishness [*polskość*]" in the eastern

borderlands. See Józef Białynia Chołodecki, *Lwów kawalerem krzyża "Virtuti militari"* (L'viv, 1992).

18 Anna Veronika Wendland, "Semper fidelis: Lwów jako mit narodowy Polaków i Ukraińców, 1867–1939," in Karolczak and Żaliński, *Lwów,* vol. 4 (2002), pp. 263–273. Such symbolism was also prominent in popular city guidebooks, including A. Medynski, *Lwów: ilustrowany prezewodnik dla zwiedzajacych miasto* (L'viv, 1937); Mięczysław Orłowicz, *Ilustrowany przewodnik po Lwowie* (L'viv, 1920; 2nd ed. 1925); and Józef Piotrowski, *Lemberg und Umgebung: Handbuch für Kunstliebhaber und Reisende* (Leipzig and Vienna, 1916). These works concentrate mainly on L'viv's "Golden Age," i.e., on its history from the Middle Ages and the early modern period. The "Kronika Lwowa, jego zabytki i osobliwości," in *M. Sonnenscheina Lwowski Skorowidz Adresowy: urzędów, handlu i przemysłu oraz wolnych zawadów,* vol. 3 (L'viv, 1927), pp. 5–11, describes the Polish-Ukrainian war of 1918–1919 as one in which the "Polish party" was said to have driven the "military party of Ukraine" out of the city. The Defense of L'viv is not mentioned separately. Lucja Charewiczowa, in her *Historiografla i miłośnictwo Lwowa* (L'viv, 1938), mentions "the unshakable faith in L'viv's Polishness, to which its history bears witness" (p. 6) as the main motive for writing a history of the city. This work is still widely consulted.

19 For Ukrainian commemorative literature, see *USS: Ukraïns'ki Sichovi Stril'tsi, 1914–1920* (L'viv, 1991).

20 See the research of Eva Rutkowska, "Wyznania i narodowości we Lwowie w latach 1857–1939 na tle ogólnej struktury demograficznef miasta," unpublished Master's thesis, Jagiellonian University (Cracow, 1993); Lidia Zyblikiewich, "Małżeństwa we Lwowie w latach 1857–1939: analiza demograficzna," unpublished Master's thesis, Jagiellonian University (Cracow, 1993); and the intellectual commemorative literature of Marian Tyrowicz, *Wspomnienia o życiu kulturalnym i obyczajowym Lwowa: 1918–1939* (Wrocław, 1991) and of Stanisław Vincenz, *Po stronie dialogu,* vol. 2 (Warsaw, 1983).

21 Joseph Roth, "Lemberg, die Stadt," in his *Werke,* vol. 2:, *Das journalistische Werk, 1924–1928* (Cologne, 1990), pp. 288–289. Among the post-World War I accounts are Jósef Wittlin, *Mój Lwów* (Warsaw, 1946); Stanislaw Lem, *Wysoki Zamek* (Cracow, 1991); and Andrzej Kuśniewicz, *Tierkreiszeichen* (Frankfurt am Main, 1991).

22 For documentation on the supra-national and anti-nationalist cooperation within the socialist movement during the 1930s, see *Istoriia L'vova v dokumentakh i materialakh: zbirnyk dokumentiv i materialiv* (Kiev, 1986), pp. 178, 180–184, 196–204.

23 For everyday life and popular culture in L'viv, including the role of radio
    and the popular programs featuring the "city originals" Szczepko and
    Tońko, see Witold Szolginia, *Tamten Lwów,* 6 vols. (Wrocław, 1991–94); and
    Habela and Kurzowa, *Lwowskie piosenki.*
24 This finding is based on a perusal of L'viv address books and local news
    and sports reports, as well as calendars of events from the main newspa-
    pers. In the 1930s Jewish sports associations were very popular for pre-
    cisely this reason. Jewish sportsmen, faced with widespread anti-Semitic
    ideology shaped by "gymnasts," avoided the general sports associations.
25 Requate, *Öffentlichkeit und Medien,* p. 15, has notes this difficulty in the con-
    text of the history of the press.
26 See the records on the "unlawful conduct of employees of the city council,"
    in DALO, f. 2/26/1083.
27 For the impact of the events of 1918 on city residents, see Kramarz, "Ze
    sceny walk polsko-ukrainskich."
28 For the relationship between internal political developments in Poland and
    increasing frequency of anti-Semitic riots, see Dietrich Beyrau, "Antisemi-
    tismus und Judentum in Polen, 1918–1939," *Geschichte und Gesellschaft,* VIII
    (Göttingen, 1982), pp. 218–219. On Poland's pacification policy, see
    Mykhailo Shvahuliak, *"Pacyfikacija: pol'ska represyvna aktsiia u Halychyni
    1930 r. i ukraïns'ka suspil'nist'* (L'viv, 1993); and Ryszard Torzecki, *Polacy i
    Ukraińcy: sprawa ukraińska w czasie II wojny światowej na terenie II Rzeczypos-
    politej* (Warsaw, 1993), pp. 12f.
29 Unsigned letter to the "Radca Stawniczy," dated Dec. 8, 1936, in DALO, f.
    2/26/1083/90.
30 Court testimony of Michał Wenk, Sept. 13, 1937, in DALO, 102 r.
31 Court testimony of Janina Jęziorska, Sept. 7, 1937, in DALO, f. 2/26/1083/
    97f.
32 Court testimony of Julia Pikas, Sept. 10, 1937, in DALO, f. 2/26/1083/101.
33 Court testimony of Janina Jęziorska, Sept. 7, 1937, in DALO, f. 2/26/1083/
    97f.
34 Reply by the Association of the Defenders of L'viv to the Aug. 24 inquiry
    from the magistrate, Sept. 2, 1937, in DALO, f. 2/26/1083/93.
35 Court testimony of Fischbach, Gradowski, and Walter, Sept. 4–7, 1937, in
    ibid.
36 Military prison of the Lemberg garrison to the municipal authorities, Sept.,
    1937, in DALO, f. 2/26/1083/100.
37 Court testimony of Janina Jęziorska, Sept. 7, 1937, in DALO, f. 2/26/1083/
    97f.
38 Record of the interrogation of Karolina Zimmermann, July 24, 1937, in
    DALO, f. 2/26/1083/91.

39 Court testimony of Józef Chrzymeda, Sept. 9, 1937, in DALO, f. 2/26/1083/99.
40 Court testimony of Julia Pikas, Sept. 13, 1937, in DALO, f. 2/26/1083/101.
41 Court testimony of Michal Wenk, Sept. 10, 1937, in DALO, 102r.
42 Record of the interrogation of Franciszek Witeusz [or Witensz], Sept. 14, 1937, in DALO, f. 2/26/1083/102–103; file memorandum of the city administration, Department I, dated Sept. 14, 1937, in DALO, 2/26/1083/104. In January 1938, the Association of the Defenders of L'viv attempted to have the investigation reopened. They sent confidential letters to the mayor of L'viv, containing yet more second-hand accounts of the events of 1918 at the Podzamcze train station, and the allegation that a certain Stanisława Lechka, an employee of the city administration, had incriminated a Polish prisoner, who was later executed.
43 Eliyahu Yones, *Die Straße nach Lemberg: Zwangsarbeit und Widerstand in Ostgalizien 1941–1944* (Frankfurt am Main, 1999); Dieter Pohl, *Die nationalsozialistische Judenverfolgung in Ostgalizien 1941–1944: Organisation und Durchführung eines staatlichen Massenverbrechens* (Munich, 1997); Thomas Held, "Vom Pogrom zum Massenmord: Die Vernichtung der jüdischen Bevölkerung Lembergs im Zweiten Weltkrieg," in Fässler et al. pp. 113–166; Jan Tomasz Gross, *Neighbors: The Destruction of the Jewish Community in Jedwabne, Poland* (Princeton, N J, 2001).

9 Back to *Galicia Felix*?

LUIZA BIALASIEWICZ

The revolutions of 1989 brought with them a profound re-ordering of the spatial imaginary of Europe. The fall of the Berlin Wall and the disintegration of the Soviet bloc have rendered necessary new geographical stories and new spatial representations to capture and codify the cartographical chaos that remained of the former "Eastern" European space. Jubilant pronouncements in the early 1990s heralded "the return to Europe" of countries and peoples who had been unnaturally wrenched away from it for years by Communist domination.[1] In fact, the 1990s were hardly a return to an idealized, unbounded Europe. The collapse of the Iron Curtain gave rise to a whole new set of divides and boundary demarcations. Michael Heffernan identifies "some remarkably persistent geopolitical instincts of the European idea through the ages" that have now been given new life. One such instinct is the evidently enduring need to signify the borders of belonging against a threatening Other. In the post-1989 era, the Other is Orthodox, Russian, East.[2]

Drawing the Boundaries of Europe

Post-Soviet space today is rendered in shades of "European" belonging. Increasingly the divide is between those countries anointed as bona fide Europeans and fast-tracked for incorporation into the European Union – the Czech Republic, Hungary, Poland, Slovakia, Estonia, Latvia, Lithuania – and the rest. At best the latter are relegated to the margins of the New Europe, if not entirely denied the right to material as well as symbolic membership in the "European family of nations."

Identifying Europe's "proper" boundary has assumed enormous political significance.

A particularly salient site for the examination of the discourses of European belonging is the Polish-Ukrainian border. Policy-makers and geostrategic analysts alike are increasingly designating this border as one of the "hard" frontiers of the emergent European space. It has also become a locus of struggle between the post-Communist Polish and Ukrainian states. Indeed, it is one of the key symbolic sites where Polish national elites have attempted to affirm Poland's post-1989 European credentials. The Polish-Ukrainian border has become a marker of distinction and a divide between Europe (and Europeans) and the non-European Other.

Throughout the 1990s the Polish Ministry of Foreign Affairs in its policy rhetoric distanced itself from its post-Soviet neighbors. The ministry pointed to a "deep economic but also sociopolitical chasm" that separates Poland from the countries to its east. The differential "success rates" of these countries' transitions to liberal democracy and a free market economy were proof of this chasm.[3] Such differentials have been documented by numerous experts in observing the transition process in central and eastern Europe.[4] Significant here, however, is how these apparent indicators of economic and political progress have made their way into the identity discourse of Poland's elites. For one thing, successive Polish governments have all been quick to assert their willingness to police the European Union's future eastern boundary. There has been a progressive fortification of the check-points along the Ukrainian and Belarusan borders, paid for in large part with European Union funds. The Polish government introduced a new and highly restrictive visa regime with the 1998 Act on Foreigners, Migrants, and Border Traffic. Visas and work vouchers are required of all citizens of the former Soviet republics. These restrictions were tightened in the spring of 1999. The particular target was the almost six million Ukrainian workers and shuttle traders who cross the border into Poland each year.[5]

This border has enormous symbolic significance for both countries as they work out their national re-signification. The demise of the Soviet era unleashed national tensions that had been suppressed for more than forty years. As elsewhere in the ex-Soviet bloc, the fall of communism in 1989 in Poland and the advent of political independence in 1991 in Ukraine brought questions of national identity to the surface. Redefining the contours of Polish national identity has inevitably involved facing the contentious and symbolically loaded issue of Poland's "lost Eastern Territories." Ukrainian national identity formulation has had to address the residual impact of historic Polish colonialism in eastern Galicia. Both Ukraine and Poland have had to come to terms with the memory of the brutal struggles for these borderlands in the years before the Communist era.[6] The Polish-Ukrainian border has in many ways become a locus of division, one of the new "velvet curtains" that have descended on the former "Eastern" Europe. Both post-Communist Poland and Ukraine have actively adopted the international border that separates them as a point relative to which they are defining their national and geopolitical identities, as well as their relationship and putative belonging to the "European project" and European institutions.

The competing geographical imaginary of these lands is to be seen not so much as a border *line* delimiting competing national perceptions of belonging, or as the "end of Europe." Rather, these borderlands constitute the center of an extensive historical border *space* marked by a multi-national and fully European coexistence. The historical imaginary to which this geographical narrative appeals is that of Habsburg Galicia.

The Habsburg legacy has been rediscovered in a number of post-Communist contexts. In cities such as Budapest, Cracow, Ljubljana, and Prague, revalorization of the Habsburg imperial heritage provided grounds for numerous public interventions into the urban landscape, and savvy tourist entrepreneurs promptly cashed in on the fashion for the former empire.[7] The "Habsburg model" has also enjoyed a revival as a viable alternative for cross-national political organization in place of the former Communist bloc. Some of the collaborative projects launched in eastern and central Europe after 1989, such as the Visegrád group or the Central European Initiative, drew their inspiration precisely from this source. Indeed, there was the widespread sense that "the Habsburg legacy, especially in the early years of the transition, came to represent all that was true, good, beautiful and, above all, European."[8]

In examining alternative narratives regarding the Polish-Ukrainian borderlands, my focus is the idea of European belonging in the Habsburg legacy. In particular, I will discuss the ways in which the alternative geographical imaginary of recent years aims to subvert and negate the cartographical representation of these territories as the boundary of the space called Europe. It does so by appealing to the iconography of a liminal space of multinational coexistence in what was once the Austro-Hungarian Empire. My interest here is the Polish experience; for an analysis of comparable processes transpiring in Ukraine, see Yaroslav Hrytsak (Chapter 10) in this volume.

The spatial ideology and iconography that depicts historical Galicia as an open, multinational, ethnocultural *oikumene* denies, in many ways, the strategies of national and geopolitical boundary-making of both Poland post-1989 and the new Ukraine. The "rediscovery" of Galicia can be seen as a revolt against the new walls and as a discourse counter to the attempts of *national* political elites to draw hard boundaries for the New Europe. It closely echoes the ways in which the imagination was manipulated in Soviet days. During the Cold War, the geographical imagination of a *Mitteleuropa* enabled Polish, Czech, and Hungarian dissidents and literary dreamers to leap outside of the closed spaces of the bipolar divide and place themselves in the West.[9] Re-signifying the Polish-Ukrainian borderland as a historical space of coexistence and contentment, as Habsburg Galicia, is being actively promoted as a means to subvert the legitimacy of the international boundary that now cuts through the region – a border-line that is symbolically coterminus with those of central Europe, Europe, and the West.

This geographical re-signification is still in its nascent stages. Thus far it has been limited to local and regional cross-border cultural initiatives and a flourishing market for books documenting the history of the Habsburg period. Nevertheless, this re-signification is important. The very act of giving an alternative name to these border territories is a first step in re-imagining them and in crafting a new regional coexistence. Finnish geographer Anssi Paasi has examined what he calls the "institutionalization" of a border region. One of the first steps in the formation of the conceptual shape of any regional entity, according to Paasi, is precisely the establishment of a distinct set of territorial symbols. The most important of these symbols is the name "which connects its image with the regional consciousness of the inhabitants and outsiders." The name itself concretizes the regional whole, and makes it "real."[10]

Naming places territories and their inhabitants in a geopolitical, civilizational, historical, and cultural space. Recalling the name Galicia not only evokes a series of nostalgic associations of a "lost home" and "tradition." It also *locates* that home and that tradition. Naming the territories "Galician" immediately places them within a broader spatial

framework and a wider set of geopolitical representations. The re-evo-
cation of Habsburg Galicia suggests an alternative way of organizing
the space called "Europe" and thereby carries with it a whole set of nor-
mative assumptions about the post-Cold War European project.

The Habsburg Myth

According to Roland Barthes, myth-making may be defined as the
manner in which a civilization attempts to reduce its many social,
political, and cultural realities into a unity; the chaos of the world into
an order; fragmented and accidental existence into essence; and his-
torico-political contradictions into a harmonious whole capable of unifying if not resolving those contradictions.[11]
    The role of myth for a society was particularly pronounced in the
case of the Habsburg Empire. The Habsburg myth was not so much an
alteration or deformation of reality or even an attempt to extract some
supposed metahistorical "truth." The Habsburg myth was about "the
sublimation of an entire society into a picturesque, safe and orderly
fairy-tale world."[12] It derived from an ideal time-space, but the Habsburg myth also *actively built* that time-space upon itself in practice. In
the words of Robert Musil's protagonist, it was the time of the "good
old days when there was still such a place as imperial Austria, [when]
one could leave the train of events, get into an ordinary train on an
ordinary railway line, and travel back home."[13] This "home," writes
Stefan Zweig, another master narrator of the Habsburg myth, was one
where "everything appeared long-lasting and the State itself appeared
as the guarantor of such continuity ... Everyone knew how much he
possessed or how much was owed to him, that which was allowed,
and that which was prohibited: everything had its norm, its precise
weight and measure."[14] Austria-Hungary was an ideal – and idyllic –
place, Musil tells us:

> Whenever one thought of that country from some place abroad, the mem-
> ory that hovered before the eyes was of wide, white, prosperous roads
> dating from the age of foot-travelers and mail-coaches, roads leading in
> all directions like rivers of established order, streaking the countryside
> like ribbons of bright military twill, the paper-white arm of government
> holding the provinces in firm embrace. And what provinces! There were
> glaciers and the sea, the Carso and the cornfields of Bohemia, nights by
> the Adriatic restless with the chirping of cicadas, and Slovakian villages

where the smoke rose from the chimneys as from upturned nostrils, the village curled up between two little hills as though the earth had parted its lips to warm its child between them.[15]

Imperial Austria was a place and a time indelibly marked by what Franz Werfel would term its *superior ideal*: the Austro-Hungarian Empire was the attempt to re-instate "God's reign upon the Earth, in the unity of all peoples" and the antithesis of "the nation-state which is, in its very essence, demonic and, as such, idolatrous and menacing."[16] The Austro-Hungarian Empire – Musil's *Kakania* – was an ideal beyond time and beyond history, if history is taken to be equivalent to progress and modernity. Indeed, this was the rightful heir of the spirit of the Holy Roman Empire, embodying the universalism of European culture as well as serving as mediator between East and West. Habsburg Austria's paternalistic myth of the "peoples" went against the very ideals upon which nationality and nationhood were grounded. Emperor Franz Josef addressed his subjects collectively as *meine Völker* (my peoples). This invocation had tremendous symbolic effects. It was the fundamental ideological basis of the imperial project. These two words served both as spiritual support and as propaganda tool in the empire's struggle against the new ideal that was emerging, the ideal of the modern territorial nation-state.

The Habsburgs, above all, provided an alternative vision of governance and community. They exemplified a dynastic ideal and a "historical unity [representing] an organic pluricultural, pluri-ethnic and multinational totality, cemented by the legitimacy of the ruling house and a web of geopolitical alliances."[17] The Habsburgs offered a sharp contrast to the emergent Prussian statist ideal with its particularism, its romanticization of the one and only (German) *Volk*, and its idealization of the ties of blood, soil, and belonging. *Meine Völker* were instructed "that they not only be Germans, Ruthenians, or Poles, but something more, something higher"; of them was required "a true *sacrificium nationis*."[18] Austria-Hungary was a supra-national ethnocultural *oikumene* striving to transcend the *nation* as the exclusive territorial ideal and as exclusive marker claimant of identity. The Habsburg Empire was "an indefinable call binding Bohemia and Galicia, Hungary and Moravia, bringing together all origins into a harmonious unity." The empire had many crowns and many languages which intoned together the *Gott erhalte*. In this land "everyone was born with twelve tongues and twelve souls."[19]

In the decades after 1867 Galicia was granted more privileges than any other province in the Austrian half of the Habsburg Dual Monarchy.[20] This helps to explain the allure of that period, which in myth became an Arcadian space in which, at the peripheries of the empire, could be found the felicitous coexistence of a whole host of peoples, cultures, languages, and faiths. Galicia, in this representation, is a microcosm of multilingual, multicultural Habsburg co-existence. Thus, Galicia becomes a vital, emblematic piece necessary in the construction of this vision of the empire and the emperor's "peoples." Some important parallels can be drawn between the idealization of a *Galicia Felix* (Happy or Fortunate Galicia) and the Habsburg myth writ large. [21] As in the imperial myth, Galicia's imaginary also came to symbolize a "being beyond history," a being subsumed under an ideal and idyllic chronotype of *tam i kiedyś* (there, once upon a time) and in opposition to the determinate "here and now." To its inhabitants and narrators during the years of Habsburg rule (as well as its later bards), Galicia represented the antithesis to the traditional Polish national(ist) historicist and romantic-messianic tradition, which presented the high-moral vision of Poland as the "Christ of nations." Following its demise, Habsburg Galicia was depicted, rather, as a lost "private homeland,"[22] where "one could be what one wanted to be" and where the prevalent definition of one's belonging was described vaguely as *tutejszy* (one from here).[23]

The prevalent topos of the Galician myth was that of a landscape of childhood, seen both as an ideal and as an indeterminate time and/or space. The Galician territories were borderlands marked by an "unstable geography" (a phrase used by Günther Grass in characterizing the Gdańsk/Danzig of his youth). In the narrative of the myth, History – identified with the advent of the modern nation-state – forcibly froze this flux. History enforced absurd categorical choices, whether cultural, ethnic, or national. History robbed the peoples of these borderlands of even the right to name the places of their birth.[24] Accordingly, Galicia – and the Habsburg Empire in its dying days – became "the last Europe."[25] Galicia represented the last expression of a multinational cosmos enjoyed by all before the chaos of the two world wars and before the imposition of categorical choices.

The Spatial Ideology of the Empire

What ideals bound together the unique multinational creation that was late imperial Austria? Two guiding representations may be identified in the ideology of the imperial project. The first was the "reconciliation of difference," which permitted the coexistence of "shared institutions and private homelands."[26] In *Imagined Communities*, his work on the emergence of modern nationalism, Benedict Anderson pointed out that the "ease with which [the Habsburg] Empire was able to sustain its rule over immensely heterogeneous, and often not even contiguous, populations for long periods of time" relied precisely on the "porosity" and "plurality" of the imperial identity.[27]

The imperial identity demanded only partial allegiance and never strove to impose the bounded and historicized homogeneity of national belonging. The inhabitants of Habsburg Galicia were contemporaneously citizens of Europe as well as "locals" (*tutejszy*). Regardless of social status, they were all versed in the common cultural code. Every individual who passed through the doors of any of the imperial *gymnasia* – from the postal clerk to cabinet ministers – had acquired "a knowledge of both European as well as national history, of the Bible and Greek mythology, of all branches of philosophy, literature, art, all that which, through the ages, formed what we term "modern civilization."[28] Both Benedict Anderson and Eric Hobsbawm have remarked on the key role of Habsburg institutions in creating imperial commonality, including the educational system, the armed forces, and the famous Habsburg bureaucracy entrusted with the execution and policing of the empire's manifold rules and regulations.[29]

The empire's institutions and regulations coexisted with a multitude of local contexts and "private homelands." The emperor's many subjects may well have all shared the same official *lingua franca* and cultural reference points, but they were equally proficient in whatever happened to be the *Geschäftssprache* of their everyday life. In Galicia, this was often a fluid mixture of Polish, Yiddish, Ukrainian, and German that was incomprehensible to outsiders.

The mythologized Habsburg ideal of the "unity in diversity," which in the empire's later years ossified into so-called Austrian legalism (the conviction that all disputes could be addressed and resolved through the appropriate channels and appointed legal representatives), was a glue that held together disparate local realities. The imperial bureaucracy reached into all corners of the empire, even into the remote *shtetls* of the Galician plains. Bruno Schulz, in a memoir of his childhood, draws an evocative picture of the small Galician towns and villages, where the locally employed imperial bureaucrats were seen as direct emissaries of the emperor, "the Divine Father of his peoples" who "sent out into the world a heavenly contingent, clothed in symbolic celestial blue uniforms, divided into ranks and orders: angelic personnel in the form of postmen, officials and tax inspectors. Even the most petty of these celestial messengers reflected in his eyes the Creator's eternal wisdom and the jovial, sideburn-framed smile – even if, as a consequence of his earthly toils, his feet stank of sweat."[30]

Imperial statutes and regulations embodied the guarantee of individual and local freedoms, albeit under the emperor's watchful eyes. Using a wonderful anecdote, Ewa Wiegandt tells us how one Galician mayor (wójt) understood the constitution that had been devised in 1867 for the Dual Monarchy. Article 19 pronounced the equality of all peoples within the empire and their rights to the protection and cultivation of their nationality and language. The mayor translated the proclamation to his small-town subjects in the following manner:

> Our Emperor says and writes in bold letters that are black on white and gold on silver: My peoples, be what you wish to be, whether of divine or human faith, peasant or noble, baptized or Jewish, Latin or Uniate, Turkish or Bosnian, Armenian, Gypsy – whatever you wish. If it suits you, it suits me. Do not worry about your faith nor that of anyone else; faith is like skin, no one can be blamed for their own skin. I, the Emperor, like your skin. I ask you kindly only for one thing: do not bring shame to the Emperor. Believe one another, this is the most ancient faith. And do well, do your best. I know you are capable of it. That would be very nice and will make me quite happy. Signed, your Emperor, Franz-Josef.[31]

This mythical, paternal vision extended to matters of identity. Although the Dual Monarchy's "nationality policy" was made explicit only in the 1867 constitution, the empire had never put a high premium on national belonging. National identification in Austrian Galicia, as in the Empire's other provinces, was never overly clear. It appeared, as Wiegandt terms it, faded: "an outline of official belonging [the Austrian one], within a chiaroscuro of variously fading and emerging shades of other belongings."[32] One of the characters in Jozef Wittlin's novel, The Salt of the Earth, provides a case in point: "Piotr Niewiadomski was a Ruthenian, although his father was Polish. Well, his faith decided. National consciousness was never Piotr's strong point. Actually, Piotr always stopped short of national consciousness. He spoke Polish and Ukrainian, he worshipped God according to the Greek Catholic rite, he served the Austro-Hungarian emperor."[33]

Indeed, for the Empire's Galician subjects, national or ethnic belonging did not constitute the primary focus of identification. Nor did they guide everyday existence or determine an individual's life chances and "place" in Galician society. Habsburg Galicia was the epitome of a liminal community characterized by unstable belongings and identities that combined and recombined daily in an endless tangle of reconfigurations and re-representations that shifted from one conversation to the next depending on the interlocutor.[35] "I am a public employee, an Austrian, a Jew, a Pole – all in the space of an afternoon," Bruno Schulz wrote in one of his notebooks.[35] Belonging, when delimited, was traced along class and religious divides – peasant, noble, Uniate, Jewish – but it was the attribute of *tutejszy* that traced the sharpest boundaries. It was as though the Babel of languages and cultures in eastern Galician towns, suggests Wiegandt, symbolized the primeval state of harmony and perfection, so that only those "not from here" were considered to be Others (although, if imperial subjects, they still formed part of a broader commonality as one of the "emperor's peoples").[36]

Jewish Galicia

The Galician chiaroscuro of identities and its "theorization" by elite intellectuals – and also its "practical theorization" in daily life – would have been inconceivable without the province's significant Jewish presence. This is also true for the Habsburg Empire more broadly, whose enormous intellectual contribution to what we consider "modern" European culture derived to an important extent from a Jewish cultural elite which, according to Milan Kundera, represented "its intellectual cement, a condensed version of its spirit, creators of its spiritual unity."[37] Claudio Magris, the foremost scholar of the Habsburg myth, takes this assertion a step further. Magris argues that German culture alone would have never been capable of crafting the Habsburg dream without Judaism and secular Jewish thinkers.[38]

The Jewish presence in Galicia dates to at least the first large-scale eastward migration of Ashkenazi Jews to these lands in the twelfth century. This migration was a result of their persecution in the lands of the Holy Roman Empire. Most of these Jews settled in what was then the Kingdom of Poland and remained there into the thirteenth and fourteenth centuries. Poland subsequently expanded eastward, and when the Polish-Lithuanian Commonwealth was formed Jews were encouraged to settle in its eastern territories – in present-day Lithuania,

Belarus, and Ukraine. The Zaporozhian Cossack revolt of 1648 in Ukraine sowed terror among the Jewish population. Thousands were killed or forced to flee. Over the next century, however, many returned, and after them new waves of Jewish settlers. Poland was partitioned at the end of the eighteenth century, and most of its areas of heaviest Jewish settlement came under Russian rule. The tsarist regime restricted the movement of Jews to other parts of the Russian Empire, and the lands where they were obliged to remain came to be known as the Pale of Settlement, or simply the "Pale."[39] At the beginning of the twentieth century an estimated 7.5 million Jews were living in central and eastern Europe. More than 70 percent of them lived in "Russia's" Pale and in Galicia. Jews made up 30 percent of the population in Cracow and L'viv, and more than half the population of other key Galician towns such as Brody, Sanok, Ivano-Frankivs'k/Stanislawów, and Ternopil'/Tarnopol was Jewish. With pogroms in the Russian Empire in the 1880s and early 1900s, many Jews sought refuge in neighboring Galicia and Bukovina.[40]

The Jewish community made up a vital part of multinational and multicultural Galicia. Outstanding political figures and scholars among them include Isaac Deutscher, Karl Radek, and Martin Buber; all three were born or raised in Galicia. Significant Zionist and Jewish socialist movements also originated in Galicia. To Le Rider Galician Jews were the quintessential citizens of the Habsburg Empires, the "*shtetl* and the world." This diverse community brought together conservative Hasidim, progressive intellectuals, Polonophiles, ardent Germanophiles, and those Jews who, following Emil Byk's Shomer Israel movement, declared with pride: "We are Austrians."[41] Jewish artists and intellectuals such as Emil Franzos, Joseph Roth, Manes Sperber, Bruno Schulz, and Andrzej Kuśniewicz were the first to raise the cry of alarm in face of the dismemberment of the Galician Babel. They expressed the greatest regret as the Habsburg dream slid into what subsequently became a nightmare of language laws, ethnic registers, and violent nationalist conflicts.[42]

The Nationalization of the Empire

How did it happen that I became the author of "Polish" books, good or bad, but "Polish"? Why was I forced into this role? Me – a European, no, a citizen of the world, an Esperantist cosmopolitan ex-citizen of the Universal Empire – who transformed me, as though by wicked spell, into but a close-minded, stubborn, ignorant "Pole"?[43]

At this point, that damned Rózkowski from the Security Services comes up to the cart and screams at the peasant: "You, you a Pole?" The peasant: "I don't know, Sir, I just came to see the doctor"; and Rózkowski: "Idiot! Pole or not?" The peasant, getting scared, slurred his words: "What you mean Sir, Pole? I am coming to the doctor"; and Rózkowski: "Ukrainian?" The peasant: "Devil may take me, I am no Ukrainian"; and Rózkowski, grabbing his arm: "So what the hell are you?" The peasant, almost in tears: "I am from here, I'm a Roman Catholic." So Rózkowski pushes him away "Ehhh ... you people"[44]

Most historical observers trace the first institutional attempts to mark off the Galician space along national and ethnic lines to 1896. Austrian electoral reform that year triggered the slow death of the Habsburg ideal of "unity in diversity" among "the emperor's peoples." The reform marked a sea-change in the empire's nationality politics. The national balance in the Austrian parliament was thereby significantly transformed, giving rise to new alliances and facilitating the appearance of a plethora of national(ist) organizations, including those of the Ruthenians. Enactment of this electoral reform was the very first time that the Habsburg regime had sought to delimit ethnic groups. In provincial and imperial elections double constituencies could now be constructed, drawn along ethnic lines. Ethnically and linguistically separate voters' registers (the infamous *nationale Kataster*) were created. In Moravia, for example, this enabled the organization of elementary education on a strictly separated ethnic and linguistic basis. Gerald Stourzh has termed this process, which began in 1869, the "ethnicizing of Austrian politics."[45]

The new primacy of the ethnic factor had the effect of de-emphasizing, and to some extent delegitimizing, the traditional roles enjoyed by the provinces and the imperial government. This new arrangement also "reduced the position of the individual as citizen of the state, stressing, instead, the individual's role as a member of an ethnic group."[46] The emperor's *meine Völker* ceased to exist as a historical, organic, pluri-cultural unity cemented together by dynastic right. Instead the Emperor's subject were now "nationals" divided up along ethnic lines.[47] Individuals, wrote Joseph Roth, were increasingly "constrained by the nationalism of others to become a nation." [48] They were obliged to limit their belonging to one *Volkstamm* – nationality, people, nation, or ethnic group – and this had a number of consequences.

First, this new arrangement tended to serve the interests of persons who not merely acknowledged a national affiliation but who were, in fact, "nationally minded." These people were deemed particularly qualified, for example, to serve on provincial school boards in Moravia and in other provinces.[49] Second, the imperial state now went about "objectively" attributing ethnic membership to its subjects on the basis of evidence acquired from official questionnaires.[50] All this gave impetus to the modern ideal of a nationality bound to a distinct territorial base. This conception of nationality subverted the Habsburg vision. It also went against Austro-Marxist conceptions of nationality being "freely chosen," and "nationality [that] could attach to persons, wherever they lived and whoever they lived with, at any rate if they chose to claim it."[51]

Purifying the Galician Space

The Austro-Hungarian Empire collapsed at the end of World War I. The violent national struggles and the re-partitioning of the Habsburg lands that ensued did not have the effect of fully "purifying" central and eastern European spaces, and certainly not those of Galicia.[52] Nazi Germany addressed this task and the victors of World War II completed it. The Holocaust had eliminated 5.4 million central and eastern European Jews, leaving no trace of the vibrant Ashkenazim communities of Galicia and the Pale. Nine to ten million others – Roma, Poles, Ukrainians, Belarusans, Russians – died in the Nazi and Soviet sweeps through these territories. The multinational dream of the Habsburgs expired at Auschwitz.

After the war the Allies carried out their project for re-ordering what they referred to as the eastern borderlands of Europe. Clothed in the rhetoric of peace and political stability, in epistemological terms this project was completely in line with the politics of "pure geometry" as articulated by Carl Schmitt and applied by Nazi geopoliticians.[53] At Teheran, Yalta, and later Potsdam, the members of the Grand Alliance expressed their aim to "secure eastern Europe's frontiers on the basis of practical considerations."[54] By the end of the war, common dogma held that one of the major destabilizing factors during the interwar years had been the presence of large populations of ethnolinguistic minorities within the countries of central and eastern Europe.

The space comprising central and eastern Europe was to be "cleaned up," and populations were to be realigned in conformity with the newly drawn postwar frontiers. Between 1944 and 1948 this project was responsible for uprooting no fewer than thirty-one million people.[55] Next to the mass resettlement of Germans living in what had been the eastern territories of the Reich, Galicia was the chief focus of the population transfers of the years immediately following the war. The new boundary between Poland and the Soviet Union cut through the middle of Galicia, prompting forced transfers in both directions. From this area alone, more than 1.4 million people were uprooted and forcibly resettled. Among them were 810,000 Polish inhabitants of former eastern Galicia and Volhynia and 630,000 individuals identified as belonging to the Ukrainian "ethno-linguistic community."[56]

Back to *Galicia Felix?*

> Cracow: a town located 210 metres above the Adriatic Sea. This confirms Cracow's role as cradle of Mediterranean customs north of the Carpathians.

> L'viv: ... through L'viv runs the principal European continental divide ... There is, in fact, a particular house in Kortumówka that appears quite ordinary when the sun shines. Yet even the slightest drizzle betrays its unique position; water from one side of its roof flows into the Baltic; from the other, the raindrops proceed into the Black Sea.[57]

Galicia was born of myth, and from myth it would rise again. When new myths were so sorely needed, in the years after 1989, *Galicia Felix* proved particularly attractive. The re-materialization of Galicia first became apparent in the early 1990s through the sudden proliferation of its name. Shops, restaurants, and bars in the principal towns of the province (at least those on the much more prosperous Polish side of the border) carried the name *Galicia*.[58] Evocations of Galicia and the Habsburg past were used in promoting a variety of new consumer goods. There was mineral water from Przemyśl called *Galicja* blessed by the emperor's smile (*es hat mich sehr gefreut*). A Cracow micro-brewery produced a beer called K. & K. (*kaiserlich und königlich* – the "imperial and royal" of the Dual Monarchy). Various assortments of "Galician-era" sweets appeared on the market.

The designation "Galician" was made part of the names of a wide variety of public as well as private institutions and associations in Cracow, Rzeszów, Nowy Sącz, and the surrounding areas.[59] Associations for the preservation of Galician history, Galician literary organizations, and Galician cultural groups sprang up. Today there is an active Galician Television Association (Galicyjskie Towarzystwo Telewizyjne), presided over by the prominent Cracow journalist Leszek Mazan. It is funded by leading "Galician" entrepreneurs and corporations.[60] Numerous Galician advertising agencies, travel bureaus, radio stations, banks, and even brokerage firms are now flourishing concerns. Portraits of the Emperor Franz Josef adorn the offices of *Tygodnik Powszechny,* Poland's oldest and most distinguished progressive Catholic political weekly, as well as Cracow's daily *Dziennik Polski.* The emperor's visage also graces the walls of bars, restaurants, and coffeehouses.

Under the title "Galicia and Its Heritage," a conference was held in in 1992 in the cities of Rzeszów and Łancut. Attendance vastly exceeded expectations, and the eight-volume work that emerged from the proceedings quickly went through several printings.[61] As one of the conference organizers, Kazimierz Sowa, wrote in his introduction to the series: "Galicia is a powerful, still-living myth in the culture of two nations: the Polish and the Ukrainian. Certainly, it is not a unitary or homogeneous myth, yet in both cultures it is viewed first and foremost as an 'ideal' past, as a lost Arcadia" and, by extension, "as a path toward the future."[62] According to Sowa, two key elements characterize the present-day Galician myth. The first is an idealization of the lost time and space of the local, whether this be the familiar Galician village or *shtetl,* or the urban magnificence of turn-of-the century Cracow or L'viv. The second is a resurrection of the ideal of social and ethnic peace, of the peaceful coexistence of the "many peoples, many nations" who inhabited "these lands" since time immemorial. Both elements, notes Sowa, are predicated upon the idea of a unitary and/or unified Galicia and, therefore, upon a *negation* of the increasingly rigid border that cuts through it.[63]

The Politics of Spatial Representation

We should not be overly hasty in equating this recent fashion with the resurgence of "Galician" identity. Yet the trend is revealing. The names that we give to our social world, to ourselves, and to the institutions to which we belong are hardly accidental. They emerge from a complex negotiation of meanings and mark not only *who* we are but also *where* we are. The names we give to "our places" and to ourselves as social actors matter in two distinct ways. First, the act of naming concretizes the "reality" of a spatial representation. Naming is vital to the creation of togetherness and shared representations of spatial belonging. The act of naming a Galician region thus "gathers together [the region's] historical development, its important events, episodes, and memories, and [it] joins the personal histories of its inhabitants to this collective heritage."[65]

Naming also acts to "place" territories and their inhabitants within a set of broader representational containers – whether geopolitical, civilizational, historical, or cultural. Recalling the name Galicia not only evokes a series of nostalgic associations reminiscent of "home" and "tradition," it also serves to *locate* that home and that tradition, both within the mytho-poetic space of the past and vis-à-vis the spatial and political containers of the present. In the case of Galicia, the evocation of the historical region rests on denying legitimacy to present-day national-spatial divides.

No re-territorialization, not even symbolic re-territorialization, is possible without a prior de-territorialization. The "institutionalization" of a new spatial representation is always predicated upon the "de-institutionalization" of some other territorial unit or spatial representation.[66] However, as Denis Cosgrove and Mona Domosh have stressed, our representations of space are "not to be judged by a theory of correspondence but in terms of their value as moral/political discourses."[67] Defining the region named Galicia is thus a micro-strategic as well as macro-strategic exercise that is coterminus with a whole series of political and geopolitical choices about what constitutes the "proper" organization of this part of Europe.

From this perspective, the resurgence of Galicia in post-1989 Poland is best seen as an ironic politics of opposition that plays with space and spatial representations in order to contest the formal politics of the state. One of the first public "Galician" actions came in the wake of the 1995 presidential elections. The Polish Supreme Court was asked to ratify the results, since their legality had been put into question by revelations that the newly elected President Aleksander Kwaśniewski had lied about his educational qualifications.[68] In disgust over the scandal, prominent Cracow journalists and cultural figures joined local parliamentary deputies in erecting mock border crossings along the historical boundary between Austro-Hungarian Galicia and what had once been Congress Poland, proclaiming it "a *cordon sanitaire* separating us from the barbarians."[69] The event was playful in tone, intended to ridicule the political and spatial integrity of the Polish state and, above all, its institutions. As one of the participants wrote: "It is finally time to admit that the people who live here [Galicia] are different, have different traditions, a different way of thinking ... There was a time when the peoples of central Europe lived together in unity, within a common democratically governed state, taking the best from their respective cultures. This was before the onset of the disease of nationalism. Think about what Cracow and Kielce [a town less than 100 km north of Cracow] have in common. Nothing, besides the language, a couple of elected monarchs, and a common history that ended three hundred years ago."[70]

The Cracow City Council has also become increasingly vocal in recent years on matters normally considered to be national prerogatives, especially foreign policy. The council has sent numerous directives to the Polish parliament since 1990, covering everything from demands for President Kwaśniewski's resignation to condemnations of the Russian intervention in Chechnia. The council has been particularly active in contesting Polish state policy towards Ukraine, and over the past decade has established a wide-ranging network of exchange and aid programs with cities in western Ukraine.[71]

Such "scale-jumping" strategies[72] of empowerment have also been put into practice quite successfully by Galician business figures. Numerous local entrepreneurs and chamber of commerce leaders have launched cross-border trade initiatives and capital investment networks long before competent state bodies began to regulate such ventures. A Galician regional economic space has come into being – despite the lack of institutional or formal administrative ties and in spite of increasingly restrictive border policies.[73]

Conclusions

What do these recent events and strategies tell us about the relevance of the Galician myth in the present? The idealization of the historical region of Galicia raises two sets of questions. The first concerns the very nature of regions and regional identities. The second pertains to the ongoing construction of the "common European home" and the ways in which it is being imagined.

Is it even appropriate to speak of a Galician region today? If we consider regions, above all, to be geographical representations, we can claim that such representations are "real" (and thus politically, socially, and culturally "relevant") from the moment they are shared and constitute a referent for political action, for the articulation of identity, and for the forging of economic networks. The Galician regional representation, at present confined to the sphere of limited cultural and economic exchanges, is important as an alternative spatial imaginary and identity for the region stretching across both sides of the Polish-Ukrainian border.

Care must be taken, however, not to conflate this new regional identity, that is, the re-evoked identity of the historical Galician region, with the potentially endless identities of the region's inhabitants. The latter may or may not coincide with the identity of the region.[74] In this sense, "regional identity" is best conceived as a shared or dominant territorial idea or representation (of the region) that is shaped and articulated by particular social actors. Such actors are those "specialized" in the production and maintenance of territorial distinctions and identities and include politicians, journalists, cultural elites, business elites, and so on. In other words, we mean here people with the power to craft representations of territorial identity because of their social rank and their assigned role in reproducing the hegemonic structures of society. Regional identity is a shared geographical representation that induces coherent behavior and that, over time, can serve to consolidate the region.[75] The myth of *Galicia Felix* can plausibly play this role in the near future.

The revival of the Galician imaginary also raises some key questions surrounding the construction of identities in the new Europe. Adoption of the Habsburg myth within the post-Communist states is paradoxical. On the one hand, imperial belonging has been adopted by state elites as a marker of "Europeanness" and, thus, in *contradistinction* to an obviously non-European Other. On the other hand, the Habsburg myth (or at any rate its popular reincarnation) is situated within an idealization of multicultural and multinational *diversity and inclusion*, envisioned to be fundamental "European" values. This paradox speaks to a more fundamental paradox inherent in the European project itself. It speaks particularly to the question of "European citizenship."[76] How does one reconcile a necessary delimitation of the boundaries (political, symbolic, and territorial) of European belonging while at the same time proclaiming Europe's "unity in diversity"? For many in this part of the world, the "pluricultural, pluri-ethnic, multinational totality"[77] represented by the Habsburg Empire and its multiple, porous belongings provides an ideal model.

Notes

This is a revised version of an essay that first appeared under the title "Another Europe: Remembering Habsburg Galicia" *Cultural Geographies*, X (London, 2003), pp. 21–44.

1 Dennis Shaw, "The Chickens of Versailles: The New Central and Eastern Europe," in Brian Graham, ed., *Modern Europe: Place, Culture and Identity* (London, 1998), p. 14.

2 Michael Heffernan, *The Meaning of Europe: Geography and Geopolitics* (London, 1999), p. 239.

3 Ministry of Foreign Affairs of the Republic of Poland, "Annual Foreign Policy Statement," Warsaw, March 5, 1998. See also the Ministry's "Annual Foreign Policy Statement," April 8, 1999, and its "Security Strategy of the Republic of Poland," Jan. 4, 2000.

4 An excellent overview is provided in Valerie Bunce, "Postsocialisms," in Sorin Antohi and Vladimir Tismaneanu, eds., *Between Past and Future: The Revolutions of 1989 and Their Aftermath* (Budapest and New York, 2000), pp. 122–152.

5 For a more detailed discussion, see Luiza Bialasiewicz and John O'Loughlin, "Re-ordering Europe's Eastern Frontier: Galician Identities and Political Cartographies on the Polish-Ukrainian Border," in David Kaplan and Jouni Hakli, eds., *Boundaries and Place: European Borderlands in Geographical Context* (London, 2002), pp. 217–238.

6 See the discussion in Chris Hann "Ethnic Cleansing in Eastern Europe: Poles and Ukrainians beside the Curzon Line," *Nations and Nationalism*, II, 3 (Cambridge, 1996), pp. 389–406. See also C. Hann, "Postsocialist Nationalism: Rediscovering the Past in Southeast Poland," *Slavic Review*, LXII, 4 (Champaign, Ill., 1998), pp. 840–863. On the role of historical memory in post-1989 Poland, see Jerzy Jedlicki, "Historical Memory as a Source of Conflicts in Eastern Europe," *Communist and Post Communist Studies*, XXXII (Los Angeles, 1999), pp. 225–232.

7 For a discussion of urban transformations in Budapest, see Judit Bodnár, *Fin de Millenaire Budapest: Metamorphoses of Urban Life* (Minneapolis, 2001). For Prague, see Lily Hoffman and Jiri Musil, "Culture Meets Commerce: Tourism in Postcommunist Prague," in Dennis Judd and Susan Fainstein, eds., *The Tourist City* (New Haven, Conn., 1999).

8 The quotation comes from Predrag Matvejvic, *Mondo "Ex"* (Milan, 1996). See also the postscript to the 1999 edition of Ralf Dahrendorf, *Reflections on the Revolution in Europe. In a Letter Intended to Have Been Sent to a Gentleman in Warsaw* (London, 1996).

9 The notion of *Mitteleuropa* carries diverse connotations, many far from positive. It should be noted that the *Mitteleuropa* fondly recalled by Habsburg-era nostalgics stands in clear opposition to the Prussian understanding of *Mitteleuropa*. The Habsburg multi-national vision is a negation of the Prussian state-centric ideal first promoted by Friedrich Naumann and others, and later adopted by Nazi geopoliticians. See Arduino Agnelli, *La Genesi dell' Idea di Mitteleuropa* (Milan, 1971); Jacques Le Rider, *Mitteleuropa: storia di un mito* (Bologna, 1995); Claudio Magris, *Il Mito Absburgico*

nella Letteratura Austriaca Moderna (Turin, 1963) and his *Danubio* (Milan, 1986); Hans–Dietrich Schultz, "Fantasies of *Mitte*: *Mittellage* and *Mitteleuropa* in German Geographical Discussion in the 19th and 20th centuries," *Political Geography Quarterly,* 8 (Boulder, Colo., 1989), pp. 315–389; and Peter Stirk, "The Idea of Mitteleuropa," in Peter Stirk, ed., *Mitteleuropa: History and Prospects* (Edinburgh, 1994). For the image of *Mitteleuropa* as an "antidote" to the Iron Curtain see, especially Milan Kundera, "The Tragedy of Central Europe," *New York Review of Books*, XXXI, 7 (New York, 1984), pp. 33–38; and György Konrad, *Anti-politics* (New York, 1984).

10 Anssi Paasi, "The Institutionalization of Regions: A Theoretical Framework for Understanding the Emergence of Regions and the Constitution of Regional Identity," *Fennia*, no. 164 (Helsinki, 1986), p. 125.

11 Roland Barthes, *Mythologies* (Paris, 1957).

12 Magris, *Il Mito Absburgico*, p. 15.

13 Robert Musil, *The Man without Qualities* (New York, 1953), p. 31.

14 Stefan Zweig, *Die Welt von Gestern / The World of Yesterday* (Lincoln, Nebr., 1964), p. 12.

15 Musil, *Man without Qualities*, p. 31.

16 Franz Werfel, *Aus der Dämmerung einer Welt* (Vienna, 1936), p. 14.

17 Le Rider, *Mitteleuropa*, p. 54.

18 Werfel, *Aus der Dämmerung*, p. 19.

19 Magris, *Il Mito Absburgico*, pp. 55, 70.

20 See Stanisław Estreicher, "Galicia in the Period of Autonomy and Self-Government, 1848–1917," in William F. Reddaway, ed., *The Cambridge History of Poland*, vol. II (Cambridge, 1951), pp. 432–460; Robert Kann, *The Multinational Empire: Nationalism and National Reform in the Habsburg Monarchy, 1848–1918*, 2 vols. (New York, 1950); James Shedel, "Austria and its Polish Subjects, 1866–1914: A Relationship of Interests," *Austrian History Yearbook*, XIX–XX, pt. 2 (Minneapolis, 1983–1984), pp. 23–41; and Piotr Wandycz, "The Poles in the Habsburg Monarchy," in Andrei S. Markovits and Frank E. Sysyn, eds., *Nationbuilding and the Politics of Nationalism: Essays on Austrian Galicia* (Cambridge, Mass., 1982), pp. 68–93.

21 Ewa Wiegandt, *Austria Felix czyli o Micie Galicji w Polskiej Prozie Współczesnej* (Poznań, 1988).

22 This is the term coined by Polish sociologist Stanisław Ossowski, *Z zagadnien psychologii społecznej* (Warsaw, 1967), p. 210, who distinguishes it sharply from an "ideological homeland." The first is the home of a "patriotism" based within the direct, personal experience of a given territory; the second, of a patriotism based "within a set of constructed beliefs and assumptions," that is, within the imagined community of the modern nation-state.

23 The citation is from Wiegandt, *Austria Felix*, p. 39. See also Anne Apple-baum, *Between East and West: Across the Borderlands of Europe* (New York, 1994).

24 In Galician author Andrzej Kusniewicz's wonderful novel, *Stan niewazkości* (Łodź, 1997), the protagonists lose all trace of their identity with the forma-tion of the independent Polish state, which proceeds to nationalize their homelands narratively: "I don't even know any more where I am from, where I was born."

25 Juliusz Żuławski, *Z domu* (Warsaw, 1979), pp. 54–55.

26 Ossowski, *Z zagadnień psychologii społecznej*, p. 210.

27 Benedict Anderson, *Imagined Communities: Reflections on the Origins and Spread of Nationalism* (London, 1983), p. 19.

28 Wiegandt, *Austria Felix*, p. 27.

29 Anderson, *Imagined Communities*, p. 19; Eric Hobsbawm, *Nations und Nationalism since 1780* (Cambridge, 1990), p. 97.

30 Bruno Schulz, *Sanatorium pod Klepsydrą* (Warsaw, 1994), p. 233.

31 Cited in Wiegandt, *Austria Felix*, p. 33.

32 Ibid., p. 39. See also Józef Buszko, *Galicja 1859–1914: Polski Piemont?* (War-saw, 1989); Robert Kann and Zdeněk David, *The Peoples of the Eastern Habs-burg Lands, 1526–1918* (Seattle, 1984); and Henryk Wereszycki, *Historia Polityczna Polski 1864–1918* (Wrocław, 1990).

33 Józef Wittlin, *Sól ziemi* (Warsaw, 1995), p. 42. It should be noted that even faith divides were far from rigid. Children of mixed marriages, for exam-ple, generally followed the faith tradition of their same-gender parent, a practice that helped combat exclusive religious demarcation.

34 Józef Chlebowczyk, *Procesy narodotwórcze we wschodniej Europie środkowej w dobie kapitalizmu* (Warsaw, 1975).

35 Bruno Schulz, *Z listów odnalezionych* (Warsaw, 1993), p. 21.

36 Wiegandt, *Austria Felix*, p. 39.

37 Kundera, "The Tragedy of Central Europe," p. 35.

38 Magris, *Il Mito Absburgico*, pp. 277–286. On the role of the Jewish cultural and intellectual elite in fin de siècle Vienna, see Carl Schorske, *Fin de Siècle Vienna: Politics and Culture* (Cambridge, 1981); Allan Janik and Stephen Toulmin, *Wittgenstein's Vienna* (New York, 1973); and the exhibition volume *Le Vie del Mondo: Berlino, Budapest, Praga, Vienna e Trieste: Intellettuali Ebrei e Cultura Europea dal 1880 al 1930* (Milan, 1998).

39 Paul Robert Magocsi, *Historical Atlas of East Central Europe* (Seattle, 1993), p. 107.

40 See Marsha Rozenblit, "The Jews of the Dual Monarchy," *Austrian History Yearbook*, XXIII (Minneapolis, 1992), pp. 160–180; and Wolfdieter Bihl, "Die

Juden," in Adam Wandruszka and Peter Urbanitsch, eds., *Habsburgermonarchie 1848–1918: Die Völker des Reiches*, vol. 3 (Vienna, 1980), pp. 880–948.
41 See Le Rider, *Mitteleuropa: storia di un mito*. The Shomer Israel movement, formed in L'viv in 1867, was the first registered Jewish political organization in Austria. See Piotr Wróbel, "The Jews of Galicia under Austrian-Polish Rule, 1869–1918," *Austrian History Yearbook*, XXV (Minneapolis, 1994), p. 115. The opposition of a "good" Austria to a "barbaric" Russia formed a common theme in Galician Jewish prose, as did the paternal figure of the benevolent Franz Josef, who "watched over" Galicia's Jewry. As Julian Stryjkowski noted in his autobiographical novel, *Austeria* (Warsaw, 1966), p. 45: "This is Austria, and not Chişinău [the site of a horrifying pogrom in 1903, ordered by Nicholas II]. And thank God, such things will never happen here as long as the Emperor looks over us. There isn't a Jew who does not wish him long life and health. And the Rabbis pray for him so that his interests prosper, and that all his family live long as well... Pity only that he's not a Jew."
42 For an overview of the Galician Jewish experience in late-Habsburg Austria, see Leonard Prager, "Galicyjsko żydowska historia w zwierciadle trzech biografii: Mordechaj Gebirtig, Ignacy Schipper i Dow Saddan," in Jerzy Chłopecki and Helena Madurowicz-Urbańska, eds., *Galicia i jej Dziedzictwo*, vol. 2 (Rzeszów, 1995), pp. 137–156; and Wróbel, "The Jews of Galicia," pp. 97–138.
43 Tadeusz Konwicki, *The Polish Complex* (London, 1982), p. 100.
44 Włodzimierz Odojewski, *Zasypie wszystko, zawieje ...* (Warsaw, 1995), p. 335.
45 Gerald Stourzh, "The Multinational Empire Revisited: Reflections on Late Imperial Austria," *Austrian History Yearbook*, XXIII (Minneapolis, 1992), p. 18.
46 Ibid., p. 19. It is important to note that, previously, imperial authorities considered nationality to be not "an attribute of individuals but of communities." On this point see Hobsbawm, *Nations and Nationalism*, p. 97.
47 Le Rider, *Mitteleuropa*.
48 Joseph Roth, *Ebrei Erranti* (Milan, 1985), p. 22–23.
49 Stourzh, "The Multinational Empire Revisited," p. 18.
50 The venerable Habsburg census included a linguistic questionnaire from 1880 onwards; thereafter, language served as the criterion of "national belonging." According to the 1880 census, Poles made up 51 percent of Galicia's population and Ukrainians (Ruthenians) 43 percent. As Wereszycki (*Historia Polityczna Polska 1864–1918*, p. 141) notes, the "Polish" figure included the bulk of Galicia's significant Jewish population, which for the purposes of the census tended to identify as "Poles." On the problems

posed by nationality statistics in Galicia during this period, see Paul Robert Magocsi, *A History of Ukraine* (Toronto, 1996), p. 423.

51 Hobsbawm, *Nations and Nationalism*, p. 7. This ideal was perhaps best artic-ulated by Karl Renner, who envisioned national membership as a status "freely chosen, *de jure*, by the individual who has reached the age of major-ity." Cited in ibid., p. 7 n13.

52 For more on the concept of the "purification of space," see David Sibley, *Geographies of Exclusion: Society and Difference in the West* (London, 1995).

53 See Claude Raffestin, Dario Lopreno, and Yvan Pasteur, *Géopolitique et his-toire* (Lausanne, 1995). For a thorough discussion of the Nazi project for a new ordering of spaces in the East, see Deborah Dwork and Robert Jan van Pelt, *Auschwitz: 1270 to the Present* (New Haven, Conn., 1996).

54 Bohdan Kordan, "Making Borders Stick: Population Transfer and Resettle-ment in the Trans-Curzon Territories, 1944–1949," *International Migration Review*, XXXI (Staten Island, NY, 1997), pp. 704–720.

55 Magocsi, *Historical Atlas*, p. 164.

56 Kordan, "Making Borders Stick." See also the detailed discussion of these events in Białasiewicz and O'Loughlin, "Re-ordering Europe's Eastern Frontier," pp. 217–238.

57 Mieczysław Czuma and Leszek Mazan, *Austriackie Gadanie czyli Encyklope-dia Galicyjska* (Cracow, 1998), pp. 239 and 262.

58 "Fit for imperial ministers," as announced in advertisements for the Hawelka restaurant on Cracow's main square.

59 Among the officially registered local non-governmental organizations in the "Galician" territories in 1997, over a hundred incorporated the word Galicia or Galician into their names. One example is the *Stowarzyszenie Agroturystyczne Galicyjskie Gospodarstwo Gościnne* (Agrotourism Association of Galician Farmers) which seeks to promote a "unique Galician tourist experience."

60 Among these is the Sendzimir steel mill, a principal sponsor of the afore-mentioned *Encyklopedia Galicyjska*, which advertizes how it is "building progress and civilization from iron and steel – as in the good old days." It should be noted that this steel mill is located in the socialist new-town of Nowa Huta on the outskirts of Cracow. Previously it was a symbol of Com-munist-era industrial development and later of Solidarity's struggles against the regime. Its resignification as a Galician icon is therefore particu-larly curious.

61 Jerzy Chłopecki and Helena Madurowicz-Urbańska, eds., *Galicja i jej dziedz-ictwo*, 8 vols. (Rzeszów, 1994–1996).

62 Kazimierz Sowa, "Słowo wstępne," in ibid., vol. 1 (Rzeszów, 1994), p. 6.

63 Ibid.
64 Anssi Paasi, *Territories, Boundaries and Consciousness: The Changing Geographies of the Finnish-Russian Border* (London, 1996), p. 35.
65 Ibid.
66 Denis Cosgrove and Mona Domosh, "Author and Authority: Writing the New Cultural Geography," in James Duncan and David Ley, eds., *Place/Culture/Representation* (London, 1993).
67 Kwaśniewski, leader of the post-communist Democratic Left Alliance (SLD), was re-elected president in 2000, but his support was again weak in the territories of the former Galicia.
68 Cited in Bohdan Jalowiecki, "Przestrzeń historyczna, regionalizm, regionalizacja," in Bohdan Jalowiecki, ed., *Oblicza polskich regionów* (Warsaw, 1996), p. 47.
69 Cited in Roman Szul, "Galicja: teatr czy rzeczywistość?" in ibid., p. 234.
70 A number of associations that promote dialogue and exchanges with the lands of eastern Galicia (now western Ukraine) operate in Cracow. Among these are the Foundation of St Volodymyr the Baptizer of Rus', which promotes Ukrainian culture in Poland and publishes the almanac *Between Neighbours*, and the Union of Resettlers (Związek Wysiedlonych), which publishes historical documents, works to raise awareness about the post–World War II resettlement activities on both sides of the border, and organizes exchanges and trips for the resettled and their families to "home places" now in Ukraine.
71 This notion comes from Neil Smith, "Geography, Difference, and the Politics of Scale," in Joe Doherty, Elspeth Graham, and Mo Malek, eds., *Postmodernism and the Social Sciences* (London, 1992), pp. 58–72.
72 The "reality" of these new economic territorialities has been canonized by no less than the Institut für Länderkunde in Leipzig. In 1998 the institute published an economic geography of the "Mitteleuropean West-East Axis: Saxony, Silesia, Galicia." The economic structure of each of these "regional units" was described in detail, and an outline was offered identifying the emerging linkages between them in the post-1989 space of Mitteleuropa. On the increasingly prohibitive border regimes, see the papers by Katarzyna Wolczuk, "Polish-Ukrainian Borderlands and Nation-States," and Marzena Kisielowska-Lipman, "Polish Eastern Borderlands in Turmoil?"presented at a seminar on "Fuzzy Statehood," Royal Institute of International Affairs, London, Dec. 8, 2000.
73 For an elaboration of this distinction, see Paasi, "The Institutionalization of Regions," and his *Territories, Boundaries and Consciousness*.
74 See Giuseppe Dematteis, *Le metafore della terra* (Milan, 1985). Dematteis

emphasizes that all such representations are necessarily selective. They codify collective decisions regarding what it is that the region "is," both to the regional population itself and to the external world.

75 See the discussion in Jürgen Habermas, "Why Europe Needs a Constitution," *New Left Review,* XI (London, 2001), pp. 5–26.

76 Le Rider, *Mitteleuropa,* p. 54.

10 Historical Memory and Regional Identity among Galicia's Ukrainians

YAROSLAV HRYTSAK

In May 1772, following an agreement between Austria, Prussia, and Russia, the Habsburg army crossed the borders of the Polish-Lithuanian Commonwealth and occupied new territories which, two decades later, were to border the Russian Empire. Since these agreements were rather unclear as to the future border between the two empires, the Habsburgs sought to occupy the largest possible territory. The Austrian military command received orders to stop its troops at the river Podhorce. But there was no such river – most probably, the river Seret was intended. Unable to find the Podhorce, the officers stopped, exhausted, by another river called the Zbruch.[1] Little did they know that by mistake they created one of the most enduring lines of cultural division in east-central Europe, one which has survived until our own times.[2]

From 1772 the Zbruch marked the eastern border of a new Austrian province, the Kingdom of Galicia and Lodomeria (Regnum Galiciae et Lodmeriae / Königreich Galizien und Lodomerien). Its title was a Latin-German rendering of the name of a medieval Rus' state, Halyts'ko-Volyns'ke kniazivtsvo (Galician-Volhynian principality). That principality had come into existence in 1199 as a result of the disintegration of Kievan Rus'. It reached its zenith under Prince Danylo (1201–1264), who claimed control over large swathes of southern Rus', Kiev included, and was crowned *Rex Russiae* by the pope. The Danylo dynasty was related through marriage to other Rus' princes, as well as to Polish and Hungarian kings. But the dynastic line expired in 1340. The Danylo patrimony was claimed by various scions and relatives, and for a short period between 1370 and 1387 it was controlled by the Hungarian crown. In 1387 Galicia was annexed by the Kingdom of Poland, which after 1569 was known as the Polish-Lithuanian Commonwealth. Four centuries later the Habsburgs invoked the existence of the Galician-Volhynian principality to legitimize their new annexation of areas to the east: The Habsburgs laid claim to the lands that had once been the Galician-Volhynian principality as a part of their patrimony, by virtue of holding the Hungarian crown.[3]

The new Habsburg province and the medieval principality were, however, by no means territorially congruent. The Habsburgs had Volhynia (Lodomeria) in name only. In 1793 this province had, in fact, been passed to the Russian Empire. However, the Principality of Galicia-Volhynia had never included Little Poland (Małopolska), the historic core of the Polish-Lithuanian Commonwealth. This in no way prevented the Habsburgs from adding Little Poland to their new acquisitions and calling it West Galicia. From 1849 its center was Cracow. These manipulations of history and territory were criticized by local intellectuals, both Ruthenian (Ukrainian) and Polish, who were uncomfortable with the new shape of their homeland. In the mid-nineteenth century, Maurycy Dzieduszycky, a Polish noble man and Catholic writer, lamented that the Habsburgs were out "to create some kind of non-historical Galicians."[4] Iakiv Holovats'kyi, a leading Ruthenian patriot, echoed these views. In his geographical, statistical, and ethnographic description of Galicia (1875–1878), Holovats'kyi stressed that the "non-organic character" of Habsburg Galicia reflected the fact that it had come into being "in the absence of any historical background."[5]

Yet the fall of Communism showed Austrian Galicia to be one of most enduring inventions of the Habsburgs in central and eastern Europe. Having compared electoral behavior in five post-Communist countries – the Czech Republic, Hungary, Poland, Slovakia, and Ukraine – Thomas Zarycki came to the conclusion that Austrian Galicia "is one of the few places ... where one would like to extend the map beyond the present day political boundaries and present differentiation of the Polish-Ukrainian political space in order to show the persistence of the nineteenth-century Galician borders."[6] Both in contemporary Poland and Ukraine, Galician attitudes are conservative and strongly marked by religious and anti-Communist sentiments.[7] Moreover, in both countries, Galicians are very actively engaged in building what is being called a civil society.[8]

Defining the Problem

It is not easy to describe the essence of a Galician subjective identity. Here we face a set of paradoxes which are difficult to resolve. One of them stems from contemporary academic discourse. In Ukraine and

Poland, there is a lot of discussion about regionalism, with an emphasis on its political significance. Still, few scholarly projects have dealt with this phenomenon specifically, and those that have, address the subject in often very speculative terms and lack any serious empirical data.[9]

This chapter is an attempt to correct these shortcomings. It is partly based on projects carried out between 1994 and 1999 (with supplemental data from 2001 and 2004) by the Institute for Historical Research at the University of L'viv. These projects considered both objective and subjective aspects of regional identity in post-Soviet Ukraine. Our explicit goal was to transcend the limited scholarly agendas of those unable to conceptualize beyond the framework of national identities or, at least, to locate these identities within a wider range of possibilities for collective identification. The projects could not, however, avoid a degree of simplification. First, the spatial focus was limited (although not exclusively) to L'viv and Donets'k, respectively the centers of Ukraine's two large historic regions of Galicia and the Donbas. These regions are considered to represent opposite poles on the political map of contemporary Ukraine. Today, Galicia is one of the most ethnically Ukrainian regions of Ukraine, in terms both of its demographic make-up and its cultural self-presentation. It is very western-oriented and provides continual support to the Ukrainian democratic opposition. By contrast, the highly industrialized and russified Donbas, which used to be a stronghold of Ukraine's Communists, has recently come under the control of local oligarchs aspiring to power in Kiev. We began our work with the following two suppositions: (1) Other Ukrainian regions fall somewhere in between Galicia and Donbas.[10] (2) The cities of L'viv and Donets'k, as regional administrative centers and cultural capitals, are to a large extent responsible for, and representative of, regional identities and attitudes.

The study has another obvious shortcoming. During and immediately following World War II, both L'viv and its surrounding region lost their traditional multiethnic character. Poles, Jews, and smaller numbers of Germans were replaced by a steady increase in the number of Russian immigrants.[11] Ukrainians formed a large majority in L'viv (79.1 percent in 1989) and their dominance was reflected in our interviews. Our projects, therefore, present the Ukrainian perspective largely devoid of references to any multiethnic past or to alternative non-Ukrainian and non-Russian (non-Soviet) perspectives. This limitation, however regrettable, is an authentic reflection of the current political and intellectual discourses in L'viv.[12]

Explaining Regionalism

The data collected in the course of our research projects largely confirmed our initial assumptions: In terms of identity formation, L'viv and Donets'k do indeed present opposite poles. Consequently, in 1994, the most disliked group in L'viv were the Communists; in Donets'k the most disliked group were the Ukrainian nationalists. Citizens were given the possibility of selecting their most valued identities from a long list of options. In L'viv they tended to indicate Ukrainian and Greek Catholic, while in Donets'k they perceived themselves mostly as "Soviets" and "workers" – although five years later, in 1999, both of these identities in Donets'k had lost their popularity and dropped out of the "top 10"). The two cities also differed in the public use of the Ukrainian language. L'viv is predominantly Ukrainian-speaking (77.6 percent), while most people in Donets'k (80.5 percent) speak Russian as their main language. Economic problems were cited in both cities as the most serious challenge facing Ukraine, but respondents in L'viv were more inclined to think that each person should take care of himself or herself, while in Donets'k they preferred to look to the government as the guarantor of employment and a high standard of living.

Preference for the Ukrainian national version of history was evident in L'viv and for the Soviet version in Donets'k. However, both sets of respondents agreed that the starting point of Ukrainian history lay in medieval Kievan Rus'. Disagreement regarding later periods is the more pronounced the closer one comes to the present period. It can be assumed that different historical perspectives will yield different visions of the future. People in L'viv definitely saw Ukraine and Russia as two separate countries. In Donets'k more people tended to favor some form of union; however, they were not categorically against the political independence of Ukraine.

Using regression analysis these differences were investigated further. National self-identification, as either Ukrainian or Russian (some respondents chose Soviet) proved to be the most significant indicator of attitudes. The proportion of Ukrainians by self-identification in L'viv was 73.1 percent, rising to 76.0 percent in 1999, compared with 39.3 percent and 43.6 percent respectively, in Donets'k. It is evident that differences in self-identification have a regional dimension. The two popular self-identifications in L'viv were national (Ukrainian) and regional (L'vivian). Similarly, in Donets'k (although with a somewhat lower preponderance) the two leading self-identities were Soviet and "Donets'kite."[13]

Comparative history offers the only way to account for this pronounced regionalism. Polish scholar Roman Szul contends: "It was history that 'carved out' the regions in the same way that it made states and nations. The historical factor was of major importance for the making of ethnicity, as well as for the cultural, linguistic, religious, and economic situation. Thus, the historical criterion [deserves] special attention."[14]

But how exactly does history work? It is often suggested that the level of Ukrainian national consciousness, or of Ukrainian-language use, depends on how long a specific territory was under Polish rule. The highest level of Ukrainian national and linguistic consciousness is displayed by Galicia, which was under Polish political and cultural influence for six centuries. By contrast, the lowest level is found in the southern and eastern provinces, which were never (or only briefly, a mere hundred years) occupied by Poland.[15] Thus, it may be said that L'viv is in the part of Ukraine that is most Polish and Donets'k in the part least Polish. However, this line of argument does not suffice, because it treats Polish influence too loosely. It raises the need to explain why Polish Galicia differs from what were once the Prussian and Russian parts of Poland, and why in terms of a Galician identity the Ukrainian and Polish variants look so similar.

The obvious answer would seem to be that Polish and Ukrainian Galicia both were once parts of a single province in the Habsburg Empire. How does this Austrian legacy manifest itself in the long run? It is striking that today, in what used to be Austrian Galicia, people know very little about Habsburg times and they rarely invoke them. Reminiscences of "good old Austria" occupy but a marginal space in the historical memory of contemporary Galician Ukrainians. Such reminiscences persist mostly within tiny groups of intellectuals, committed to reviving and reactivating them.[16] Among ordinary people, recollections of Habsburg times have been largely overtaken by the memories of more recent times, foremost among them World War II and the Soviet period. Our empirical research thoroughly confirmed this observation.

A Galician regional identity seems able to survive regardless of what people can remember. First-hand recollection of the past is, of course, constrained by the generation factor, and the earliest period that our interview respondents could recall from personal experience was the late 1930s. Our hypothesis is that what matters is the timing and the ways in which the main paradigms of national historical memory are formed and transmitted. A starting point can be indicated rather easily. Prior to the Austrian annexation of parts of Poland in 1772, the local East

Slavic population did not use the terms *Ukrainian* or *Galician* for self-identification. At that time, their most commonly used terms for themselves were *Rus'*, *rus'kyi*, *rusyn*, *rusnak*. However, Rus' and its derivatives were very ambiguous terms. Depending on the circumstances they could invoke different meanings. In the local context, *Rus'* could mean reference to one of the earliest recorded historical names for this region (Red Rus'), or to an administrative region of the Polish-Lithuanian Commonwealth (Województwo Ruskie / the Rus' palatinate, with its center in L'viv), or to the Rus' faith (*rus'ka vira*) of the Eastern Christian Church of this region (Orthodox until 1596, with the Uniate / Greek Catholic Church rising to dominance thereafter). *Rus'* could also be used to characterize other East Slavic territories such as those located in the Polish-Lithuanian Commonwealth, those that formed the core of the Tsardom of Muscovy and later the Russian Empire, or the smaller territories that were under Hungarian rule (Transcarpathia) and Ottoman or Moldovian rule (Bukovina).

Together all of these territories were sometimes referred to as *Slavia Orthodoxa*. From the mid-1300s its population was spread among different political regimes. At no time was it homogeneous in ethnic terms. The people of *Slavia Orthodoxa* shared a single Byzantine rite, either Orthodox or Greek Catholic, with Church Slavonic as the liturgical language. Their vernacular languages were mutually comprehensible. Furthermore, wherever they might actually be, these people all had some vague memory of their common descent from Kievan Rus'. Only gradually, through the centrifugal influences of culturally strong centers such as L'viv, Kiev, Vilnius, Cracow, and others, did the people of these territories develop distinctive national identities.[17]

Rival Identities and Historical Memories

Galicia formed the westernmost borderland of this East Slavic territory. Complicated cultural, religious, and political encounters with Roman Catholics, Jews, Polish nobles, German burghers, and later, Austrian provincial officials all combined in offering local Ruthenians a wide range of possibilities for self-identification. No single identity was so compelling that its dominance was assured. However, the options were never unlimited. Identities cannot be conjured out of thin air. Identities need building blocks, such as language, religion, or other strong cultural elements. Only from these can an identity become "imaginable" and successfully adapted. In Galicia, several options were available.

The linguistic and cultural proximity of Galician Ukrainians to their potential co-nationals ("Little Russians") living in Russian ruled Ukraine made an all-Ukrainian identity seem quite natural. But alternatives, such as a common-Russian (*obshcherusskii*), or an all-Polish, or a distinct Ruthenian identity were also imaginable.

From this complex setting, it followed that historical myths about national identity were contingent. They were susceptible to multiple applications, although there were limits on the possibilities for such manipulation. Galician Ruthenian intellectuals could refer to the Galician-Volhynian principality as a precursor of nineteenth-century Galicia, as the Habsburgs did. This conceptualization could be expanded to embrace the territory of co-ethnics in Subcarpathian (Hungarian) Rus' and Bukovina. Alternatively, one might prefer a version of the past that gave pre-eminence to the historical claims of the Poles over this region. Nineteenth-century Galicians could perhaps imagine themselves united someday with the "Little Russians" of the Russian Empire. This view was easily justifiable by the assumption that historically their territory had been part of Kievan Rus', although by 1230 it was in the hands of Galician princes, who ruled it as a sovereign political entity. It was a territory which the (Ukrainian) Cossacks had sought to control in the seventeenth century. A final possibility was to regard all the lands inhabited by East Slavs as the single indivisible patrimony of the Russian Empire, and in doing so accept the idea of one common Russian identity.

These scenarios were more than theoretical possibilities. Between the revolution of 1848 and the early twentieth century they defined the principal rival national orientations held by Ruthenian intellectuals and politicians in Galicia.[18] Behind each scenario stood specific actors committed to its promotion. As a product of their interaction, different identities and versions of historical memory emerged. The debates among Galician Ruthenian intellectuals concerning self-identification necessarily had international implications. Above all these debates had an impact on relations between the Austrian (later Austro–Hungarian) and Russian empires. Vienna and St Petersburg both had interests at stake in these Galician controversies. It was not difficult to recall that in 1772 a Russian garrison was stationed in L'viv, ready to take control of the whole province and that this situation occurred again in 1809 during the Napoleonic occupation. The Galician Ruthenian imagination of themselves and their past could also affect relations between Vienna and the provinces. The local Polish nobility maintained its efforts to control the entire province and to represent Ruthenians as a part of the historical Polish nation (*gente Rutheni, natione Poloni*). Developments in Galicia always carried the potential to disrupt the balance of forces in the empire that was governed from St Petersburg. As can be seen, the self-identification of Galician Ruthenians was an issue of geopolitical significance for all of central and eastern Europe.

In focusing on the leading actors, the field, and the stakes, it should not be forgotten that there were people who for a time, at least, remained indifferent to identity politics, while recognizing that "what happens in the game matters [and] that its stakes are important ... and worth pursuing."[19] In Galicia, a significant proportion of Ruthenians did not (or did not want to) define themselves in national terms for most of the nineteenth century. Their Polish opponents referred to them maliciously as *popy i chłopy* (priests and peasants). Indeed, as late as 1910 not even 2 percent of Ruthenians were living in towns or cities. Moreover, 61 percent of them were illiterate, a proportion that in the entire Habsburg Empire was exceeded only by Serbs (61 percent) and Croats (63.4 percent).[20] In Galician-Ruthenian folklore occasional allusions to Kievan Rus' and Cossack Ukraine could be found, and belief in the Holy or White (Russian) Tsar was widespread among local peasants.[21] The Ruthenian peasant memory was outstripped by that of the Protestant German peasants in Galicia, who were able to specify some names and events of ancient history.[22] However, for a long time, Ruthenian peasants in Galicia simply did not participate in discussions about historical identity.[23]

The educated Ruthenian elites who first took it upon themselves to change this apathy consisted mostly of Greek Catholic priests. Their main concern was the status of their Greek Catholic Church relative to the Roman Catholic ("Polish") Church. The Habsburgs actively promoted their status, and the Greek Catholic clergy reciprocated with expressions of unswerving loyalty to Vienna. Before 1848 the Greek Catholic hierarchy steadfastly refrained from any engagement in the national question for fear that this would prejudice good relations with the Habsburg imperial court. This caution seemed stifling to the vanguard of the "national awaking," recruits from the Greek Catholic seminary in L'viv and from the lower clergy.[24]

The only available publication presenting the imperial interpretation of Galicia's history before that time appeared in 1796. It was written by a Habsburg official, Johann Christian von Engel, and entitled *Geschichte von Halitsch und Vladimir* (History of Galicia and Volhynia).

The Ruthenian authors of two other accounts restricted themselves to the history of the church[25] and to the medieval period,[26] thus avoiding more recent politically sensitive secular issues.

The national question in Galicia evolved as a by-product of Austrian-Polish rivalry. Habsburg policy-makers wanted to modernize a province that to them seemed virtually destitute. It was a peculiar kind of modernization, however, because the main agent of change was the state official.[27] In the early 1800s, Habsburg officials were one of largest social groups in L'viv.[28] These bureaucrats, mostly Germans and germanized Czechs, took the Polish nobility to account. They held the Poles directly responsible for the drastic decline of the region and considered it their mission "to re-educate the Sarmatian beasts [the Polish nobility] into human beings."[29] Most positions were occupied by a foreign elite, and until 1849, for example, no native Galician was appointed to the office of vice-governor. In 1825 German replaced Latin as an official language and became the language of instruction at L'viv University. By the 1840s L'viv looked like a German city, not unlike Magdeburg, Nürnberg, or Frankfurt-am-Main.[30] This apparent Germanness stemmed from the layout of the city, the feeling that it was being protected by a just government, the general emphasis on order, and last but not least, the presence of "German" coffeehouses.

The growing germanization provoked resistance from the Polish elite. The political class of high society in L'viv was by mid-century divided into two antagonistic parties, German and Polish – "the party of Schiller" versus "the party of Mickiewicz." The principal political aim of Polish nationalism was the restoration of the Polish-Lithuanian Commonwealth within its old, "historical," borders. Various attempts to take advantage of major political upheavals and re-establish Polish rule, from Napoleon's offensive in 1809 through the national uprising of 1846 and the revolution of 1848, were all unsuccessful.

To counter Polish national ambitions Austrian bureaucrats needed to activate the Ruthenian issue. At the end of 1847 and the beginning of 1848 Austrian Governer Count Franz Stadion summoned before him several Galician-Ruthenian intellectuals. Stadion wanted to know whether or not they had an account of their own history. Thus it was that, given the urgency of the moment, in July 1848 the Supreme Ruthenian Council – the highest representative body of Galician Ruthenians and controlled by the Greek Catholic Church hierarchy – commissioned the young priest Antin Petrushevych "to write a history of Galicia."[31] The first such histories began to appear in the 1850–1860s, written by Petrushevych, Denys Zubryts'kyi, Izydor Sharanevych, and Bohdan Didyts'kyi. They all sought to prove the historical primacy of Ruthenians over Poles in Galicia and to present Ruthenians as "a historical" state or nation that had its own tradition whose roots were to be found in Kievan Rus' and the Principality of Galicia-Volhynia.[32] With little exception, their visions of what they called Ruthenian history did not imply a definitely national orientation for the future. As to the different interpretations of what Rus' was and should be, they remained equivocal. The two editions of Bohdan Didyts'kyi's *Nachal'naia istoriia Rusy ot nachala do noveishykh vremen* (Elementary History of Rus' from Earliest to Most Recent Times) published in 1868 and 1885, presented two different trajectories of Rus' history after the fall of the Kievan and Galician-Volhynian princes. In the 1868 edition the trajectory led to the Muscovite tsars, while in 1885 Rus' history produced the Ukrainian Cossack hetmans.

Major changes ensued in the late 1860s, when as the result of the Austro-Hungarian *Ausgleich*, the empire was transformed into a dual monarchy. On the provincial level, the Ausgleich was supplemented by an Austro-Polish compromise. Galicia was granted autonomous status, including permission to set up its own provincial parliament (the Galician Diet). This autonomy radically transformed the parameters within which different historical memories could be shaped. In the new constellation, the polonization of Galicia became the sine qua non for continued Austrian-Polish cooperation.[33] The result, in short, was that the Habsburgs abandoned their loyal Ruthenian supporters to the mercy of the Polish ruling elite. An Austrian minister at the time reportedly pronounced: "Whether and to what extent the Ruthenians may exist is left to the discretion of the Galician Diet."[34]

At almost this same time repressive measures were being taken against the Polish and Ukrainian national movements in the Russian Empire.[35] In response, both sets of nationalist agitators relocated in Galicia, where they had hoped to carry on their work under the auspices of a more liberal Habsburg regime. As a result, Galicia became the "Piedmont" of both partitioned "historical Poland" and "imagined Ukraine." Within Galicia symbols of Polish and Ukrainian nationalism were in opposition not so much to each other but to Austrian and Russian domination from outside Galicia.[36] Eventually, however, Polish-Ukrainian conflicts did erupt. The Russian government started to nurture "Russian irredentism" within the province to counter rival nationalisms and, thus, provide a pretext for the future annexation of Galicia. L'viv became a major center for the publication of modern national historical narratives. Inevitably, social groups in Galicia grew ever more exclusionary in terms of Polish-Ruthenian/Ukrainian rivalry. This also had implications for Austrian-Russian relations.

The Victory of a Ukrainian Identity

In the new circumstances, the old, ambiguous, and largely church-based concept of Rus' stood little chance. It came under fire in the 1860s, when a new generation of Ruthenian intellectuals with a Ukrainian orientation merged the concept Rus' into the idea of a Cossack Ukraine. This appropriation of the Cossack period had the psychological impact of a religious conversion. It was, however, formulated in entirely secular modern terms of national time and space. In this way the historical and spatial imagination of early Ukrainophiles was consolidated. More systematic accounts by scholars began to appear as the nineteenth century drew to an end.[37] This was an enormous shift that had long-term consequences: The regional history of Galicia was replaced by the national history of Ukraine. After the 1860s and until the outbreak of the World War I, approximately three-quarters of all the historical works written and published in Galicia focused on all-Ukrainian issues. Only one-quarter were dedicated specifically to the history of Galicia.[38] Many of the writings promoting the new shift were produced by the "dean" of modern Ukrainian historiography Mykhailo Hrushevs'kyi, and his disciples. Hrushevs'kyi was a Ukrainian from the Russian Empire who was appointed to the new chair (*katedra*) of Eastern European history at L'viv University in 1894. He remained in L'viv until 1914. During this period Hrushevs'kyi published several volumes of his *Istoriia Ukraïny-Rusy* (History of Ukraine-Rus'). This work had a tremendous impact on Ukrainian nation-building and, regardless of its academic merits, laid the foundations of the modern Ukrainian national myth.[39]

The Hrushevs'kyi School and its role in establishing a Ukrainian national paradigm of history is well known and will not be examined in detail here (see Chapter 6, by Volodymyr Potul'nyts'kyi, in this volume).[40] However, two points deserve emphasis. First, the Ukrainian idea in Galicia was largely an intellectual import, but an import aptly suited to Ruthenian needs. The possibility of inviting a historian from the Russian Empire to L'viv University was first advanced in 1863. The expectation was two-fold: the professor from Russia was to write a Ukrainian national history and this history was to be an instrument to be used by proponents of the Ukrainian idea to overcome their rivals.[41] The main rivals were Galicia's Russophiles, who identified themselves with the "ready-made" Russian culture and language and, in doing so, considered themselves to be more sophisticated.[42] The balance of intellectual resources in Galicia finally gave the Ukrainian idea an edge. As Roman Szporluk has put it: "By joining with Ukraine, Galicians were becoming members of a nation larger than Poland; not by accident did they call it *Velyka Ukraïna*, 'Greater Ukraine.' Without an affiliation with Ukraine, the Galician community was roughly the size of the Lithuanian or Slovak nationalities. Perhaps it was the sense that Ukraine offered them the best hope of survival vis-à-vis Poland that made it possible for [Greek] Catholic Galicians to unite with the Orthodox Eastern Ukrainians – against Catholic Poles."[43]

Second, even though the Ukrainian idea was largely imported into Galicia, it underwent a major transformation there. The final result differed substantially from its (Russian or Eastern Ukrainian) original, indeed, so much so that the two versions of Ukrainian identity and historical memory frequently clashed with each other. The Galician, or as it proponents would call it, Western Ukrainian version, is much more exclusionary with respect to Russians and Russian history. This may be the result of the direct influence of rival Polish national narrative in Galicia that was both bellicose and exclusionary.

For Poles, the prime target of exclusion was all manner of German or Austrian influence in Galicia, and their aim was to reassert the Polish character of the province. During the period of Galicia's status as an autonomous province in the Habsburg Empire, the alleged dangers posed by the presence of Ruthenian (Ukrainian) and Jewish people in their midst became an increasingly common theme in the Polish nationalist discourse. Poles feared the emergence of a new secular Ruthenian-Ukrainian elite, the mass migration of Ruthenian peasants to the cities, and the introduction of a universal franchise. Such developments, they feared, were likely to undermine the Polish domination of Galicia. The Poles articulated these fears in historical terms. Frequent references were made to the seventeenth-century Cossacks and eighteenth-century Haidamaks (social rebels), describing them as people who had opposed the civilizing and westernizing mission of Polish culture in the commonwealth's "eastern borderlands" (*wschodnie kresy*). The short

Russian occupation of 1914 and the Polish-Ukrainian war over L'viv and Galicia in 1918–1919 added fat to the fire. They provided rich material for further historical and political mythologies that sprang up in the interwar period, during which Galicia was included within the "reborn" Polish state and referred to as *Małopolska Wschodnia* (Eastern Little Poland). These mythologies were bolstered by carefully planned historical commemorations of the heroic defense of the "Polish borderlands" from "eastern hordes," "Cossacks,", and "Haidamaks." All this was heavily reliant on prewar narratives. The tone of Polish patriotism became increasingly aggressive. Ukrainian patriots constructed their historical narratives according to similar exclusionary patterns, often ignoring completely Galicia's obvious Polish heritage.[44]

A new, radical, and right-wing Ukrainian nationalism in the first-half of the twentieth century gained ground steadily.[45] In the Galician version of the Ukrainian national discourse, Poles were replaced by Russians and Soviets as the primary "national enemy." Intellectual patterns, however, remained the same. It was now a Ukrainian and highly westernized L'viv and Galicia that allegedly led the resistance against the "Communist and Russian hordes." The persistence of patterns of antagonism is graphically evident in the history of renaming streets. In this respect the post-Soviet Ukrainian L'viv of 1999 is no different in essence from the Polish L'viv of 1939.[46]

In accepting an exclusive version of the national past, the Galician-Ukrainian elite dissolved their regional history into a history of the Ukrainian nation. This radical appropriation of the national paradigm is perhaps the most striking feature of the regional historical memory, as manifested in the dissemination of the Ukrainian historical myth to the masses. A study of naming patterns among villages between the 1830s and the 1930s, for example, reveals a shift away from the traditional names of popular Christian saints to the adoption of new names taken from the Ukrainian "national Pantheon" – which includes Kievan and Galician princes, Ukrainian Cossacks, and nineteenth-century Ukrainian patriots.

The new pattern of names was invented by Ukrainian intellectuals in L'viv in the 1830s. Gradually, it found its way into the countryside, where it had become a kind of fashion by the eve of World War II. To be sure, with the imposition of Soviet rule after 1945, the Galician countryside would have been ukrainianized anyway, as were other regions of Ukraine in the 1920s. Nevertheless, a comparison of naming patterns in Galicia and the rest of Ukraine indicates that in the former case ukrainianization developed much deeper roots. In Galicia, ukrainian- ization was the result of long-lasting and organic work "from below" that characterized the local Ukrainian national movement in Habsburg Galicia, as well as in interwar Poland. These features were absent in other ethnic Ukrainian territories, which were sovietized and ukraini- anized "from above."[47]

Regional History Imagined and Re-imagined

Every victory has its price. In the case under discussion, this price was the suppression of all the subtleties and vicissitudes that accompanied the insertion of modern Ukrainian identity into Galicia. It would seem that, as Ernest Renan once put it, "forgetting, I would even go so far as to say historical error, is a crucial factor in the creation of the nation."[48] The Galician Ruthenians who transformed themselves into Galician Ukrainians had to silence some moments of their own regional history in accommodating themselves to a more general Ukrainian perspec- tive. Historical records inform us that during the 1648 siege of L'viv by Hetman Bohdan Khmel'nyt'skyi and his Tatar allies, the Ukrainian Cossacks themselves desecrated St George's Cathedral. But by the Habsburg period, St George's Cathedral had become the seat of the Greek Catholic metropolitan and a symbolic stronghold of Rus' iden- tity. At that times, church-based Ruthenian nationalism was even referred to as the St George Circle. Thus, in 1833–1834, when Markiian Shashkevych, both an early Ukrainophile and a Greek-Catholic priest, wrote verses about the 1648 siege, he was entirely sympathetic to the besieger and careful to avoid any mention of the Cossack-led pillage.[49]

For early generations of Ukrainophiles, the poetry of Taras Shev- chenko was read as if it were a kind of national Bible. In L'viv Shevchenko commemorations were among the main public manifesta- tions of the Ukrainian orientation.[50] Indeed, Shevchenko is very largely responsible for integrating Cossack history into the modern Ukrainian national myth.[51] True to the Cossack perspective, Shevchenko's verses had some anti-Uniate (Greek Catholic) overtones, and his interpreta- tions of religious issues did not adhere strictly to Christian orthodoxy. Thus, it was no easy task for Galician Ukrainophiles – many of whom, like Shashkevych, were Greek Catholic priests or scions of priest fami- lies – to reconcile the poetry of Taras Shevchenko with their own Greek Catholic identity.[52] But they did the best they could, and Shevchenko has remained a central symbol of national identity in both Galicia and Ukraine.

In all eastern Galician towns and many villages there are streets and squares named after Shevchenko and Shashkevych, and monuments to them are common. Statues and streets commemorating leading Russophile heroes such as Bohdan Didyts'kyi, Denys Zubryts'kyi, and Antin Petrushevych are almost non-existent. From the perspective of Ukrainian nationalism, these men made the wrong choice, and as "national renegades" they do not deserve to be remembered. Local post-Soviet historiography has been very slow to reappraise the Russophile movement, and it was left to western scholars to reintroduce the Russophiles into the academic discourse as a legitimate part of the Ukrainian nation-building project.[53]

Other targets for selective forgetting have been the non-Ukrainian ethnic groups of Galicia, the Poles and the Jews with whom Ukrainians share common Polish-Lithuanian as well as Habsburg legacies. Until World War II, Poles and Jews made up a large proportion of the population. In the capital of Galicia both were more numerous than the Ruthenians/Ukrainians.[54] Nonetheless, Poles and Jews remain grossly underrepresented in historical symbols and sites of memory in contemporary Galicia. Public memory of the Poles and the Jews is being tolerated only to the extent that such memorials "do not harm the national pride of Ukrainians" – to quote a principle elaborated by an expert group set up to rename city streets in post-Communist L'viv.[55] Application of this principle has led to attempts to marginalize historical events and figures that are central for Jewish historical memory, particularly of the Holocaust.[56] Similarly, in the Polish case, the Orlęta Lwowskie, Polish heroes of the Polish-Ukrainian war of 1918–1919 – who were buried at the Polish military cemetery in L'viv – have been expunged from local memory.[57]

The main targets of the latest outburst of historical amnesia are the ethnic groups that are relative newcomers in Galicia, the Russians and people of other former Soviet republics who arrived in conjunction with the Soviet annexation of Galicia after World War II. Residents from former Soviet republics are often treated as one group, since they are mostly Russian-speaking, even though a significant number of them are actually eastern Ukrainians, Belarusans, Kazakhs, etc. In the local Ukrainian intellectual and political discourse, they are all "eastern barbarians" who endanger Ukrainian identity – just as Galician Ukrainians endangered Polishness in interwar Polish discourses. Galicia was one of the first parts of the former Soviet Union to start removing symbols of Soviet domination, such as statutes of Lenin and other state symbols, and replacing them with Ukrainian historical symbols.[58] In some cases these activities had dramatic effects. In December 1990 and June 1991 three newly erected nationalist monuments were blown up in Galicia. Allegedly this was the work of the same KGB unit involved in an assault on the TV tower in Lithuania's capital city Vilnius in January 1991.[59] The publication of new historical textbooks that make explicit reference to the "Hrushevs'kyi scheme" of Ukrainian history, which was harshly repressed under Soviet rule, has been less dramatic.[60] It has, however, had a profound effect on the re-emergence of Ukrainian historical memory in Galicia.[61]

The de-sovietization and the de-russification of historical memory in Galicia has been very successful, as demonstrated by our opening comparison between L'viv and Donets'k. The irony is that this has not happened on a national scale. The Ukrainian historical myth is still perceived as essentially exclusionary and, therefore, unacceptable by most Russian-speaking Ukrainians and Russians. These so-called Russophones together comprise half of the population of Ukraine.[62] Recent survey evidence reveals that post-Communist Ukrainians are blending Ukrainian, Russian, and Soviet narratives in new ways. It is interesting to note that the Ukrainian nationalist leader Stepan Bandera – who is venerated in Galicia on the national scale – is among the three historical figures who evoke the most negative attitudes in the country as a whole (the other two are Iosif Stalin and Mikhail Gorbachov).[63]

In contrast to Galicia, which for the most part sacrificed its regional history for the sake of an all-Ukrainian national interpretation, the dominant historical discourses in the Donbas region give priority to the regional past.[64] There is, however, some common ground on which L'viv and Donets'k are able to reconcile their versions of history. Both share negative attitudes towards Stalin and his repressive policies, especially collectivization and the Ukrainian famine of 1932–1933.[65] There seems also to be a tendency in Donets'k to view Ukrainian independence more positively than was the case just few years ago, in 1994. But it will take much longer to reach a comprehensive reconciliation, and there is no certainty that this will ever be possible.

Contemporary Ukraine offers very little to satisfy the expectations of Ukrainians in Galicia. Their region seems to derive little benefit from Ukrainian independence, just as for Poles interwar Galicia lost out as a consequence of Polish independence. In both cases, the homeland lost the special status of a "national Piedmont," which it could only enjoy as long as it existed under a "foreign yoke." In interwar Poland, "Austrian" L'viv and Cracow lost ground to "Russian" Warsaw. In contemporary Ukraine, it is Kiev and Donets'k , not L'viv, that dominate the political landscape. Highly industrialized and russified Eastern Ukraine, rather than conservative and ukrainianized western Ukraine, seems to exemplify the image of the Ukrainian nation for the present and the foreseeable future.

Under such circumstances it is interesting to note that a group of young Galician intellectuals have been trying to develop a new cultural and political program. They are calling for Galician autonomy within the Ukrainian state.[66] They support their claims with historical arguments that emphasize the elements that divided western and eastern Ukrainians in the past.[67] L'viv artist Volodymyr Kostyrko currently is probably the most outspoken Galician autonomist.[68] He is best known as a cartoonist for the influential Ukrainian newspapers *Postup* and *Krytyka*. In one of his pictures, popularized in a mass-produced pocket calendar for the year 2000, Galicia is presented as a young woman – not unlike Joan of Arc perhaps – clad in shining armour. In her hand she holds the Ukrainian national flag, while at her feet lies a sleeping lion (symbol of L'viv). Encircling her image are the portraits of Galician historical horoes King Danylo and Stepan Bandera. And to be very clear and blunt for those Ukrainians who do not follow the Galician version of history the picture bears the words: *"Na kolina, khamy!"* ("On your knees, you rogues!").[69]

The image promoted by these Galician autonomists is very exlusionary toward other regions of Ukraine. This does not mean, however, a complete denial of the national, Hrushevs'kyi, scheme of history. On the contrary, in the autonomists' view, Galicia is *the* one and only Ukraine – after all, the Galician Stepan Bandera fought for Ukrainian and not Galician independence. In this view, Galicia is the one and only pro-democratic, pro-western, and market-oriented region of Ukraine; only Galicia is ready and eager to be accepted into the European Union, in sharp contrast to "Russian" Ukraine.[70]

The autonomists have been successfully reviewing elements of Galicia's multiethnic legacy by popularizing the works of Leopold Sacher-Masoch and Bruno Schultz and by celebrating in L'viv, in 2000, the 170th anniversary of the birth of Austrian Emperor Franz Josef. The

Habsburg period is particularly significant in these new manipulations of historical memory. In the nineteenth century, Galicia was one of the least industrialized and most impoverished regions of the Austrian Empire. Indeed, "Galician misery" (nędza galicyjska) was a trademark description throughout central Europe and beyond. For today's Galician autonomists, however, the Habsburg period represents "the good old days." References to those "golden days" under the Habsburgs are partly a reflection of disappointment in the new realities of present-day Ukraine. Equally important, however, in motivating this new construction of Galician identity is a desire to "return to central Europe."[71] In the autonomist view, now is the last chance for a part of Ukraine – or, in their imagination, the only "true" Ukraine – to step onto a rapidly departing European train, and this precisely at the moment when a new "velvet curtain" is descending on the western borders of what was formerly Soviet territory.

Conclusions

Galician identity in its Ukrainian form is full of paradoxes. According to a self-deprecating anecdote that one may still hear in the region, Galicia used to be a peaceful, God-fearing land. Then Ukrainians from Greater Ukraine, that is, the Russian Empire, arrived and managed to persuade the inhabitants that, in actual fact, they – the Galicians – were the real Ukrainians. That is when all the problems started. The Ukrainians from Greater Ukraine soon forgot that they themselves were Ukrainians and so they put all the burden of responsibility for preserving a Ukrainian identity onto the Galicians. In their naiveté, the Galicians accepted this great challenge, although neither they nor their compatriots from Greater Ukraine seemed to be happy with this solution. Instead, both are   still suffering from the after-effects of trying to fulfill this "mission impossible."

As with every anecdote, this one contains a grain of truth. The Galician-Ukrainian identity now seems to have been "carved in stone." Yet, studies of historical memory prove that this identity emerged as a result of historical contingency. With every new development in the twentieth century, this identity formation became the focus of new controversies. Indeed, the making of historical memory is a continuous process, and the further clarification of problems and formulations of identity will remain a necessary part of the research agenda for a long time to come.

Notes

1 Zbigniew Fris, *Galicja* (Wrocław, 2000), p. 8.
2 The Zbruch thereby forms part of Samuel Huntington's eastern boundary of western civilization. See his *The Clash of Civilizations and the Remaking of the World Order* (New York, 1996), p. 159.
3 On the Galician-Volhynian principality, see Ivan Krypiakevych, *Halyts'ko-Volyn'ke kniazivstvo*, 2nd expanded ed. (L'viv, 1999); Iaroslav Isayevych, *Halyts'ko-Volyns'ka derzhava* (L'viv, 1999). For a concise treatment, see Paul Robert Magocsi, *Galicia: A Historical Survey and Bibliographic Guide* (Toronto, 1983), pp. 46–64.
4 Fris, *Galicja*, p. 89.
5 Iakov Golovatskii, "Karpatskaia Rus': geografichesko-statisticheskie i istoriko-statisticheskie ocherki Galichiny, severo-vostochnoi Ugrii i Bukoviny," in *Slavianskii sbornik*, vol. II (St Petersburg, 1878), p. 55.
6 Tomasz Zarycki, *The New Electoral Geography of Central Europe: A Comparative Study of Regional Political Cleavages in the Czech Republic, Hungary, Poland, Slovakia, and Ukraine* (Lund and Warsaw, 1998), p. 58.
7 Martin Åberg and Janusz Korek, "Mosaic of Change: Institutional Trajectories in Transitional Wrocław and L'viv," paper presented at the conference, Institutionalizing Democracy: Poland and Ukraine in Comparative Perspective, University College of South Stockholm, Nov. 13-16, 1998; Dominique Arel, "The Parliamentary Blocks in the Ukrainian Supreme Soviet: Who and What do They Represent?" *Journal of Soviet Nationalities*, I, 4 (1990-91), pp. 108-154; Taras Kuzio and Andrew Wilson, *Ukraine: Perestroika to Independence* (Edmonton, 1994), p. 89; Roman Szporluk, "Reflections on Ukraine After 1994 Elections: The Dilemmas of Nationhood," *Harriman Review*, VII, 7-9 (New York, 1994), pp. 1-9; Andrew Wilson, *Ukrainian Nationalism in the 1990s: A Minority Faith* (Cambridge, 1997), p. 121, 133, 140; Roman Szul, "Perspektywy regionalizmu Galcyjskiego w Polsce na tle tendencji międzynarodowych," in Jerzy Chłopiecki and Helena Madurowicz-Urbańska, eds., *Galicja i jej dziedzictwo*, vol. 2, *Społeczeństwo i gospodarka* (Rzeszów, 1995), pp. 86-88.
8 A similar pattern, although to a lesser degree, can be found in Ukraine's far western region of Transcarpathia, also a former part of the Habsburg Empire. For statistics, see *Counterpart data on Ukrainian NGOs (2000):* http://www/viaduk.net/cp/cpk e.nsf/. This appears as Table 3 in Iaroslav Hrytsak, "Dylemy ukraïns'koho natsiotvorennia, abo shche raz pro stare vyno u novykh mikhakh," *Ukraïns'kyi humanitarnyi ohliad*, no. 4 (Kiev, 2000), pp. 11–33.

9 See, for example, Oleksandr Fil'ts and Oleh Neveliuk, "Halyts'ka mental'nist': shche odna sproba rozhliadu problemy (proekt Politilohichnoho
tsentru 'Heneza')," *Stavropihion–politolohichnyi tsentr "Heneza"*: *shchorichnyk*
(L'viv, 1997), pp. 20–31.

10 This hypothesis was partially proven by other studies of regionalism in
Ukraine; see Louise Jackson, "Identity, Language, and Transformation in
Eastern Ukraine: A Case Study of Zaporizhzhia," in Taras Kuzio, ed., *Con-
temporary Ukraine: The Dynamics of Post-Soviet Transformation* (Armonk, New
York, and London, 1998), p. 101.

11 Ivan Terliuk, *Rosiiany zakhidnykh oblastei Ukraïny* (L'viv, 1997).

12 On these discourses, see the special issue "Strasti za L'vovom," *Krytyka*, VI,
7–8 (Kiev, 2002).

13 See Y. Hrytsak: "National Identities in the Post-Soviet Ukraine: The Case of
L'viv and Donets'k," in Zvi Gitelman, Lubomyr Hajda, John-Paul Himka,
and Roman Solchanyk, eds., *Cultures and Nations of Central and Eastern
Europe* (Cambridge, Mass., 2000), pp. 269–277; "Ukrainian Nationalism,
1991–2001: Myths and Misconceptions," *Central European University History
Department Yearbook: 2001–2002* (Budapest, 2002), pp. 241–245; and "Die
kommunistische Vergangenheit in der Gegenwart," in Gerhard Simon, ed.,
Die neue Ukraine: Gesellschaft-Wirtschaft-Politik (1991–2001) (Cologne,
Weimar, and Vienna, 2002), p. 47.

14 Szul, "Perspektywy," p. 78.

15 Ihor Ševčenko, *Ukraine between East and West* (Edmonton, 1996), pp. 116–
117; Szul, "Perspektywy," p. 80.

16 For an example of such a reactivation, see the special issue dedicated to the
Habsburg monarchy of the L'viv journal *Ï: nezalezhnyi kul'torolohichnyi chasopys*, no. 9 (L'viv, 1997).

17 John A. Armstrong, "Myth and History in the Evolution of Ukrainian Consciousness," in Peter J. Potichnyj, Marc Raeff, Jaroslaw Pelenski, and Gleb
N. Žekulin, eds., *Ukraine and Russia in their Historical Encounter* (Edmonton,
1992), pp. 129-130.

18 B. Podolinski, *Slowo przestrogi* (Sanok, 1848), pp. 21–22; O.A. Moncha-
lovs'kyi, *Sviataia Rus'* (L'viv, 1903), p. 4.

19 Here I follow a scheme suggested by Pierre Bourdieu, in Pierre Bourdieu
and Loïc J.D. Wacquant, *An Invitation to Reflexive Sociology* (Chicago, 1992),
pp. 94 ff.

20 Adam Wandruszka and Peter Urbanitsch, eds., *Die Habsburgmonarchie
1848–1918*, vol. 3, part 1 (Vienna, 1980), pp. 51, 77.

21 John-Paul Himka, "Hope in the Tsar: Displaced Naive Monarchism among
the Ukrainian Peasants of the Habsburg Empire," *Russian History / Histoire
russe*, VII, 1–2 (Tempe, Ariz., 1980), pp.125–138.

22 L'vivs'ka naukova biblioteka imeni V. Stefanyka NAN Ukraïny, Manuscript division, fond 206 (Vasyl' Shchurat), file 292/27, p. 10.

23 Little research has been done into the role of schools and popular enlightment societies in promoting historical memory among peasants. Most existing work focuses on the efforts of educators and institutions "from above"; see C. Majorek, *Historia utylitarna i reudycyjna: szkolna edukacja historyczna w Galicyi (1772–1918)* (Warsaw, 1990) and Jerzy Potoczny, *Oświata dorosłych i popularyzacja wiedzy w środowiskach Galicji doby konstytucyjnej (1867–1918)* (Rzeszów, 1998). How and to what extent peasants responded to these efforts "from below" is only rarely explored. A recent study from the Sambir region suggests that their impact was very limited: Andriy Zayarnyuk, "Framing the Ukrainian peasantry in Habsburg Galicia: 1846–1914," Doctoral dissertation, University of Alberta. Edmonton, 2003.

24 Jan Kozik, *The Ukrainian National Movement in Galicia 1815–1849* (Edmonton, 1986), passim; *"Rusalka Dnistrova": dokumenty i materialy* (Kiev, 1989), passim.

25 Michael Harasiewicz, *Annales ecclesia ruthenae* (L'viv, 1862).

26 Denys Zubrycki, *Rys historyi Narodu Ruskiego w Galicyi i hierarchii cerkiewnej w temże królewstwie* (L'viv, 1837).

27 Waltraud Heindl, *Gehorsame Rebellen: Bürokratie und Beamte in Österreich 1780–1848* (Vienna, Cologne, and Graz, 1990); and idem, "Modernizatsiia ta teoriï modernizatsiï: pryklad Habsburz'koï biurokratiï," *Ukraïna moderna*, no. 1 (L'viv, 1996), pp. 89–100.

28 Vadym Adadurov, "L'viv u napoleonivs'ku epokhu," in Marian Mudryi, ed., *L'viv: misto-suspil'stvo-kul'tura: zbrinyk naukovykh prats'*, vol. 3 (L'viv, 1999), p. 211; Stanisław Hoszowski, *Ekonomiczny rozwój Lwowa w latach 1772–1914* (L'viv, 1935), p. 16.

29 Cited in Adadurov, "L'viv," p. 212.

30 J.G. Kohl, *Reisen im Inneren vom Rußland und Polen: Die Bukovina, Galizien, Mähren*, vol. 3 (Dresden and Leipzig, 1841), pp. 88, 103–105; Mykhailo Kril', "L'viv u opysakh inozemtsiv (kinets' XVIII–persha polovyna XIX st.)," in Mudryi, *L'viv*, p. 300.

31 Oleh Turii, "'Rus'ka istoriia' iak legitymizatsiia vyzvol'nykh zmahan' halyts'kykh ukraïntsiv," in Iaroslav Dashkevych and Iaroslav Hrytsak, eds., *Mykhailo Hrushevs'kyi i L'vivs'ka istorychna shkola: materialy konferentsiż* (L'viv and New York, 1994), p. 96.

32 Anna Veronika Wendland, *Die Russophilen in Galizien. Ukrainische Konservative zwischen Österreich und Russland, 1848–1915* (Vienna, 2001), pp. 72–78.

33 Piotr Wandycz, "The Poles in the Habsburg Monarchy," Andrei S. Markovits and Frank E. Sysyn, eds., *Nationbuilding and the Politics of Nationalism: Essays on Austrian Galicia* (Cambridge, Mass., 1989), pp. 68–93.

34 Cited in Ivan L. Rudnyts'kyi, *Essays in Modern Ukrainian History* (Edmonton, 1997), p. 324.

35 See A.I. Miller, *"Ukrainskii vopros" v politike vlastei i russkom obshchestvennom mnenii: vtoraia polovina XIX v.* (St Petersburg, 2000).

36 On the role of German-Polish antagonism in the shaping of Polish identity and historical memory in Galicia, see Viktor Lein [Victor H. Lane], "Daty na sluzhbi natsiï: pol's'ko-ukraïns'ka dyskusiia kintsia XIX–pochatku XX st. navkolo daty zasnuvannia universytetu u L'vovi," *Ukraïna moderna*, nos. 2–3 (L'viv, 1999), pp. 122–131.

37 For details,see Ostap Sereda, "Shaping of a National Identity: Early Ukrainophiles in Austrian Eastern Galicia, 1860–1873," doctoral dissertation, Central European University, Budapest, 2003.

38 This is a very rough estimation based on the selective bibliography provided in Dmytro Doroshenko, *Ohliad ukraïns'koï istoriohrafiï* (Kiev, 1996), pp. 195-200.

39 Armstrong, "Myth and History," p. 129.

40 See also Dashkevych and Hrytsak, *Mykhailo Hrushevs'kyi i L'vivs'ka istorychna shkola*, p. 96.

41 Turii, "'Rus'ka istoriia'," p. 105.

42 See the letter of Denys Zubryts'kyi to the Imperial Society of History and Antiquities in Moscow (Jan. 18, 1853), cited in Kyrylo Studyns'kyi, ed., "Korrespondentsiia Ia. Holovats'koho v lïtakh 1850–1862," *Zbirnyk filol'ogichnoï sektsiï Naukovoho tovarystva imeny Shevchenka*, VIII–IX (L'viv, 1905), pp. 519–520.

43 Roman Szporluk, *Russia, Ukraine, and the Break-up of the Soviet Union* (Stanford, 2000), p. 385.

44 See, with a special focus on L'viv, two essays and my comments: Harald Binder, "Making and Defending a Polish town: 'Lwów' (Lemberg) 1848–1914"; Anna Veronika Wendland, "Post-Austrian Lemberg: War Commemoration, Inter-Ethnic Relations, and Urban Idenities in L'viv, 1918–1938"; and Yaroslav Hrytsak, "Crossroads of East and West: Lemberg, Lwów, L'viv on the Threshold of Modernity"; in *Austrian History Yearbook*, XXXIV (Minneapolis, 2003), pp. 57–109.

45 Most historians locate the emergence of radical Ukrainian nationalism firmly in the interwar period; see Alexander Motyl, *The Turn to the Right: The Ideological Origins and Developments of Ukrainian Nationalism, 1919–1929* (New York, 1980)). This view, however, needs to be qualified because some of these tendencies were already visible at the beginning of the century, well before World War I. See Iaroslav Hrytsak. "Ivan Franko v evolutsii ukraïns'koï politychnoï dumky," *Suchasnist'*, no. 9 (Kiev, 1994), pp. 114–126.

46 See Yaroslav Hrytsak and Victor Susak, "Making a National City: The Case of L'viv," in John J. Czaplicka and Blair A. Ruble, eds., *Composing Urban History and the Constitution of Civic Identities* (Washington, D.C., 2003), pp. 140–64.

47 See Yaroslav Hrytsak, "History of Names: A Case of Constructing National Historical Memory in Galicia, 1830–1930s," *Jahrbücher für Geschichte Osteuropas*, XLIX, (Stuttgart, 2001), pp. 163–177.

48 Cited in Geoff Eley and Ronald Grigor Suny, eds., *Becoming National: A Reader* (New York and Oxford, 1996), p. 47.

49 Ševčenko, *Ukraine*, pp. 123–124; Markian Shashkevych, *Tvory* (Kiev, 1973), pp. 28–29.

50 Sereda, "Shaping of a National Identity," passim.

51 George G. Grabowicz, *The Poet as Mythmaker. A Study of Symbolic Meaning of Taras Ševčenko* (Cambridge, Mass., 1982).

52 See the discussion in Iaroslav Hrytsak, "Poshyrennia poemy 'Mariia' v Halychyni," *Radians'ke literaturoznavstvo*, no. 3 (Kiev, 1986), pp. 51–64.

53 The first instance of "rehabilitation" came in a presentation at the International Congress of Slavists held in Kiev in 1983. See Paul Robert Magocsi, "Old Ruthenianism and Russophilism: A New Conceptual Framework for Analyzing National Ideologies in Late 19th Century Galicia," in Paul Debreczeny, ed., *American Contributions to the Ninth International Congress of Slavists, Kiev 1983*, vol. 2 (Columbus, Ohio, 1983), pp. 305–324, reprinted in a revised version in Paul Robert Magocsi, ed., *The Roots of Ukrainian Nationalism: Galicia as Ukraine's Piedmont* (Toronto, 2002), pp. 99–118. More recently, this topic has been discussed at greater length by the German scholar Anna Veronika Wendland: "Rusofil'stvo: shche odyn ukraïns'kyi proekt? zauvahy pro nevtilene prahennia," *Ï: nezalezhnyi kul'torolohichnyi chasopys*, no. 18 (L'viv, 2000), pp. 113–122; idem, *Die Russophilen*, pp. 13–28; and "Die Rückkehr der Russophilen in die ukrainische Geschichte: Neue Aspekte der ukrainischen Nationalsbildung in Galizien, 1848–1914," *Jahrbücher für Geschichte Osteuropas*, XLIX (Stuttgart, 2001), pp. 389–421.

54 For a survey of the literature on Poles and Jews as well as on Armenians, Germans, and Karaites in eastern Galicia, see Magocsi, *Galicia*, pp. 224–255. See also Rudolf A. Mark, "Polnische Bastion und ukrainisches Piemont: Lemberg 1772–1921," in P. Fäßler, T. Held, and D. Sawitzki, eds., *Lemberg-Lwów-L'viv: Eine Stadt im Schnittpunkt europäischer Kulturen* (Cologne, Weimar, and Vienna, 1993), pp. 51–54; Olena Stepaniv, *Suchasnyi L'viv* (L'viv, 1992), p. 80.

55 Cited in Hrytsak and Susak, "Making a National City," passim.

56 Yaroslav Hrytsak, "The Holocaust in Historical Memory of Ukrainians,"

paper presented at the conference, The War and the Holocaust in the Collective Memory of Jews, Germans, Poles, Ukrainians, and Lithuanians,
Ben-Gurion University, Israel, May 17–25, 1998.

57 On the controversy over the Polish military cemetery, as well as on symbolic effort at Ukrainian-Polish reconciliation held on Nov. 1, 2000, and initiated by local Ukrainian intellectuals, see the website of the L'viv-based
journal "Ï" (Yi).

58 Bohdan Kravchenko, "National Memory in Ukraine: The Role of the Blue
and Yellow Flag," *Journal of Ukrainian Studies*, XV, 1 (Edmonton, 1990),
pp. 1–21; Kuzio and Wilson, *Ukraine*, pp. 101–104, pictures 24a and 24b.

59 Kuzio and Wilson, *Ukraine*, p. 155.

60 Bohdan Iakymovych, "Do istoriï vydan' tvoriv Ivana Krypiakevycha na
pochatku 90-kh rokiv XX st. (spohad-esei uporiadnyka)," in Iaroslav
Isaievych, Feadisii Steblii, and Mykola Lytvyn eds., *Ivan Krypiakevych u
rodynnii tradytsiï, nautsi, suspil'stvi* (L'viv, 2001), pp. 67–82.

61 It would be interesting to explore to what extent the new post-Soviet
national history is a continuation of the Soviet Ukrainian version. Beneath a
surface of mutual antagonism, they share some similarities. For example,
the Soviet Ukrainian version was extremely repressive toward the history
of Jews in Ukraine. A survey of Soviet writings reveals that despite the general Soviet tendency to ignore or downplay the Holocaust, the application
of this policy varied. While in Estonia one could find a rather sympathetic
and undistorted account of the Jewish tragedy during the World War II, in
Lithuania the issue was more blurred.

The Ukrainian S.S.R. was an extreme case, and a large official history
published in 1982 fails to mention Jews, not even in connection with the
Holocaust. See Zvi Gitelman, "Soviet Reactions to the Holocaust, 1945–
1991," in L. Dobroszycki and J.S. Gurock, eds., *The Holocaust in the Soviet
Union: Studies and Sources on the Destruction of the Jews in the Nazi-Occupied
Territories of the USSR, 1941–1945* (Armonk, NY, 1994), pp. 3, 9–11. The
Soviet regime tried to accommodate to local conditions and was careful to
avoid extreme russification and sovietization of western Ukraine, unlike in
western Belarus, where local nationalism was much weaker. See Szporluk,
Russia, pp. 109–138. In any case, the image of L'viv as a Ukrainian city was
strengthened in the wake of Soviet annexation.

62 Graham Smith, Vivien Law, Andrew Wilson, Annette Bohr, and Edward
Allworth, *Nation-building in the post-Soviet Borderlands* (Cambridge, 1998),
esp. chapters 2 and 6.

63 The most popular historical figures in present-day Ukraine were the Cossack hetman Bohdan Khmel'nyts'kyi and Russian tsar Peter I ("the Great"

in Russian accounts). Lilia Utkina, "Back to the USSR," *Ukrażns'ka pravda,* Jan. 14, 2003; Ivan Smishko, "Ukraïnets' – tse zvuchyt' zahadkovo," *Postup,* Jan. 16–22, 2003.

64 Andrew Wilson, "The Donbass between Ukraine and Russia: The Use of History in Political Debates," *Journal of Contemporary History,* XXX, 2 (Chicago, 1995), pp. 265-289.

65 The research projects described at the outset of this chapter consisted of six focus groups, three in L'viv and three in Donets'k. The groups were balanced according to gender, age, and language differecnes. Participants were asked by the end of the discussion to select historical figures and events that they thought were important for their understanding of history and to evaluate them positively or negatively.

66 See *Ï: nezalezhnyi kul'torolohichnyi chasopys,* no. 23 (L'viv, 2001), a special issue dedicated to the idea of a Ukrainian federative republic.

67 Vasyl' Rasevych, "Avstriis'ki ukraïntsi mizh natsional'noiu ideieiu ta impers'koiu loial'nistiu," *Postup,* May 30, 2000.

68 See the catalogue of his recent exhibition, *Ares ta Eros: vystavka Volodymyra Kostyrka* (Leopolis [*sic*], 2002).

69 *Personofikatsiia Halychyny* (L'viv, 2000).

70 The issue to what extent the image of democratic and market-orentied Galicia represents the everyday reality is beyond the scope of our study. The recent study claims, however, that social capital both in L'viv and Donets'k is very similar. See Martin Åberg, "Putnam's Social Capital Theory Goes East: A Case Study of Western Ukraine and L'viv," *Europe-Asia Studies,* LII, 2 (2000), pp. 295–317.

71 Andriy Zayarnyuk, "On the Frontiers of Central Europe: Ukrainian Galicia at the Turn of the Millennium," Spaces of Identity (http://www.univie. ac.at/spacesofidentity/Vol_1). For a similar reinterpretatation of the Habsburg past in post-Communist Polish Galicia, see Jadwiga Kowalikowa, "Słowo – Galicja – dawniej i dziś, czylo habent sua fata verba," in Halina Kurek and, Franciszka Teleszkiewicza, eds., *Inteligencja południowo-wschodnich ziem polskich* (Cracow, 1998), pp. 211–219.

11 The Limits of Galician Syncretism: Pluralism, Multiculturalism, and the Two Catholicisms

CHRIS HANN

The last two chapters have addressed the continuing significance of Habsburg Galicia, both mythical and non-mythical, more than three-quarters of a century after its collapse. Since the 1940s, which saw genocide, the establishment of a new frontier between Poland and Ukraine, and massive population transfers, the ethnic composition of this region has been basically stable. To all appearances, the principle of the nation-state has triumphed. On the Polish side of the border the population declares itself overwhelmingly to be of Polish ethnicity, while on the Ukrainian side the self-identification is Ukrainian. The Jews have all but disappeared from both states.

Yet in spite of communist destruction, visible markers of the multicultured past remain, for example, in neglected cemeteries and dilapidated churches and synagogues now used for secular purposes. Moreover, a few pockets of ethnic diversity have survived the perturbations caused by violent nationalism. This final chapter concentrates on one such locality, the city of Przemyśl, whose role in the Ruthenian national movement was explored by Stanisław Stępień in Chapter 4. Since 1945 this city, previously always a kind of center, has been rendered marginal: it is located a mere twelve kilometers from the Ukrainian border. The analysis derives from a field project in social anthropology, but the microstudy is intended to illuminate the larger issues raised throughout this volume. The nature of Galician society before 1918 is of more than local, antiquarian significance. What does it mean to speak of Galicia as a multicultured land? What kind of intermingling or cohabitation of peoples does this describe?

A precise answer would vary from one district to another and from one historical period to another, and would depend on who was asked. In very general terms it seems reasonable to begin with some negative observations. The linguistic, religious, and general cultural profile of Galicia developed over centuries. This took place under conditions quite different from those pertaining in, say, North America or western European countries, which today have large immigrant minorities – the sort of states with which the term multiculturalism is currently associated. There are some resemblances, of course, especially if attention is concentrated on major urban centers. However, in the centuries preceding the era of nationalism the basic social context for the intermingling of groups was different.

Pluralism may be a less value-laden term than multiculturalism. Habsburg Galicia during the period in which modern nationalisms emerged resembled more an Ottoman province than, say, contemporary Canada or the Netherlands. The pluralism of Ottoman society was rooted in religious rather than other cultural or ethnic differences. Muslims were the dominant *millet* (religiously defined collectivity), and the case of Ottoman Bosnia-Herzegovina illustrates the advantages that came through belonging to it. But alongside this dominant *millet*, other groups were able to sustain their non-Muslim identities over the centuries. Anthropologist Michael E. Meeker has argued that the diverse peoples of the Ottoman Empire were united by a common political culture and "common philosophy of citizenship."[1] Might it be possible, by analogy, to identify a common Habsburg philosophy of citizenship and to see how it played out in Galicia?

Alternatively, it can be argued that deep and irreconcilable differences precluded any possibility for the establishment of a single overarching, or unifying political culture in the empire of the Habsburgs. Samuel Huntington follows a long line of scholars in taking Eastern and Western Christianity to be the two sides of a fundamental civilizational divide in Europe.[2] Habsburg Galicia, of course, straddles this divide. While Huntington himself classifies the province as a whole as belonging to the West and emphasizes the significance of the church unions, Paul Robert Magocsi reminds us (this volume: Chapter 1) that "historic Galicia" was predominantly Orthodox. What light does the disintegration of Habsburg Galicia in 1918, followed by the dramatic consolidation of more homogenized national cultures in Poland and Ukraine in the 1940s, shed on Huntington's theses? Now, at the beginning of the twenty-first century, Poland's admission to the European Union and the extension of the "Schengen boundary" to the frontier with Ukraine is threatening to entrench a sharp line of division in a territory that, until the 1940s, was a zone of interstitial fuzziness.[3]

Under Communism, Ukrainians and Poles could not easily visit each other's countries. They were brought up to imbibe national narratives in which the history of cities like L'viv and Przemyśl was played out in the shadows of Kiev and Warsaw respectively. These developments would seem to support a view that is both less fashionable in the social sciences and less attractive morally. After the disappearance of Galicia, its East Slavs eventually found their way into an East Slavic state (Ukraine), its West Slavs into a West Slavic state (Poland). Its Jews were killed, and the few who managed to survive moved to other continents. Contrary to those who emphasize the importance of common political and administrative structures in the formation of modern states, what happened after the demise of the Habsburg regime in Galicia seems to confirm that linguistic and other cultural factors are more significant. Was the cohabitation of peoples that characterized Galacia somehow fake or, at best, a thin veneer? If, over the long run, Habsburg political and administrative institutions did not manage to bridge the pre-existing "cultural fault line," was any other force capable of doing so?[4]

The Greek Catholic Church was the principal candidate for the role of unifying cultural agent. Before, during, and after the lifetime of Habsburg Galicia it provided a unique bridge across the fault line between East and West. Huntington classifies this church as part of the civilization of the West, on the basis of four centuries of institutional integration and exposure to "western values." Indeed, he entertains the possibility that Ukraine could split along the east-west axis defined by the historical border between the Greek Catholics and the Orthodox.[5] Whereas the recent revival of "Galicia" is largely a matter of myth-making and irony, with the re-emergence of the Greek Catholics we are concerned more directly with material realities. They form the largest church in western Ukraine and the second largest in Ukraine as a whole. In Poland, Greek Catholics are a minority, numbering a total of 123,000 people nationwide (according to official statistics for 2000). Because of the deportations of the 1940s, more than half now live outside what was their Galician homeland, scattered across western and northern Poland. Nevertheless the Greek Catholic Church, now known as the Ukrainian Catholic Church of the Byzantine Rite, has been reconstituted under a new metropolitan with his seat at Przemyśl, where it tends to be viewed by some local Poles as a manifestation of an unwelcome eastern civilization.

These recent developments will be examined below, drawing on research in and around Przemyśl in the 1990s. First, however, we will briefly consider the history of this religious community, not only in the context of its unique position between East and West but also in terms of a continuous tension between its elites and the mass of the faithful, most of whom not all that long ago were peasants.

Two Kinds of Catholics: Difference, Hybridity, and Inequality in Historic Galicia

In his comparative study of South Asia and the Balkans, Robert Hayden uses the term *antagonistic tolerance* in characterizing how different communities in these societies share the same places of worship.[6] He demonstrates that the presence of elements of syncretism, mutual borrowing of religious practises, and even beliefs, does not entail a spirit of multiculturalism in the modern sense. It is possible to share a common religious space and to worship at the same shrine, while preserving a certain distance, competition, and even antagonism toward groups other than one's own. In examining the history of peaceful coexistence in Bosnia, Hayden notes the measures taken by successive new rulers to privilege their own faith. Tolerance can develop in such settings. But this tolerance is not the positive embracing of the Other, in the modern liberal sense, which Hayden traces back to John Stuart Mill. Rather, this is a "negative tolerance," a concept which he links to John Locke. Communities do accept one another's right to be where they are and to worship as they do. Syncretism is common. But there is also a keen awareness of boundaries and a reluctance to intermarry.

Hayden's analysis concentrates on shared shrines at the interface between Islam and other religious traditions. The specifics of his work are not directly pertinent to the case of Galicia, but his broader themes certainly are. The mobilization of religion in the service of modern nationalism ruptures traditions of pluralism everywhere. More specifically, the old forms of coexistence and sharing seem to be incompatible with the new ideal, which holds that the coexisting communities should be *equal*. Let us now turn to explore these suggestions in the context of the two – or two and a half – Christian traditions of Galicia.[7] The long-term background has already been examined in this volume in Chapter 2, by John-Paul Himka. Little is known about the early centuries of Christianity in the Przemyśl region. Perhaps there was a fluid period of missionization in which Eastern and Western churches were genuinely balanced. Nevertheless, Himka reminds us that Galicia originated as a Rus' state, oriented to the east. Over the centuries there was an ebb and flow of tolerance and antagonism, depending on the political circumstances of the time, but it would appear that, put in Hayden's terms, such tolerance as existed was always of the negative type.

In 1596, the Union of Brest brought many Eastern (Orthodox) Christians of the region into communion with the Catholic Church of Rome. The Catholic Church uses many rites, and it was not the intention of either the statesmen or clergymen who promoted the Union to require the Orthodox faithful to change their religious practices. For Eastern bishops in the negotiations that preceded Brest, conservation of the traditional forms of worship was the most important consideration.[8] The only changes required of them were acknowledgement of papal authority and a few changes on points of theology (notably concerning the *Filioque*) which were of no concern to the masses.[9] However, our immediate concern is not theology but, rather, the importance of religion for group identity and for popular culture. We will proceed from the assumption that, in a borderland region such as Przemyśl, processes of exchanging religious ideas and practices were under way all the time. This was so long before the Union of Brest, before the Union of Florence (1439), indeed, before 1054 and the Great Schism itself.

In Galicia, loyalty to Orthodoxy ensured that the Union of Brest was not fully implemented for approximately a century. The Commonwealth of Poland and Lithuania was dominated by Roman Catholics, and incentives were offered to Orthodox bishops to accept the Union. Undoubtedly, church union was perceived by some Orthodox as unwelcome, but nonetheless preferable to the most likely alternative, which would have been pressure to convert to the Latin rite. Resistance was considerable, and the Eparchy of Przemyśl did not definitively accept the Union until 1692. Through the years, Orthodox churches have consistently viewed all church unions as an attack on the Eastern tradition, designed ultimately to lead to conversion to the Latin rite. This interpretation was reiterated in Marxist terminology by Soviet historians in justifying Stalin's liquidation of the Greek Catholic Church in 1946.[10] It was also accepted in the Communist period by many former Greek Catholics. They defended their new allegiance to the Orthodox Church on the ground that this is the original church of all East Slavs. More than a decade after the collapse of Communism, there are still many people who upheld this principle (cf. Jepsen: this volume, Chapter 5).

One of the many fascinations of the Greek Catholics is the following.

Their church was obviously established "from above," as a result primarily of the political and material calculations of elites at the time, although certainly some of them may also have been motivated by deeply held aspirations to Christian unity. Over the centuries, however, the Greek Catholic Church has been modified and continuously reshaped "from below." The loyalty that this church has attracted, which has been abundantly demonstrated in the post-Communist years, proves that it has deep roots in particular cultural communities. Successive elites have attempted to channel this evolutionary process. Yet, always, in addition to facing the prevailing institutional and political constraints, in Greek Catholic communities elites also had to contend with the accumulated loyalties and sentiments of the masses who were the cultural carriers of this confessional tradition. This applies to all those who have tried to influence or to standardize the traditions of the Greek Catholic Church. Whatever the particular direction desired by the elite – whether towards western, Latin practices, purer eastern forms, endorsement of Ukrainian national aspirations, or integration into the Polish state, the outcome necessarily depended on the reactions and "agency" of other groups.

The basic conditions of unequal power within which processes of interaction unfolded in Galicia after 1596 are found in many other parts of the world. Anthropologists tend to speak of acculturation rather than imperialism and to use terms such as *syncretic* and *hybrid* to describe the outcomes. There is the danger that these terms may be taken to imply that, at some point before the interaction began, pure forms of an unchanging religious culture existed on either side.[11] Neither Polish Roman Catholicism nor East Slav Orthodoxy was an unadulterated religious culture; rather, both were complex evolving traditions that had influenced each other over centuries before the Union of Brest. Provided we recognize this fact, it may nonetheless be useful to speak of syncretism and hybridity in the particular case under examination. The crucial question is the following: to what extent was the Greek Catholic Church able to establish a body of practices that it could claim as its own, distinct from both Orthodox and Latin traditions, and thus form a "culture in between" capable of transcending that dualism?

Power disparities, particularly regarding the status and educational levels of the clergy, favored the Roman Catholics. Thus, perhaps it was inevitable that the popular religious culture of the Eastern tradition would come under pressure, particularly in areas of mixed population such as Przemyśl. To describe these processes, I follow historian August Fenczak in preferring the term *occidentalization* to the more familiar *latinization*.[12] It was not just a question of the Latin rite displacing the Byzantine rite, but one of increased exposure to western influence having diffuse insidious effects on the beliefs and practises of the Eastern Church. István Molnár provides many examples from the seventeenth and eighteenth centuries. These include changes to church buildings both internally (such as removing the iconostasis) and externally (such as the addition of steeples).[13] Molnár pays particular attention to the role played by the Basilian Order and the many priests who, on returning from their studies abroad, imported western cultural elements. The Basilian Order was popular with Poles because it could offer them quicker career advancement than the Roman Catholic monastic orders could. The language of communication among Greek Catholic clergy until well into the nineteenth century was most often Polish. Moreover, ethnic Poles were prominent at the highest level of the church even in the first half of the twentieth century. Ecclesiastical vocabulary changed to conform to normal Western usage: the Eastern *vladyka*, for example, became the *biskup*. Pressure on the clergy to adopt celibacy, which became widespread only in the twentieth century, can also be seen as an example of occidentalization.

Yet western cultural imperialism is not the whole story. A closer scrutiny of the processes of reception and reaction reveals a more complex picture. In addition to the actions and reactions of clerical elites, we need to recognize the agency of the peasant masses. How else can one explain the rapid dissemination of many distinctive features of Western Catholicism, including pilgrimages, cults of relics, popular icons, and miraculous images of Mary? Top-down directives do not account for these, which spread because they met pastoral needs. Indeed, the clergy disapproved of popular icons – such as those produced in large numbers in the eighteenth century at Rybotychi/ Rybotycze, near Przemyśl.[14] Yet these and other "folk" traditions appear to have acquired their own authenticity for the masses. Meanwhile, at the "high culture" end of the spectrum, it seems hardly likely that Greek Catholics believed the Rococo style of their most famous building, St George's Cathedral in L'viv, to be a foreign imposition.

Unequal power relations led continuously to competition and conflict between Roman Catholic and Greek Catholic clergy, as a reading of Hayden's comparative material would lead us to expect. In the seventeenth century, Roman Catholic clergy were reluctant to recognize the sacraments administered by Greek Catholic clergy.[15] The Synod of Zamość (1720) addressed the feeble condition of the latter. Thereafter, their educational standards improved significantly and a sort of modus vivendi developed at all levels. For example, baptism and marriage were expected to take place within one's own church, but confession and communion could readily be made in the other rite. The use of different calendars allowed for participation in each other's main religious holidays, although we do not know how widespread this practice was. We do know that some Christmas carols mixed the Polish and Ukrainian languages, or existed in two forms. This allowed carollers to perform in the language of the household they were in.[16]

The emergence of Greek Catholicism meant that Eastern and Western Christian communities had a common leader in Rome and shared both Catholic theology, and many religious practises. Yet the Greek Catholics had a perennial dilemma, and some of the seventeenth-century protests against occidentalization resembled those put forward at the end of the twentieth century. Basically, the position was this: if union with Rome means attenuation of the distinctive rite of the Eastern Christian tradition, then the Orthodox will be repelled by such union. This problem challenged even the most celebrated of Greek Catholic clergymen. Some of them felt obliged to reaffirm ideal forms of Eastern practice, but this exposed them, in turn, to the criticism that they were copying the Orthodox and perhaps even substituting Russian influence for Polish.

In the years between 1596 and 1772 Eastern and Western Catholics in Galicia did not come to share shrines. But, like the communities examined by Hayden, the two Catholicisms in Galicia coexisted in structural inequality. The Greek Catholics were the "second class Catholics." As a symbol of the inequality of the communities, we may note the geographical segregation of the congregations. In places such as Przemyśl (see Chapter 3 in this volume, by Jerzy Motylewicz) the local Greek Catholic Church was displaced to a site outside the city walls. Meanwhile, the Roman Catholics dominated the historic center, even adding several monastic foundations to their old cathedral. Nevertheless, despite political opposition to the Union, in the period that followed "syncretism from below"[17] continued on the pattern of previous centuries, probably at an accelerated pace. The details of this community coexistence remain, however, poorly researched. Little is known concerning intermarriage or participation in the rituals of the other congregation.

Habsburg Antisyncretism: The Politics of Confrontational Equality

Syncretic tendencies initially continued after Galicia came under Habsburg rule in 1772. As in earlier centuries, when impositions by the elite were not welcome they could be rejected, modified, or transformed. The Cracow ethnographer Roman Reinfuss described a case of syncretism from below in which Greek Catholics in the Lemko region, which is the southwestern part of the Przemyśl eparchy, appropriated their church. In 1805 a new stone church, designed in the Western style, was erected. It had been commissioned by the dominant local landowner, who was a Polish noble. This building was imposed on the people in place of earlier Greek Catholic wooden church. In a major reconstruction in 1864, however, the priest and the parishioners moved the main altar away from the church wall and also added three cupolas and an iconostasis to the church.[18]

Similar processes unfolded regarding the structure and form of services. Over time, many Latin forms entered the Greek Catholic liturgy and the Polish language crept into hymn singing. Despite a continuing trend to hybridity, in their ritual calendar liturgies, and buildings, Greek Catholics remained distinct from the Roman Catholics and largely indistinguishable from the Orthodox.

Habsburg rule brought with it a new political constellation. It set set in motion forces that reaffirmed the cultural fault line as the strength of nationalist movements and "antisyncretists" increased.[19] When the eighteenth century ended, no one was yet thinking in modern national terms. No nationalist tendencies were to be seen among Greek Catholics in the Lemko region. They sang hymns imploring the miraculous image of the Mother of God at the Franciscan Monastery in Przemyśl to protect them from the depredations of invaders from the East – such as Khmel'nyts'kyi's Zaporozhian Cossacks. This indicates that they seem to have identified with the West.[20] By the end of the nineteenth century a different picture had emerged and the Greek Catholics of Central Europe were condemned to follow one of three paths. In the Russian Empire, they lost their religion to tsarist violence but were otherwise able to preserve their language and culture. In the Kingdom of Hungary the situation was more complex. There Greek Catholics were able to preserve their religion, but many sacrificed their language as they assimilated into Hungarian society. Only the Greek Catholics of Galicia managed to preserve and consolidate both their religion and their language. This can be largely explained in terms of the political context.

The Austrian regime found it convenient, even before the "ethniciza-tion" which set in at the end of the nineteenth century, to play off the new East Slav nationalism against the more developed nationalism of the Poles in Western Galicia, while at the same time clamping down heavily on Russophilism. Thanks in particular to the work of John-Paul Himka, the role of the Greek Catholic Church in the development of Ukrainian nationalism is relatively well understood.[21] The develop-ment of Ukrainian as a literary language gave the clergy an alternative to Polish (see also chapter 4 in this volume, by Stanisław Stępień). In many localities, at least in the early period, the crucial disseminators of the new nationalism were the clergy. I the new context, certainly from 1848 onward, such cultural bases as may have existed for a unifying Habsburg philosophy of citizenship became progressively weaker. No possibility remained for a single transethnic movement to liberate a *region*, Galicia, in face of a plurality of monoethnic movements seeking to liberate *nations*.

Initially, the new secular movements had little impact on the long-term syncretic tendencies of the Greek Catholics. This hybridization peaked in 1891, when the Synod of L'viv approved a "Ruthenian rite" incorporating many Latin customs. The spread of Sacred Heart cults among Greek Catholics is the clearest illustration of the continued pop-ularity of the West in the East. However, over the half century following the Synod of L'viv the forces of differentiation asserted themselves with ever more vigor.[22] The church of Andrei Sheptyts'kyi (metropolitan between 1900 and 1944) reaffirmed its Eastern character. At the same time, it continued to perform a careful balancing act. Sheptyts'kyi was aware that many of the elements alleged to be Latin were not seen to be "alien intrusions" by the masses. On the contrary, at the grassroots level these elements had been thoroughly appropriated. Practises such as devotion to the Blessed Mother were not to be seen as latinizations, he argued, but as manifestations of universal messages for which ap-propriate Eastern forms could be found. This made Sheptyts'kyi an in-between figure. On one side were men like Cyrille Korolevskij (Korolevs'kyi), who were strident in their criticisms of Uniatism. On the other, bishops Hryhorii Khomyshyn (Stanyslaviv) and Iosafat Kotsylovs'kyi (Przemyśl) were no less opposed to what they called "Byzantinism" and the unnecessary (as they saw it) removal of the accu-mulated Latin elements.[23]

The Greek Catholic Church's increasing entanglement with Ukrai-nian nationalism led to new problems, new reactions, and new local appropriations. An added complication was that there were Greek Catholics who considered themselves to be ethnically Polish; some of them had made major contributions to Polish intellectual life.[24] Eventually, however, this combination of identities became untenable. The Latynnyky (Ukrainians who practised the Latin rite) also disappeared, because non-compatible religious orientations could not withstand the growing influence of secular nationalism. There was, however, much local variation. In the Lemko Region west of the San River, for example, many thousands of Greek Catholics, in their vigorous espousal of an "Old Ruthenian" identity and in their conversions to Orthodoxy, showed distaste for the new nationalism. Influences coming from emigrants in North America, not to say from anti-Ukrainian circles in interwar Polish society, also played a role here. There can be little doubt that the intensifying association of the Greek Catholic Church with a national cause was an alienating experience for some of the faithful.

In mixed communities such as Krasiczyn, close to Przemyśl, at the grassroots level the Greek Catholic hybrid of Christian culture continued to have a genuinely "interethnic" character. In these communities, "ethnic division did not indicate an absolute cultural barrier."[25] High rates of intermarriage between Roman Catholics and Greek Catholics persisted right down to World War II. Religious differences could persist inside mixed households, with children following the confession of their same-sex parent. This suggests more than a modus vivendi, more than simply a "mosaic" of cultures.[26]

It is ironic that the practical intertwining of the two Christian communities probably reached its peak at precisely the same time in history when their elites, especially the new secular elites, were emphasizing irreconcilable differences. The nature of Galician pluralism underwent a fundamental change during the Habsburg period. Galician pluralism was no longer based on the structural supremacy of the West but rather, in keeping with modern, liberal understandings, on assumptions of equality. Eastern-rite Catholics were now accorded the same rights and status as Roman Catholics, including the right to speak for and to mobilize a nation. Unlike its hierarchical predecessor, however, this late Habsburg model of pluralism was inherently unstable. Symbolic evidence of this change can be found in Przemyśl. Emperor Joseph II had expressed his sympathy for the second-class Catholics of this city in 1784, when he transferred to them a "prime site" baroque church, confiscated a few years earlier from the (Roman Catholic) Carmelite order. The Greek

Catholics proceeded to consolidate their presence in the center of the old town. They constructed a magnificent palace for their bishop, and other fine buildings as well, right beside the long-standing ecclesiastical complexes of the Roman Catholics. Confessional intertwining could hardly have been more complete. Yet, in 1918, in hand-to-hand street battles, comparable to those that took place on a larger scale in L'viv (see Chapter 8 in this volume, by Anna Veronika Wendland). The two types of Catholics fought each other on the streets for control of the city.

Post-pluralist Aftershocks in Przemyśl[27]

The Polish victory in 1918 was the opening act in the outright dismemberment of Galician pluralism. Tensions mounted during the interwar decades. The two Catholic churches remained locked in an uneasy embrace in the center of Przemyśl, but the relationship ceased to be one of even nominal equality. By no means were all Greek Catholic clergy were committed nationalists. Indeed, a perceived lack of strong national identification made Bishop Kotsylovs'kyi of Przemyśl unpopular with some of his own priests in the interwar period.[28] The general trend, however, was clear. The Warsaw authorities secured the establishment of a separate apostolic administration for the Lemko region, in an effort to prevent the further dissemination of Ukrainian nationalism.

In the space of a few years, in the 1940s, Przemyśl was transformed from what had long been a city with three ethnoreligious components, roughly equal in strength, into a city that was – at least theoretically – exclusively Polish and Roman Catholic.[29] The Greek Catholics lost all of their property, as they did in Ukraine. After the crisis of 1956, however, the Polish People's Republic de facto tolerated small communities that, by now, were scattered all over the country. This negative tolerance allowed some Greek Catholics to return to their homeland in the southeast. Przemyśl's Greek Catholic parish was re-formed. Under Roman Catholic auspices, the congregation could gather at what had formerly been the Jesuit church, also known as the Garrison church. This was the only period in which the two Catholicisms shared the use of one and the same building. As in Hayden's model, this sharing was predicated on structural inequality. The building, after all, was unambiguously owned by the Roman Catholics alone. Also in 1956, a branch of the Ukrainian Civic and Cultural Society was established in Przemyśl by those who somehow had managed to avoid the deportations or arrange an early return to their home region. Together, parish and club made the city a popular choice for later returnees. Their number has increased steadily. Even so, this minority comprises nowadays no more than about 2,000 among a population of approximately 70,000 for the city as a whole. The extent to which the Ukrainian language can be used in the public sphere has remained extremely limited, even after the end of the Communist period.[30]

Few among the new Ukrainian minority are natives of Przemyśl. What used to be their village homes were allocated to Polish settlers. In any case, many who settled in the city after 1956 were no longer peasants but well-qualified professionals. They included Orthodox as well as Greek Catholics. In 1985, the Communist state helped an Orthodox parish establish itself. It was based at a former Greek Catholic church on the outskirts of town. But Greek Catholics predominated, and they were identified by the majority surrounding them strongly with the Ukrainian national cause. At least some of the people deported from this region in the 1940s still had no pronounced national self-identification at that time. Those who chose to return to Przemyśl, however, generally had a strong commitment to the Ukrainian nation. To them, the Greek Catholic Church was a vital component in their national culture.

Their attitudes and aspirations could not be articulated in the public sphere while the Communist regime was in power. After the transformations of 1989, however, Greek Catholics joined the general campaigns for retribution and compensation. In doing so, they quickly provoked controversy and opposition from the Roman Catholic majority, some elements of which were unwilling to agree to any revival of pluralist traditions in Przemyśl. The Ministry of Culture in Warsaw decided, for example, to relocate the biennial Festival of Ukrainian Culture from the Baltic coast to Przemyśl. This would make it much more accessible to visitors from Ukraine. This move was opposed by Polish nationalists at the local level, who wanted no such opening. The festival did take place in the city in 1995 and 1997, but against an unpleasant backdrop of anti-Ukrainian campaigns and a strong security presence. The efforts of both sides to honor their dead from the 1940s – the kind of commemoration that had not been possible during the four decades of Communist rule – also contributed to a sharpening of hostilities. Greek Catholic property claims were obstructed. Their former seminary was returned to them. A church that had been confiscated, and that for decades served as a secular archive, was handed back to the Basilian Order. The return of the Greek Catholic bishop's palace, however, was long delayed. Przemyśl municipal officials argued that the new Ukrainian Catholic bishop had no binding claim to a building that had been erected in the "Galician period," when no Ukrainian church as such existed.[31]

At the center of the struggles for a new multiculturalism in Przemyśl was the contestation of a particular church. Here I shall only summarize a complicated story that I have told in more detail elsewhere.[32] Early in 1991, the pope appointed a new Greek Catholic bishop to the See of Przemyśl. Local Greek Catholics pressed their claims for the restitution of the cathedral church, taken from them by force in 1946. These claims – and even a compromise negotiated by bishops of both rites, which would have involved the old cathedral church being returned for a five-year period until a new one was built – were rejected outright by Roman Catholic Polish nationalists. This building had been originally constructed in 1630 for the benefit of the Carmelite Order, they argued, and used by the Roman Catholics for a long time before its transfer to the Greek Catholics by Joseph II in 1784. Therefore, according to this argument, the Carmelites were entitled to keep their property, even if it had only come back into their possession because the Communists took it away by force from the Greek Catholics. No one suggested that the two sister churches might share the building.

The controversies were resolved not by historians or an ethics committee. Instead, by a Roman Catholic activist group set up barricades and led hunger strikes. These extremists succeeded in preventing the pope from fulfilling the wish he had expressed to worship with the Greek Catholics in their former cathedral church during his pilgrimage to the city in June 1991. Nevertheless, John-Paul II took local Roman Catholics by surprise. He made the former Jesuit church, dedicated to the Sacred Heart of Jesus, a permanent gift to the Greek Catholics. This was the church that Greek Catholics had been using, on an unofficial basis, ever since the re-establishment of their parish under Roman Catholic protection in 1956.

The Carmelite church occupies a conspicuous hilltop site in the center of Przemyśl. It remained at the center of tense minority-majority relations for several more years. The main bone of contention was the church's large central tower and cupola, which dominates the city skyline (see Plate 1). The same Roman Catholic activists who had prevented the building from being returned to the Greek Catholics now argued that certain nineteenth-century alterations to the church were alien intrusions. They called them "eastern" symbols and launched a campaign for restoration of the building to its authentic "western" design.

1 The church of the Carmelites in Przemyśl, which between 1784 and 1946 served as the cathedral church of the Greek Catholics (photo by C. Hann, 1994).

Some of the activists brought forward spurious technical arguments to the effect that the tower and cupola were structurally unsound. It is clear, however, that their motivation was to rid their city of what they considered to be polluting eastern elements. As with the ownership claims, the issue was eventually settled through complex political maneuvering and force majeure. In flagrant breach of instructions from the national conservation officer, the local conservation officer (a former Communist who was working closely with the Polish nationalists) authorized the destruction of the tower and cupola. His superior in Warsaw had made the observation that, far from being an intrusion from the East, the tower and cupola were additions modeled on Saint Peter's Basilica in Rome. In other words, the additions were, in fact, an example of occidentalization. But that is not how they were understood – by either side – in Przemyśl. The destruction of the tower and the cupola was completed in 1996, in the 400th anniversary year of the Union of Brest (see Plates 2 and 3). There were no large-scale celebrations of this anniversary in Przemyśl. Even though the city is the principal center of a Greek Catholic rite for all of Poland and since 1996 the seat of the metropolitan, its community of 400 families was not strong enough to counter the weight of the Polish nationalist groups.

Later, the controversies shifted to the former Jesuit church, which has been converted into the Greek Catholic Cathedral Church of Saint John the Baptist. This process involved painstaking discussions with the local conservation officer. Redecoration of the interior was completed in 1997. Eastern paintings, stained glass, Cyrillic inscriptions and a large iconostasis were introduced without altering the fabric of the building. The Baroque exterior proved to be more contentious. The Greek Catholics wanted to remove the prominent symbol of the Jesuit Order from the center of the facade, as well as the Latin inscription *Gloria Sacratissimo Cordi Jesu*. (See Plates 4 and 5). Now that the church was no longer dedicated to the Sacred Heart of Jesus, a cult which has no place in Eastern Christianity strictly speaking (although as already noted, it later grew popular among Greek Catholics), the Greek Catholics wanted to substitute a text in Cyrillic proclaiming the new name of the church and revealing its religious affiliation. They also proposed changes in the color of the roof tiles, the positioning of new statues of the Eastern saints – and medieval "Ukrainian" political heroes – Olga and Volodymyr, and a new belltower.[33] The Greek Catholics pointed out that this would not be the first time that changes had been made to the building: the inscription and Jesuit symbol were themselves additions made during a major

2 The tower is demolished, 1996 (photo courtesy of Stanisław Stępień).

3 The Carmelite church with its new "western" spire, 1997
(photo courtesy of Stanisław Stępień)

4 The former Garrison church in Przemyśl, originally built by the Jesuits
(photo by C. Hann, 1998).

5 The same façade after renovation, following the transfer of this church to become the new Greek Catholic Cathedral (photo by C. Hann, 2000).

renovation carried out in 1904. But the Polish media cited Polish academics, who expressed their conviction that these proposals would have an "aggressive" impact on the Przemyśl skyline.[34] Polish nationalists argued that to remove the inscription would be to insult the people, all Roman Catholic Poles, who had funded and worked on the earlier renovation. One "expert" presented the conflict as one between "Catholics" and "Uniates." This person was apparently oblivious of the fact that the latter are also Catholics.[35] Professor Jerzy Kowalczyk of the Polish Academy of Sciences came out against the Greek Catholic proposal, reportedly arguing that "a cathedral cannot be a hybrid, a mixture of Eastern and Western elements."[36]

These very recent struggles to establish multiculturalism in post-Communist Przymśl bring us back to the heart of the matter. In the Galician past, the Greek Catholic Church had been able over a long period to develop as a hybrid, a genuine and creative syncretic fusion of Eastern and Western elements. But from the mid-nineteenth century and throughout the course of the twentieth, it grew increasingly difficult to defend hybrids of any sort. Within the Greek Catholic Church pressure again built up, now with support even in Rome, calling for a return to the "pure" Eastern forms of ritual. The use of bells and the monstrance, as well as other "western" practices such as kneeling during mass and to receive communion have, over the centuries, become part of the religious *habitus* of Greek Catholics. Imagine the dismay of elderly people who, when their church could finally emerge from the catacombs in western Ukraine, found that its clergy had been instructed not to allow these features – but instead to be even more "Eastern" than their rival Orthodox churches. In these circumstances, it is hardly surprising that some divisive splits have emerged within the church. In large cities such as L'viv it is possible to choose one's preferred style. Those who care about the *Filioque* can attend a church where a Basilian priest is sure to include it. This church is likely to have some features distinguishing it from an Orthodox church; but, externally at least, one *tserkva* resembles another, and all are readily distinguished from western churches.[37] By contrast, in Przemyśl and elsewhere in Poland, the vulnerable minority status of the church has helped to keep such conflicts in check. The liturgy is now standardized, although here, too, there is local variation in singing, seating, and kneeling customs. Some priests show more tolerance than others concerning these centuries-old accretions.

The most important characteristic of the Greek Catholic Church in the Przemyśl region, from the later Habsburg period to the present day, is its identification with the Ukrainian nationality. It does not matter that in Poland, as in Ukraine, more Ukrainians are Orthodox than Greek Catholic. What does matter is that a Greek Catholic is a Ukrainian. In Ukraine this continues to contribute to a significant East-West division (see Chapter 10, by Yaroslav Hrytsak). There are still some links between the Greek Catholic Church and the extreme nationalist currents that flourished down to the 1940s. In Poland this relationship is now expressed in the name itself, the Ukrainian Catholic Church of the Byzantine Rite, even if informally everyone continues to speak of Greek Catholics. In both countries the national identity of the church is expressed through the general use of literary Ukrainian, although there is some variation at the parish level, particularly in the Lemko region. Many adherents in Przemyśl express dismay at any suggestion that their priests should switch to Polish for the sermon. They do know, of course, that this would make the message more accessible, especially to the youngest generation, many of whom have only a weak command of Ukrainian.[38] Throughout what used to be Galicia, as well as further afield, whether in Canadian Toronto or Polish Gdańsk, the Greek Catholic Church is today a symbol of the Ukrainian people and their national and cultural aspirations.

The old pluralism of Galicia has gone, and a new multiculturalism has yet to establish itself. Yet, it is not as if no possible basis for ecumenism exists in the lands that once constituted Galicia. Despite the politicking over various church buildings in the 1990s, it is now common for Roman Catholics in Przemyśl to join members of the Greek Catholic congregation in its procession through the city and to the banks of the River San for the annual *Jordan* (Epihany) rituals on January 19. The Roman Catholic archbishop sets an example by joining his Greek Catholic counterpart as a co-celebrant throughout this feast. This gesture is reciprocated by the Greek Catholic metropolitan on Corpus Christi Day, when many Greek Catholics join Roman Catholics in their public procession to mark the city's most important patronal feast. This sort of reciprocal courtesy may formerly have been common in Galician regions that had mixed populations. Today it is the exception rather than the rule, because the context is determined not by a common Habsburg philosophy of citizenship but by highly sensitive majority-minority relations in two sovereign states. The present Roman Catholic archbishop in Przemyśl is committed to improving relations with Greek Catholics. But the Greek Catholics can remember that his predecessor did not participate in the Jordan processions, even when it became legal to hold them once again, after 1990. Greek Catholics say that Roman Catholic clergymen, with few exceptions, do not encourage participation in the rituals of the other Catholic rite. In these circumstances it is hardly surprising that the minority community developed something resembling a siege mentality in the years after the collapse of Communism.

Conclusions

István Molnár concluded his history of the Greek Catholic Church in Poland by recalling an observation made by Volodymyr Mokryi in the 1980s. Mokryi is one of perhaps the most widely known Galician-Ukrainian intellectuals in contemporary Poland. He referred to an ethnographic exhibition at which someone sawed off the head of a Lemko wooden sculpture of Christ "because it was a Ukrainian God."[39] Molnár commented that such attitudes no longer prevailed in the 1990s. Yet, as we have seen, in Przemyśl at this very time, Polish nationalists succeeded in destroying the cupola of the building that had for many years symbolized the presence of the Greek Catholic Church in that city.

Molnár also cites a celebration of the Greek Catholic Church by the Polish literary historian Ryszard Łużny. Despite all the problems it brought, Lużny hails the Union of Brest as an "exceptional civilizational experiment."[40] This "experiment," argues Łużny, led to more substantive contacts between the mainstreams of Eastern and Western Christianity than have a myriad of modern ecumenical initiatives. In some obvious and important ways the experiment was, indeed, successful. That the church survived half a century of Communist repression is testimony to its fundamental importance in the lives of many latter-day Galicians. The Greek Catholic Church continues to provide Eastern-rite Christians with links to the West, in terms of theology and education, as well as – although this has always been contested – in terms of practical, popular religion. But syncretism in practical religion and relations of polite reciprocity add up to "negative tolerance," which is a good deal less than the positive variant demanded by modern multiculturalism. The Greek Catholic experiment complicated the earlier East-West divide, but it did not fundamentally alter it. On the contrary, recent events in Przemyśl show clearly that Poland's Ukrainian Catholic Church of the Byzantine Rite is firmly identified, both by its own members and by the Polish mainstream, with the East and with the cause of Ukrainian nationhood. Similarly, the Roman Catholic

Church in Poland is firmly identified, by its own members and everyone else, with the West and with the cause of Polish nationhood. The dualism that exists between the two rites of the Catholic Church seems almost Manichean.

It should not be forgotten that Ukraine nowadays exhibits a strong division between Greek Catholics and the Orthodox (who are themselves deeply divided internally). In the historic heartland of Galicia, Greek Catholics are once again dominant. This is also, as Yaroslav Hrytsak notes in this volume, the region where Ukrainian national consciousness is strongest. The Poles may identify Greek Catholics with the East, but the majority of Ukrainians view them as a western force. Thus, Greek Catholics are in a liminal position, between East and West, belonging to both – and to neither. This brings us back to the question as to why it proved impossible to construct a modern state on the basis of its transethnic Galician traditions, based on long periods of political and economic unity. After all, the world is full of successful examples of state-building of this sort, where linguistic and cultural differences either continue, but play only a minor role in the state, or are altogether transcended. Why is it that this did not happen in the case of Galicia?

The banal explanation is that no one had any interest in trying to construct Galician identity as a basis for statehood. Compared with the Ottomans, the Habsburgs pursued a very different strategy of citizenship, as is evident in the case of the two Catholicisms of Galicia. Elevating Greek Catholics to a position of equality with Roman Catholics was important in the imperial strategy of divide and rule. Pre-existing cultural differences were not necessarily decisive. But, contrary to what is sometimes alleged in strong versions of social constructionism and postmodernism, historical factors limit the scope available to actors to manipulate collective identities. In the case of Galicia, religion was apparently a stronger constraint than language, although not necessarily an insuperable one. The convergence of numerous factors, including the maintenance of religious divisions under the Habsburgs, and the overlapping dioceses of Greek Catholics and Roman Catholics in jurisdictions such as Przemyśl and L'viv fed into the secular national movements that emerged in the nineteenth century, which in turn led to the massive social engineering and "ethnic cleansing" of the twentieth century. Competitive negative tolerance based on inequality gave way, in the later Habsburg period, to intolerance based on aspirations to equality – in both the religious and the secular domains. The old pluralist society disintegrated. Whether a new multiculturalism can emerge in its place remains to be seen. But meanwhile, suppose that Joseph II, instead of merely elevating the status of Greek Catholics, had chosen to impose Eastern-rite Catholicism on all of his new subjects in Galicia. If he had succeeded in such an ambitious project then, in 1918 Przemyśl, owing to its central location, might have been designated the capital of an independent Republic of Galicia. A substantial chunk of territory would today be defying all the attempts of academics, politicians, and bureaucrats to impose a simple East-West classification on the map of Europe.

Notes

1 Michael E. Meeker, "Concepts of Person, Family, and State in the District of Of," in Gabriele Rasuly-Paleczek, ed., *Turkish Families in Transition* (Frankfurt-am-Main, 1996), pp. 45–60; and, *Nation of Empire: the Ottoman Legacy of Turkish Modernity* (Berkeley, 2002).

2 Samuel Huntington, *The Clash of Civilizations and the Remaking of World Order* (New York, 1996).

3 Schengen is a small town in the Grand Duchy of Luxembourg which has given its name (since the original signing of an agreement there in 1985) to comprehensive policies, steadily extended from 1995 onward, aimed at controlling the movement of people into the European Union. As part of its preparations to enter the EU, Poland has committed itself to expanding the Schengen sphere to the western border of Ukraine. Although this will not happen fully until 2006, or later, the negative impact on local border traffic is likely to be considerable and leads some citizens of eastern Poland to question whether the gains they stand to make in terms of easier mobility throughout western Europe outweigh the anticipated losses in terms of the reimposition of visas for travel in the east (as in Communist times) and associated economic losses in the sector of petty cross-border commerce.

4 For the metaphor of a "fault line" see, for example, Serge Keleher, *Passion and Resurrection: The Greek Catholic Church in the Soviet Ukraine, 1939–1989* (L'viv, 1993). For an overview of the long-term historical issues, see Jaroslav Pelikan, "The Church between East and West: The Context of Sheptyts'kyi's Thought," in Paul Robert Magocsi, ed., *Morality and Reality: The Life and Times of Andrei Sheptyts'kyi* (Edmonton, 1989), pp. 1–12.

5 Huntington, *Clash of Civilizations*, pp. 165–168. In Chapter 10 of this volume, Yaroslav Hrytsak suggests that the Huntingtonian model is not so far

removed from reality, at least as perceived by some contemporary intellectuals in western Ukraine.

6 Robert M. Hayden, "Antagonistic Tolerance: Competitive Sharing of Religious Sites in South Asia and the Balkans," in *Current Anthropology*, XLIII, 2 (Chicago, 2002), pp. 205–232.

7 As far as the Jewish community is concerned, it seems evident that even here negative tolerance was by no means always to be taken for granted. Here I restrict the investigation to relations between eastern and western Christian communities, concentrating on the centuries in which both were part of the same 'universal' Catholic Church.

8 Victor J. Pospishil, "Sheptyts'kyi and Liturgical Reform," in Paul Robert Magocsi, ed., *Morality and Reality: The Life and Times of Andrei Sheptyts'kyi* (Edmonton, 1989), pp. 201–225.

9 The main theological points at issue since the Council of Florence (1439) are summarized by Donald Attwater, *The Christian Churches of the East*, vol. I, *Churches in Communion with Rome*, 2nd ed. (London, 1961), p. 12.

10 One of the last studies to provide the Soviet viewpoint is by Ivan Mihovich [Myhovych], *The Truth about the Uniate Church* (Kiev, 1988).

11 See the introduction by the editors in Charles Stewart and Rosalind Shaw, eds., *Syncretism/Anti-Syncretism: The Politics of Religious Synthesis* (London, 1994), pp. 1–24.

12 August Fenczak, "'Amplissum Chrisi Regnum' – wizja jedności Kościoła w pismach teologicznych Stanisława Orzechowskiego z lat 1544–1563," in Stanisław Stępień, ed., *Polska-Ukraina 1000 lat sąsiedztwa*, vol. IV (Przemyśl, 1994), pp. 85–96. See also Fenzak, "Latynizacja czy okcydentalizacja? W sprawie nowych kierunków badań nad rolą wpływów Zachodu na kształtowanie się tożsamości Kościoła greckokatolickiego w Polsce w latach 1595–1772." *Biuletyn PWIN*, no. 1 (Przemyśl, 1995), pp. 46–48.

13 István Molnár, *Vallási kisebbség és kisebbségi vallás: Görögkatolikusok a régi és a mai Lengyelországban* (Budapest, 1995), pp. 38–43, 50–67.

14 Ibid., p. 66.

15 Ibid., Chapter 1.

16 Jurij Medwedyk, "Z dziejów ukraińskiej pieśni religijnej," in Stępień, *Polska-Ukraina*, Vol. II (1994), pp. 397–402.

17 This concept is taken from Birgit Meyer, "Beyond Syncretism: Translation and Diabolization in the Appropriation of Protestantism in Africa," in Stewart and Shaw, *Syncretism/Anti-Syncretism*, pp. 45–68.

18 Roman Reinfuss, *Śladami Łemków* (Warsaw, 1990), p. 25, cited in Molnár, *Vallási kisebbség*, p. 99.

19 This is the term used by Stewart and Shaw, *Syncretism/Anti-Syncretism*.

20 Medwedyk, "Zdziejów," pp. 400–402.
21 On this subject see the many works by John-Paul Himka, esp. "The Greek Catholic Church and Nation-Building in Galicia, 1772–1918," *Harvard Ukrainian Studies*, VIII, 3–4 (Cambridge, Mass., 1984), pp. 426–452; and *Religion and Nationality in Western Ukraine: The Greek Catholic Church and the Ruthenian National Movement in Galicia, 1867–1900* (Montreal and Kingston, 1999).
22 Pospishil, "Sheptyts'kyi."
23 For Stanisław Stępień, Sheptyts'kyi is ultimately a westernizer, because he sought to transform practical religion with a standardized blueprint imposed "from the top down," while his episcopal colleagues in Przemyśl and Stanislaviv preferred a gradual evolution, which paid more attention to the pastoral needs of ordinary people. See S. Stępień, "W poszukiwaniu tożsamości obrządkowej: Bizantynizacja a Okcydentalizacja Kościoła greckokatolickiego w okresie międzywojennym," in Stępień, *Polska-Ukraina*, vol. 5 (2000), pp. 87–102.
24 Andrzej Zięba, "Polacy grekokatolicy: rzeczywistość historyczna czy mit polityczny?" (unpublished manuscript).
25 Jerzy Bartminski, "Szczodry wieczor – szezedryj weczir: Kolędy krasiczyńskie jako zjawisko kultury pogranicza polsko-ukraińskiego," in Stępień, *Polska-Ukraina*, vol. 1 (Przemyśl, 1990), p. 277.
26 In 1930s Przemyśl every other Christian marriage was mixed. See Anna Krochmal, "Stosunki międzynarodowe i międzyobrządkowe w parafiach greckokatolickiej diecezji przemyskiej w latach 1918–1939," in Stępień, *Polska-Ukraina*, vol. 3 (Przemyśl, 1996), pp. 219–230.
27 The research on which this section is based was funded by the Economic and Social Research Council (U.K.) as part of the project, "The Politics of Religious Identity: The Greek Catholics of Central Europe" (R 236071). I am particularly grateful to my main collaborator in this research, Dr Stanisław Stępień, for many helpful conversations, as well as help with sources; thanks also to Ewa Klekot in Warsaw.
28 Dariusz Iwaneczko, "Biskup Jozafat Kocyłowski (1876–1947): życie i działalność," in Stępień, *Polska-Ukraina*, vol. 3 (1996), pp. 247–260.
29 C. Hann, "Ethnic Cleansing in Eastern Europe: Poles and Ukrainians beside the Curzon Line," *Nations and Nationalism*, II, 3 (Cambridge, 1996), pp. 389–406.
30 The most important achievement of the post-Communist years has been the consolidation of a Ukrainian language school, in which all religious instruction is provided by Greek Catholic clergy.
31 It was finally returned to the Greek Catholics in 2000.

32 C. Hann and S. Stępień, *Tradycja i tożsamość: wywiady wśród mniejszości ukraińskiej w Przemyślu* (Przemyśl, 2000).
33 Almost all of these proposals were implemented in 2000–2001.
34 A. Niemiec, "Akt adaptacji czy wyrok zniszczenia?: spory o przebudowe przemyskiej katedry," *Architektura*, no. 2 (Warsaw, 1998), pp. 68–69.
35 Ibid., p. 69. The expert in question here was Professor Marek Kwiatkowski, Director of the Royal Gardens in Warsaw.
36 Cited in ibid.
37 Some Greek Catholic churches, including St George's Cathedral in L'viv, feature a prominent icon of Iozafat Kuntsevych (Jozafat Kuncewicz), a martyr for their church, who is of course not recognized by the Orthodox. When I attended a Sunday service in this cathedral in May 2002, I was authoritatively informed (by another visitor, Philipp Harnoncourt, Professor of Hymnology at the University of Graz) that the singing contained elements of all three local traditions: Roman Catholic, Orthodox, and Greek Catholic. I do not know how fast these nuances are noted by the congregation. But even if syncretism is an ongoing reality in sacred music, this still shows no sign of carrying over into more ecumenical confessional and political relations between the different communities. For further discussion of the domain of music, see C. Hann, "Creeds, Cultures and 'the Witchery of Music'," *Journal of the Royal Anthropological Institute*, IX, 2 (London, 2003), pp. 281–297.
38 Hann and Stępień, *Tradycja i tożsamość*, pp. 201–214.
39 Cited in Molnár, *Vallási kisebbség*, p. 234.
40 Cited in ibid., p. 240.

Contributors

Luiza Bialasiewicz is lecturer in political geography at the University of Durham, United Kingdom.

Chris Hann is director, Max Planck Institute for Social Anthropology, Halle/Saale, Germany.

John-Paul Himka is professor of history at the University of Alberta, Edmonton, Canada.

Yaroslav Hrytsak is professor of history at L'viv National University, Ukraine, and visiting professor at the Central European University, Budapest, Hungary.

Harald H. Jepsen is a former researcher at the Slavonic Institute of Odense University, Denmark.

Paul Robert Magocsi is professor of history and political science at the University of Toronto, Canada.

Jerzy Motylewicz is professor of history at the University of Rzeszów, Poland.

Volodymyr Potul'nyts'kyi is a researcher at the Institute of Ukrainian Archeography, and at the National Academy of Sciences of Ukraine, both in Kiev, and also professor of history at L'viv National University, Ukraine.

Stanisław Stępień is director of the South-East Scientific Institute, Przemyśl, Poland.

Kai Struve is a researcher at the Simon-Dubnow-Institute for Jewish History and Culture at Leipzig University, Germany.

Anna Veronika Wendland is a researcher at the Geisteswissenschaftliches Zentrum für Geschichte und Kultur Ostmitteleuropas in Leipzig, and lecturer at Leipzig University, Germany.

Index

59, 72, 74, 87, 126–127n2, 170, 185–
186, 190–191, 194, 202, 218
Russian language, 87, 188
Russian Orthodox Church, 30–31, 74,
76; conflict in, 78; defections from,
76; Exarch in Ukraine, 78; Holy
Synod, 74; merger with Greek
Catholic Church, 75; missions
abroad, 73–74; priests, 29
Russian Orthodox Moscow Patriarchate, 75; Exarchate in Kiev, 76
Russians, 3, 8–9, 29, 55, 64, 72, 84,
172, 199; as the national enemy,
197; and Ukrainians, 88
Russian-Ukrainian: patriotic celebrations, 103; population, 104; relations, 96; rite, 71
Russkaia rada (newspaper), 105, 107
russkyi (term), 88
Russophiles, 8, 60, 64, 72, 104–106,
109, 116, 126–127n2, 196, 199
Russophilism, 28, 73, 219
Russophones, 200
Rusyns, 3, 9
Ruthenian/Ruthenians, 7–8, 12,
18n8, 47, 53, 59, 64; after church
union, 44; alienation, 130n28;
crownland, 93; dialect, 55; East
Slavic population, ix; grammar, 58;
history, 194; hymnal, 58; intelligentsia, 104, 106; language, ix, 55–56,
60, 64; Liberation Festival, 106;
migration, 38; national festivals,
114–116; national movement, 53,
55, 64–65, 104, 106–107, 109–110,
113, 126; nation-building, 104;
orthography, 57; palatinate, 23, 25–
27; palatinate 1700–1772, 26–27;
patriotic celebrations, 125; peasants, 105, 192; playwrights, 63–64;

Polish relationship, 103; under
Polish rule, 110, 112; politicization
of, 111; population, 37; religious
status of, 40–44; rite, 219; Russian
relationship, 103; Russophilism of,
28–29; self-identification, 190;
streets, 46–47; term, 38, 40; and
their identity, 43; Triad, 66; and a
Ukrainian identity, 74. *See also*
Ruthenians/Ukrainians
Ruthenian Street (*vulytsia Rus'ka*),
142
Ruthenians/Ukrainians, ix, 8, 11, 26,
65; 1848 revolution, 14; eastern
Galicia, 4; Piedmont for, 13; transliteration system, ix
Rybotychi/Rybotycze, 216
Rzeszów, 37, 173–174

Saar, Matylda, 63
Sacher-Masoch, Leopold von, 16, 201
Sacred Heart of Jesus, 223, 225; cults,
219
St Barbara's Church (Vienna), 55–57,
60–61
Saint Basil the Great, 63
St George Cathedral Church (L'viv),
78, 198; Greek Catholic metropoli-
tan, 198; Rococo style, 216
St George's Circle, 72–73
St Gregory the Great, 63
St John Chrysostom, 63
Saint Peter's Basilica (Rome), 225
St Petersburg, 61, 191
Saint Stanislaus, 117
Sambir/Sambor, 37, 45–46
San River, 4–6, 8–9, 15, 17–18n5, 37,
74
Sanok, 37; Jews in, 170
Sarmatism, 27